IMAGES
of America

LYNWOOD

On the Cover: This late-1920s image shows the Long Beach Boulevard Association celebrating the opening of the newly improved Long Beach Boulevard, which was paved and widened to 100 feet through Lynwood's city limit, from Huntington Park to Long Beach. (City of Lynwood Collection.)

IMAGES
of America

LYNWOOD

The City of Lynwood
with Ilu Johnson and Chris Diaz

ARCADIA
PUBLISHING

ISBN 978-0-7385-8889-6

Published by Arcadia Publishing
Charleston, South Carolina

Printed in the United States of America

Library of Congress Control Number: 2011930434

For all general information, please contact Arcadia Publishing:
Telephone 843-853-2070
Fax 843-853-0044
E-mail sales@arcadiapublishing.com
For customer service and orders:
Toll-Free 1-888-313-2665

Visit us on the Internet at www.arcadiapublishing.com

Dedicated to Lynwood residents (past and present) who serve as a beacon of hope and to Jack Willard for his preservation of history for future generations

Contents

ACKNOWLEDGMENTS

The City of Lynwood Recreation and Community Services Department wishes to extend a sincere thank-you to all contributors who kindly shared their pictures, their knowledge, and their time to help with this book. Our special appreciation goes to countless Lynwood residents (past and present), especially the Ham family, Karen McMillian Warren, Joy McMillian Arranaga, Ron Warren, and members of the class of 1964 at the 45th class reunion, who shared their personal memories and valuable input. We are grateful to Andrea Hooper, Harry C. Gibbens, Arthur T. Dooms Jr., Roy Pryor, and Carmen Coduti, all of whom lent a helping hand and shared treasured memories and life stories to provide a glimpse into Lynwood's history over the decades. In addition, we want to thank the Lynwood High School library staff for letting us borrow its yearbook collection.

Since most of the images seen in this book came from the City of Lynwood archives, unless otherwise noted, we want to thank the city clerk's office and staff for giving us permission to peruse files of vintage images and historical documents.

We also want to thank Vanessa Garcia for research; Naeemah Campbell, Jose Trejo, and Mark Flores for the writing; Jamel Goodloe for the scanning; and Ann Llanas for her work in editing and proofing the book.

We must also acknowledge and credit J. Jack Willard's 1971 book, J. Jack Willard Recalls Lynwood All-American City 50th Year Commemorative Edition. We owe much of our information to the late Mr. Willard, who helped set a precedent of accounted information from former Lynwood residents who lived to tell their tales. Willard's book is the only comprehensive history of Lynwood, and, without it, this book would not have been possible. Other sources that were used to conduct research include newspaper columns from the Lynwood Press, Herald American, and various Lynwood Chamber of Commerce writings as well as the collection of Accolade Year Books published by Lynwood High School from 1952 through 1970. Our sincere thanks to Amy Perryman, for her professionalism and understanding when the production of the book underwent challenges, her patience and guidance is deeply appreciated. Also, special thanks goes to the Mayor and members of the Lynwood City Council – Jim Morton, Sal Alatorre, Maria Santillan-Beas, Aide Castro, and Ramon Rodriguez. Our esteem goes out to the honorable mayor and fellow city council members who continue to lead our "All-America City" toward a path of greatness.

INTRODUCTION

We live in a country that is a conglomeration of cultures and ethnicities, but where each one of us also counts on each other to live successfully. Lynwood, California, is a slice of America's melting pot, with a strong history of diversity, where residents have lived, learned, and grown from the influence of the diverse cultural heritage of our citizen-neighbors. Reflecting on its history, building in the present, and moving toward the future are critical components of Lynwood's sense of pride and unity. As a two-time winner of the All-America City Award, Lynwood, California, has prospered and been on the leading edge of greatness since it incorporated in 1921. But its provenance runs deeper still, starting two centuries ago. This pictorial history serves as a resource of valuable information about the creation and development of Lynwood.

The city's rich history starts with a settlement colonized by Spanish aristocrats, or dons, and American pioneers who purchased, settled, and formed a small communal town. It began with Don Antonio Maria Lugo, who was born in 1775. In 1810, he was awarded 11 square leagues of land in California by the king of Spain for his military service during the establishment of the Francisco missions in California. After he received these tracts of land (29,514 acres), Lugo named the area Rancho San Antonio, likely after his birthplace at La Misión San Antonio de Padua, in Jolon, California. Today, these tracts of land make up the cities of Bell, Bell Gardens, Commerce, Cudahy, Huntington Park, Lynwood, Maywood, Montebello, South Gate, Vernon, and Walnut Park. Rancho San Antonio was located just north of the Juan Jose Dominguez's Rancho San Pedro, roughly bordering today's Rosecrans Avenue in Compton. Rancho San Pedro is parallel to Pueblo de Los Angeles. The eastern boundary runs along the Los Angeles River, or as it was called then the San Gabriel River, and Rancho Santa Gertrudes. Lugo maintained a home in the Pueblo de Los Angeles, near the plaza across from a church. He was alcalde (mayor) of Los Angeles from 1816 to 1819 and a leader in most of the social functions. Lugo received a patent from the US government on July 24, 1847, that made him the undisputed owner of Rancho San Antonio, birthplace of Lynwood.

After Lugo's death in 1860, the 29,500-acre ranch was divided among his five sons and three daughters. Guadalupe Lugo inherited the area of Rancho San Antonio. She later deeded it to Isaias Wolf Hellman, a Los Angeles banker who in 1871 deeded it to M.R. Shields, wife of J.H. Shields. Mrs. Shields later deeded her land interest to Jonathon S. Slauson, an early Los Angeles banker for whom Slauson Avenue was named. Slauson deeded a portion of the land to Charles H. Sessions for a dairy barn in 1902. The dairy was located on what is now Sanborn Avenue and Long Beach Boulevard. After consulting his family on what to name the dairy, the Sessions chose Charles' wife's given and maiden names, Lynne Wood, which they abridged to Lynwood. And so their dairy became Lynwood Dairy and Creamery.

The families who first came to the Lynwood territory arrived in the late 1870s and early 1880s. The Abbott family was among the first settlers. In 1889, Haymer Abbott built a home located on the corner of Wright Road and Century Boulevard (now Martin Luther King Jr. Boulevard), where the original Lugo Park (renovated and renamed John D. Ham Park in 1965) once stood from the 1950s to 2003. This site is now home to Firebaugh High School. The home was disassembled, moved to 11832 Atlantic Avenue and Agnes Street, and rebuilt.

In 1913, H.T. Kaufin, L.G. Stone, Charles H. Sessions, E.C. Lewis, and Kingsbury Sanborn joined forces to create the Lynwood Company. Together, they brought potential buyers on excursions to Lynwood. They opened 800 acres of suburban homesites that year. Residential lots, 100 by 800 feet, were sold for $500 to $800. In 1918, the Lynwood Company closed its sales office and the building later served as the Lynwood Bank.

On July 16, 1921, voters approved the city's incorporation. The early council meetings were held in the former Lynwood Company building located at 11331 Plaza Street, which served as city hall until 1927. The building was an old wood structure that caught fire and a portion of the building was destroyed. Because repairs were deemed too costly, the Lynwood City Council voted to build a new city hall. The community voters passed a bond issue in 1927 that authorized construction. The new city hall was completed in 1928 on the same site, which is now the location of Plaza Mexico Shopping Center. The new building was an imposing two-story, redbrick structure that housed the first fire department, police department, treasurer, council chamber, building department, court clerk, and city clerk offices. In 1963, another new city hall was constructed on Bullis Road that stands to this day. The 1963 building contains offices of city council, city clerk, city manager, treasurer, finance, human resources, and council chambers for community meetings. Plans are under way to revamp and modernize the current city hall and civic center facilities.

The Lynwood School District was part of the Compton School District for 22 years, beginning in 1934. The first school built was Lugo Elementary School, located on Pendleton Street. There were several direct descendants of Antonio Maria Lugo present at the school's opening. In the 1880s, the school district bought an acre of land at the corner of what was Temple (now Bullis Road) and Cortland Streets and built a one-room schoolhouse. By 1895, a more modern two-room structure was built and equipped with a lofty tower and iron bell that rang when school began each day. The school was moved to the corner of Carlin Avenue and Bullis Road and was converted to a residence. Lynwood Junior High School was built in 1930 and has the distinction of being the only school in the Lynwood district that was not condemned after the 1933 earthquake. It later became Lynwood High School. In 1934, registration in the Lynwood School District totaled 1,282 students and 38 teachers. In 1998, the school district built a new Lynwood High School located on Imperial Highway. The old building was renamed Lynwood Middle School. There were approximately 17,206 students and 700 teachers by 2010. In 2011, the district operated 12 elementary schools, 3 middle schools, 2 high schools, 1 continuation school, and 1 adult school.

In 1946, the City of Lynwood began issuing home occupation licenses to residents and patrons. In 1952, the assessed valuation totaled $23 million. There were 8,000 dwellings and 12,000 registered voters. In 1990, Lynwood's population approached 70,000 residents and 14,432 households. The assessed land valuation for the fiscal year 1988 totaled $785,545,000. A total of 14,485 individuals were registered voters. Construction of I-105 (the Century Freeway, also called the Glenn Anderson Freeway) had been discussed since 1958 and was completed in 1993. The freeway replaced the Southern Pacific Railroad right-of-way. The Los Angeles Metro Railway extends down the center of I-105 from Norwalk to El Segundo, near Los Angeles International (LAX) Airport.

Lynwood has two large community parks and five smaller neighborhood parks located throughout the city. There is a civic center, public library, rental facility (Bateman Hall), natatorium, skate park, youth center, senior citizen center, and community center with a gymnasium. The city has gone through five phases of demographic change over the years. The first was the initial settlement colonized by Spanish-titled dons and gold-rush pioneers, who remained on the land from 1810 until the early 1900s. By this time, the population had evolved primarily to small farming families. When the Pacific Electric Railroad built a line between Los Angeles and Santa Ana in 1905, through what is now the 105 Freeway, the railway attracted new residents to Lynwood and stimulated land development—a community was forming. From 1914 to 1921, what was to be the city of Lynwood started with an active land sales promotion in Los Angeles newspapers.

They promoted the area as the new "half-way city" and brought potential buyers by excursion bus, rail, and car. As neighborhoods formed, residents saw an advantage to forming their own local government. In 1921, city founders filed articles to incorporate and the city named after Charles H. Session's dairy was established. From 1920 through 1960, the town saw an influx of working-class Caucasian suburbanites who were instrumental in forming the foundation of Lynwood's government. Then, following the civil rights movement, from the 1970s through the 1990s, African American educators and other professionals arrived, wishing to purchase homes and raise families in a safe community. The fifth and most recent shift was identified by the 1990 California census. Lynwood's population had reached nearly 70,000, and 86 percent of the residents identified their heritage as Mexican or Latin American.

The city of Lynwood is truly multicultural, and residents appreciate the unique attributes, lifestyles, values, and community spirit that made it an All-America City winner twice. The city maintains an attractive and clean environment that is safe, responsive, and well informed. There are outstanding community resources supporting social, recreational, educational, and business opportunities to residents. Lynwood's rich history was carved out by a spirit of excellence, self-reliance, hard work, and determination. The city honors these values and builds on them with an eye on what is to come. Lynwood will continue to prioritize quality services, cutting-edge activities, multicultural events, and community-involved programs.

One

A City Is Born

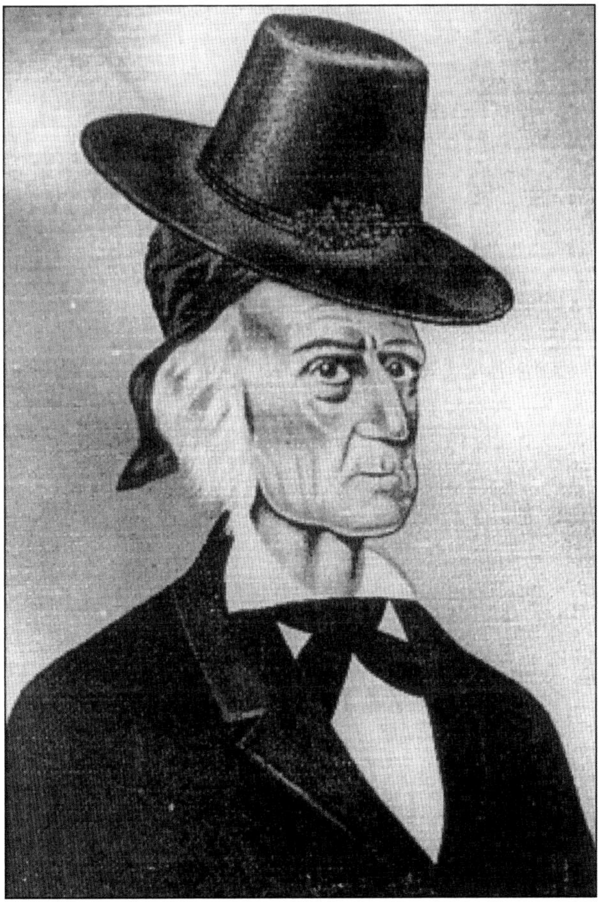

Shown is an artist's rendering of Don Antonio Maria Lugo, born in 1775 at La Misión San Antonio de Padua, California. Lugo's sobriquet, "Godfather," was based on his vast land holdings at Rancho San Antonio that today comprise Lynwood, Bell, Bell Gardens, Commerce, Cudahy, Huntington Park, Maywood, Montebello, South Gate, Vernon, and Walnut Park. In 1847, Lugo received a patent from the US government that made him the undisputed owner of Rancho San Antonio. The portion that passed to Lugo's daughter Guadalupe became the future site of Lynwood.

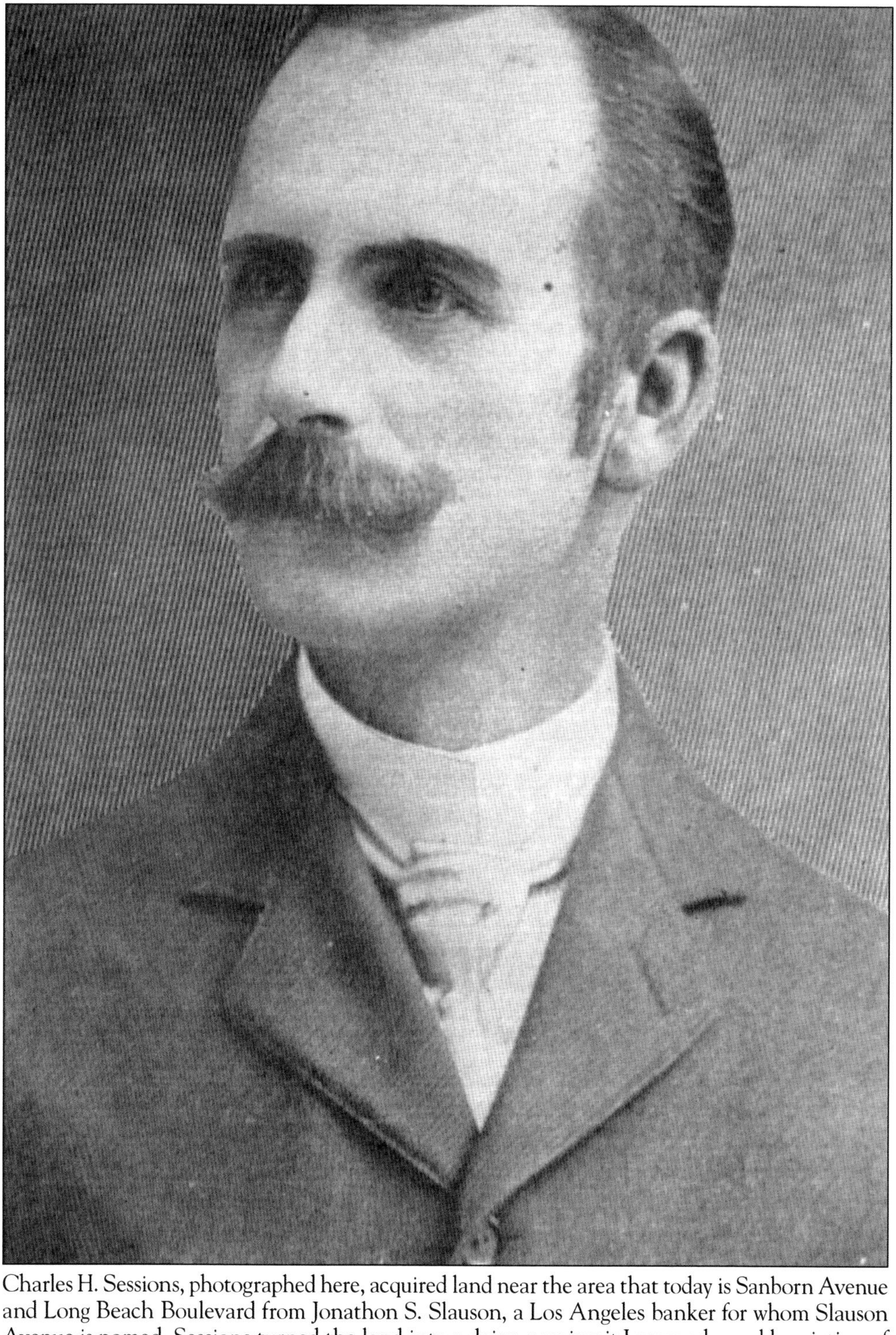

Charles H. Sessions, photographed here, acquired land near the area that today is Sanborn Avenue and Long Beach Boulevard from Jonathon S. Slauson, a Los Angeles banker for whom Slauson Avenue is named. Sessions turned the land into a dairy, naming it Lynwood, an abbreviation of his wife's given and maiden names, Lynne Wood. He was also a founder of the Lynwood Company, where he was engaged in business for many years.

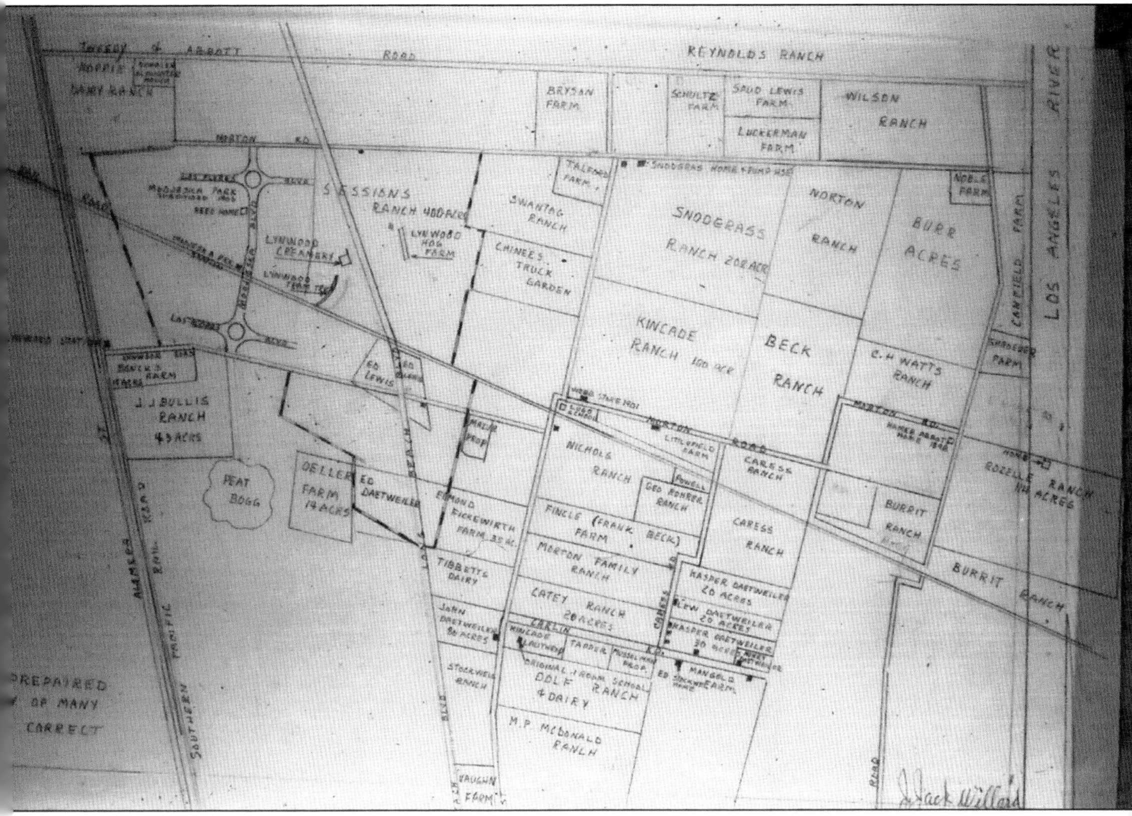

This plat map, prepared by Jack Willard from the memory of many early residents, shows the names of pioneers who settled in the area. The Modjeska Park tract, in the left corner, is the site of today's State Street, from Rosa Park to Carnation Park. It is bordered on the south by Lynwood Road, on the north by Norton Road, on the east by Peach Street, and on the west by Bellinger Avenue. This tract was subdivided by the Lynwood Company, formed by Charles H. Sessions, E.C. Lewis, and Kingsbury Sanborn.

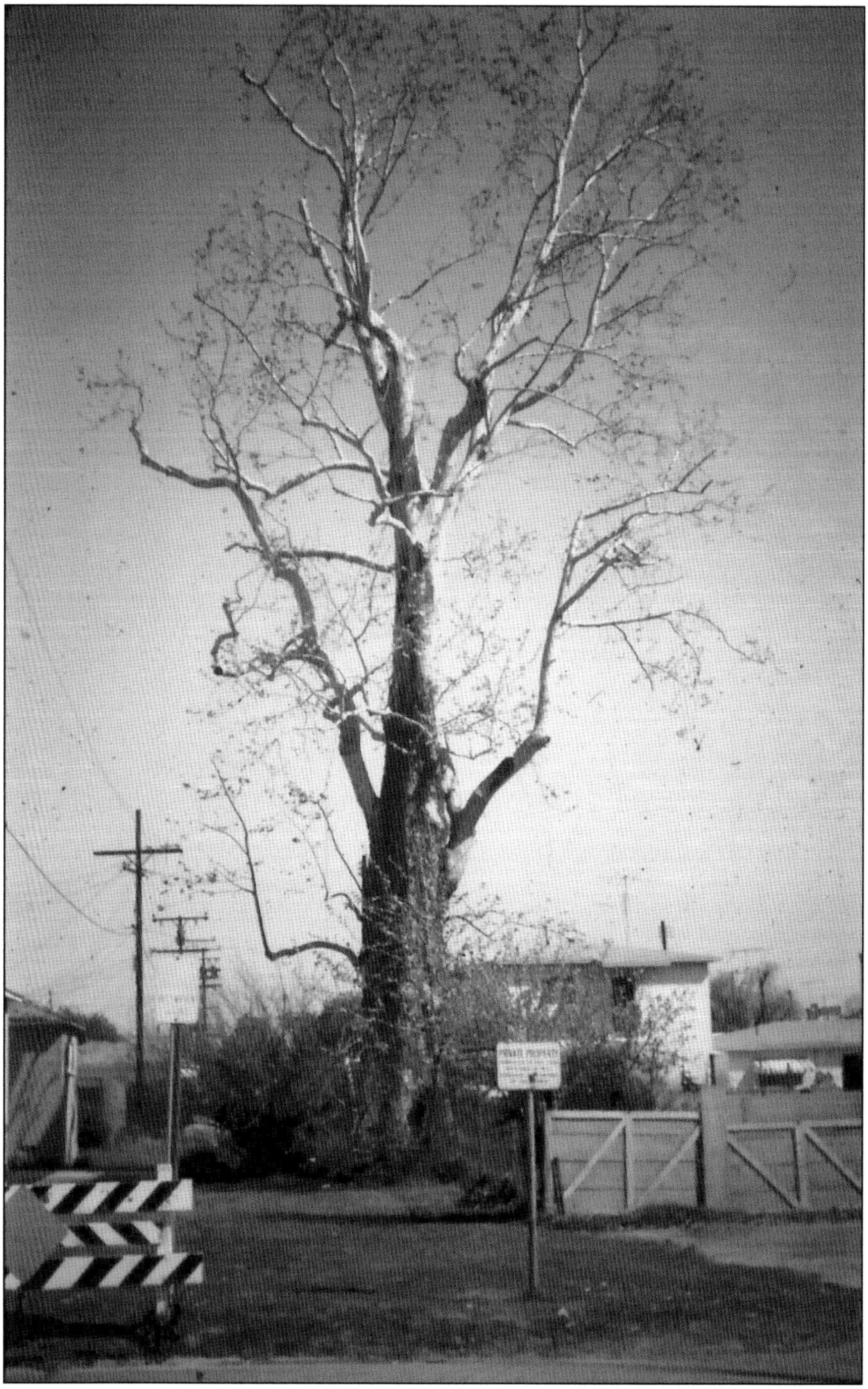

The "Eagle Tree" dates back to around 1800 and marks the southern boundary of the Rancho San Antonio, which borders Rancho San Pedro. The sycamore still lives at the corner of Poppy and Short Streets in Compton. Because the course of the Los Angeles River shifted wildly through the area, early pioneers found the sycamore tree a more reliable survey point for the ranch than creeks, rivers, and boulders.

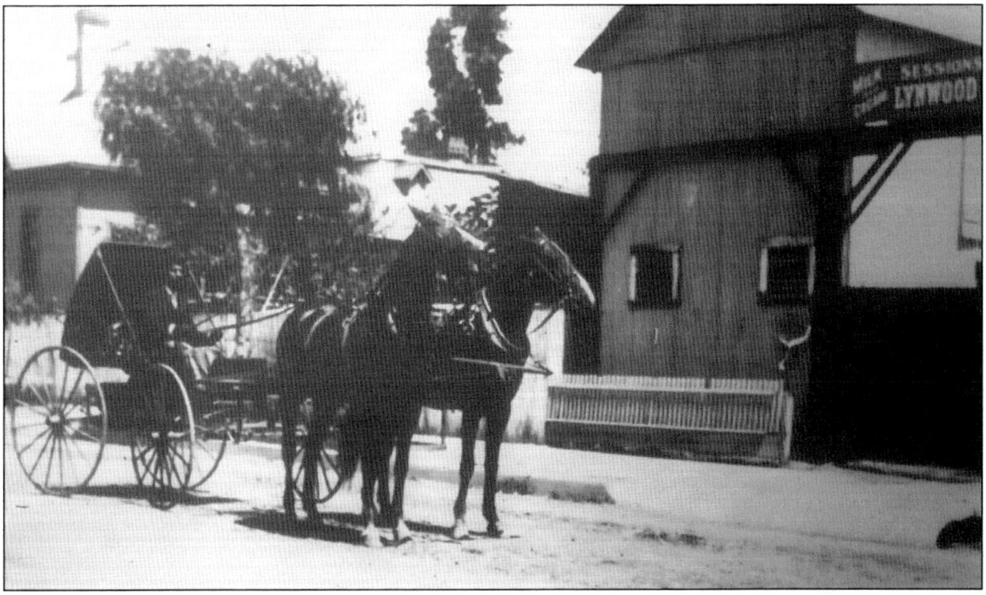

This photograph shows the front elevation of the Lynwood Dairy and Creamery barn owned by Charles H. Sessions. The barn was near northwest Sanborn Avenue and Long Beach Boulevard. Sessions processed milk from neighboring farmers, who brought the milk to him in large cans. He also raised hogs in a barn, a little farther north from the dairy. The buggy driver is unidentified.

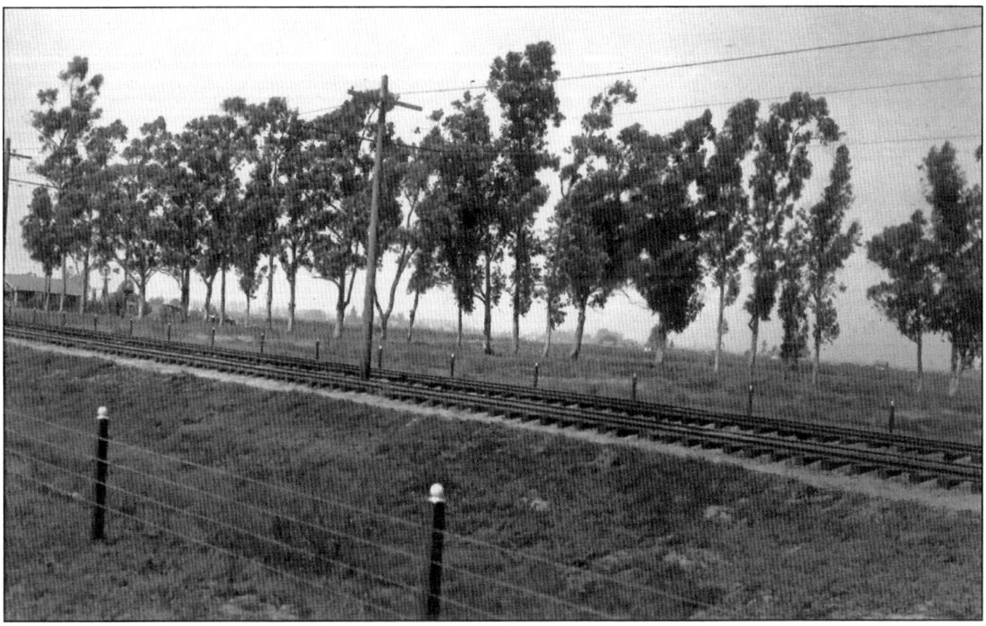

This c. 1910 photograph shows the Modjeska Park Tract facing east from what is today the corner of State Street and Imperial Highway. The Santa Ana Railroad line ran through the middle of Lynwood along Fernwood Avenue, which opened in 1905. There were very few homes built in the area, one appears here on the far left. The main boulevard, now called State Street, ran parallel north and south from the railroad tracks, marked by Circular Park sites called Gloriettas (known now as Carnation Park and Rose Park) on both ends. The parks were designed to serve as centers for the future city.

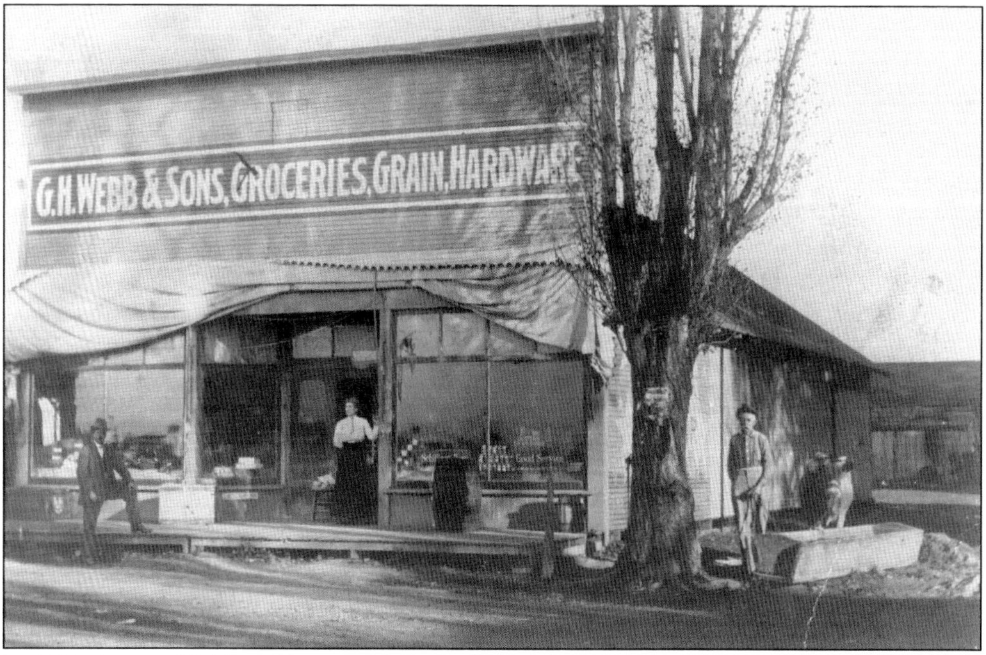

In 1909, George Webb and his parents moved from Compton into this corner store on Temple Street (now Bullis Road) and Morton Road (now Cortland Street). The store sold general groceries, grain, and hardware merchandise and was the only store in the area. It was located directly across from the Lugo District School on Morton Road.

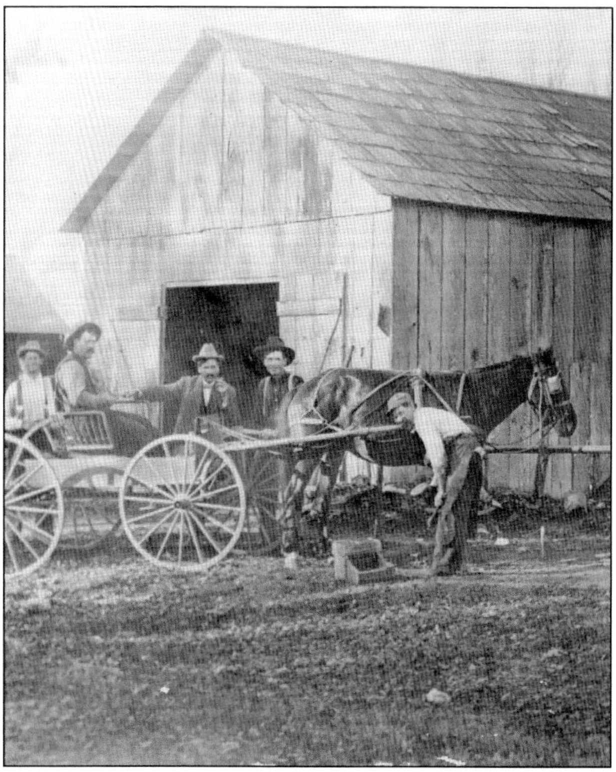

This is a 1912 photograph of a blacksmith shop located adjacent to George Webb's store on Morton Road. Across from Fernwood Avenue on the railroad was one of several sugar beet dumps in Lynwood. This shop was very close-by for ranchers making the trip. A worker is seen here tending the horse as a customer waits in the buggy.

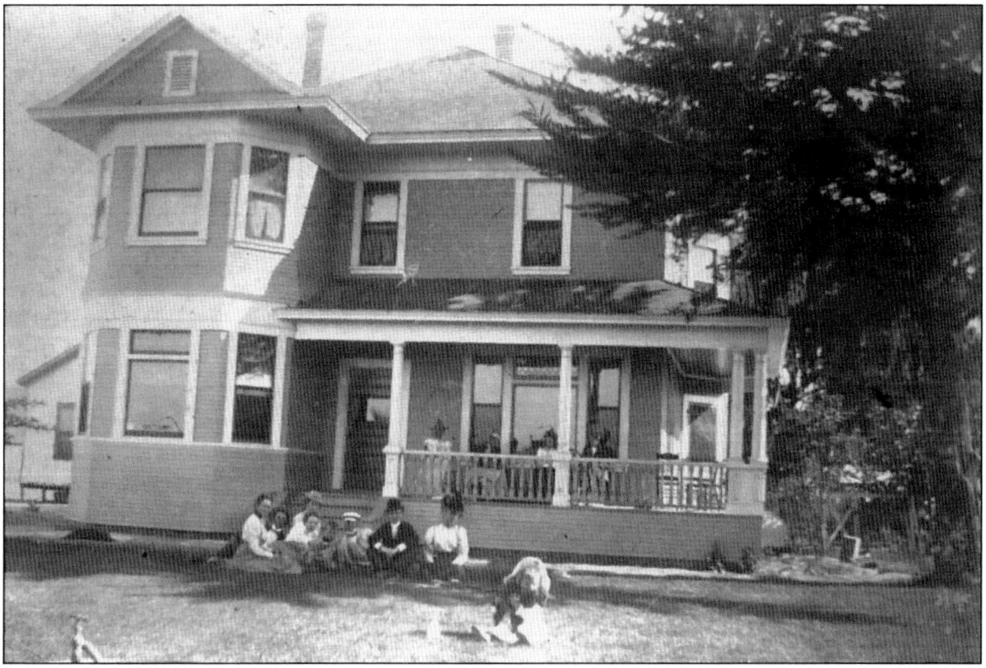

Families first arrived in Lynwood in the 1870s. Among them was the Rozelle family, whose home is pictured here on the east side of Abbott Road.

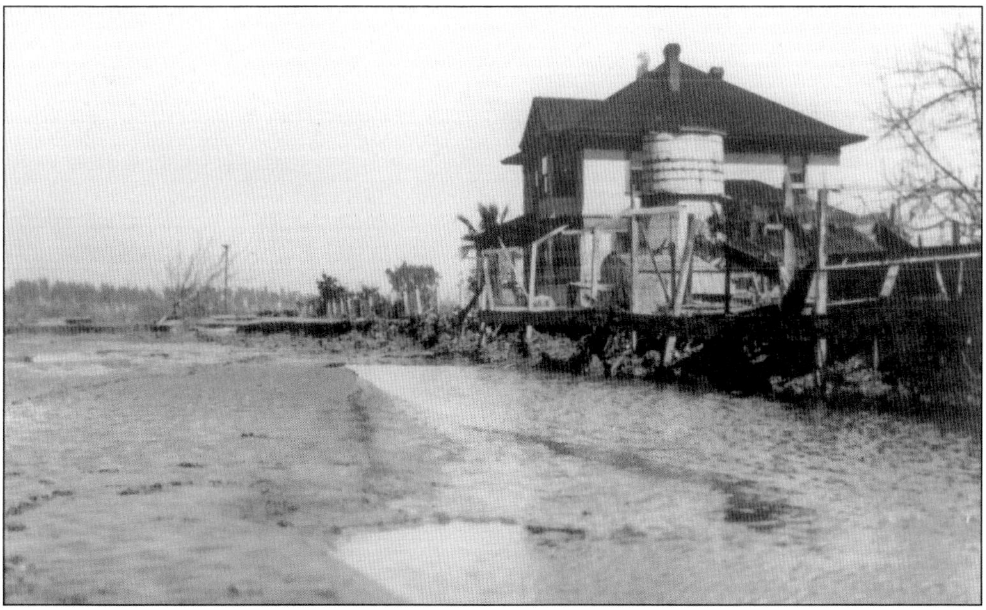

The area around Lynwood generally is flat. When floodwater came downstream, it spread wildly in the flatlands south of Lynwood. The Rozelle home is seen here after the 1914 flood washed away the family's barns and automobile. The home was completely cut off for about two weeks. The Rozelles could not get out, and no one could get in to help them. Later, when workmen excavated the river channel, the Rozelle automobile was found.

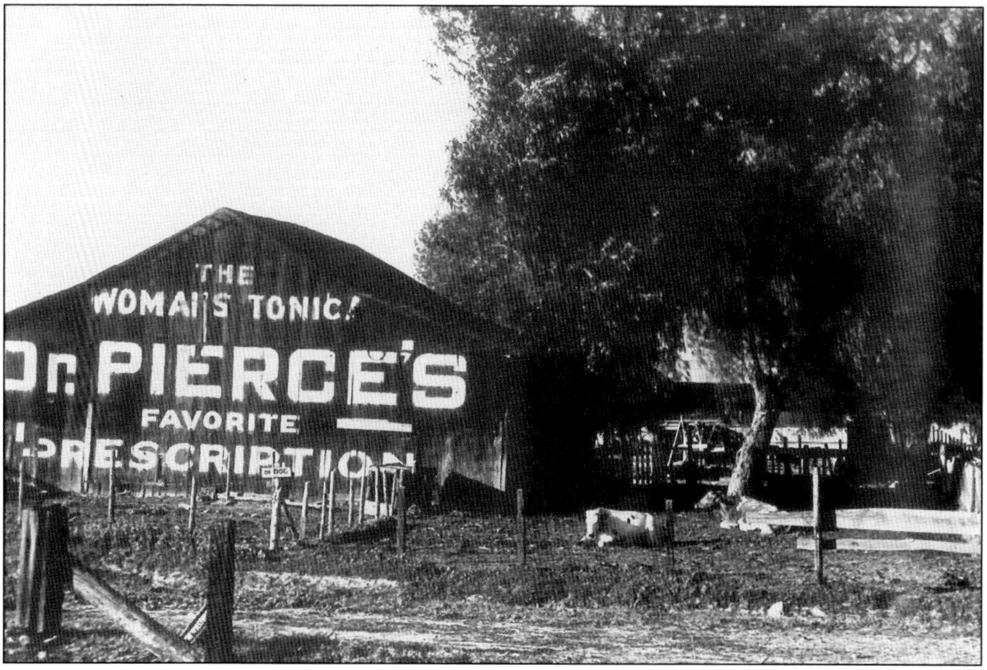

The Littlefield Farm shown here about 1912 was on Morton Road east of the Lugo District School. The painted barn here proclaims, "The Woman's Tonic! Dr. Pierce's Favorite Prescription."

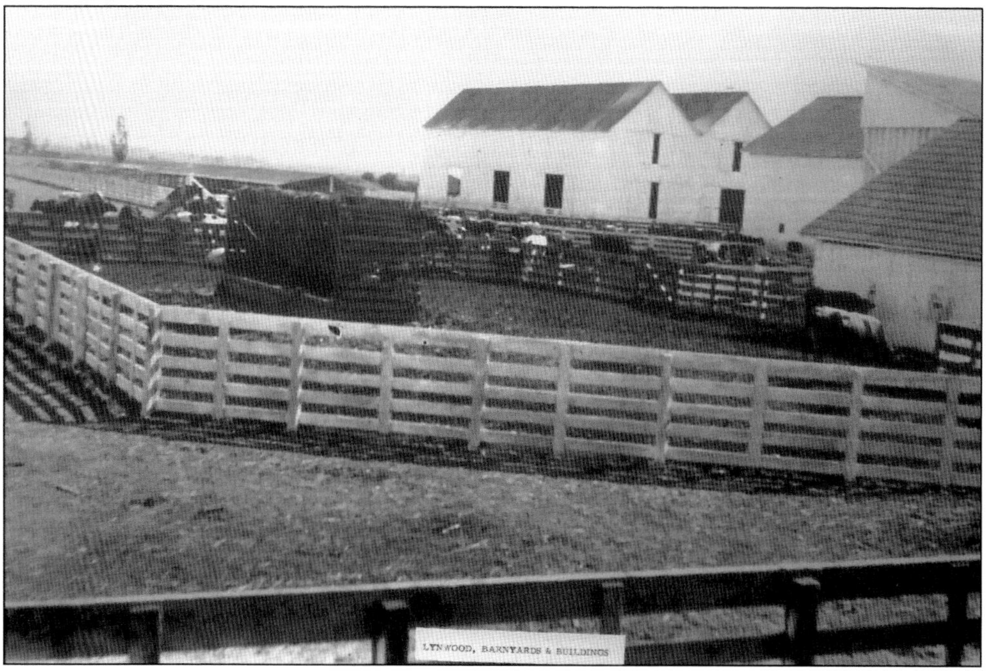

The Lynwood barns and buildings pictured here about 1910 were owned by Charles H. Sessions. The cattle and hog sheds on the 400-acre ranch are seen in the background.

This is a 1910s portrait of the Lou Daetweiler family. The Daetweilers emigrated from Switzerland, along with several of Daetweiler's brothers. They purchased 30- to 40-acre farms around Lynwood and leased them out for farming purposes.

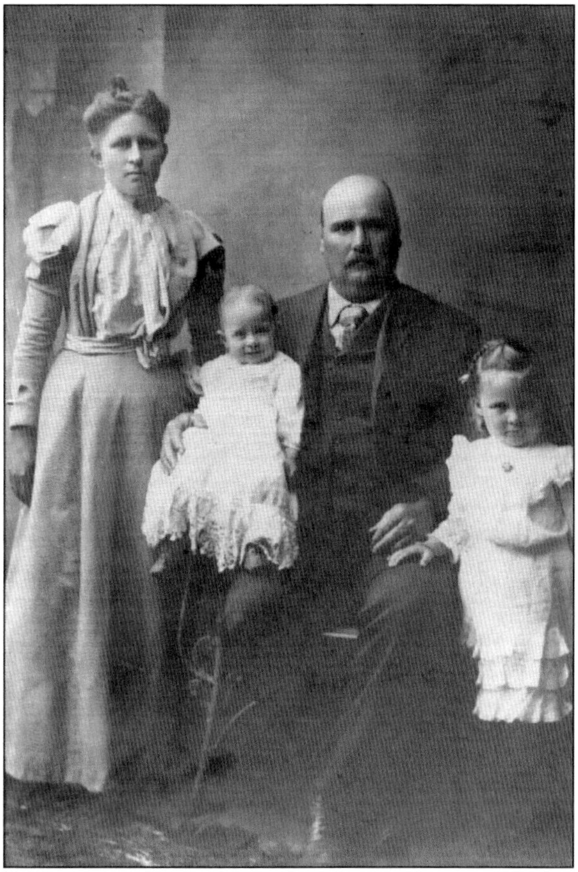

This bungalow-style home at Caress Street (now Harris Street) was home to the Daetweiler family.

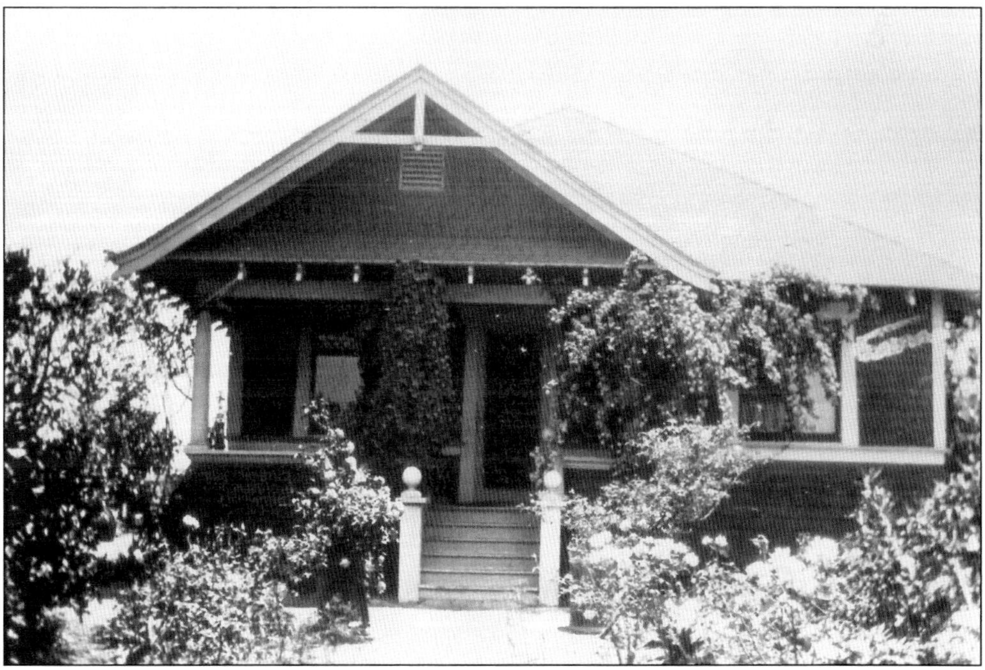

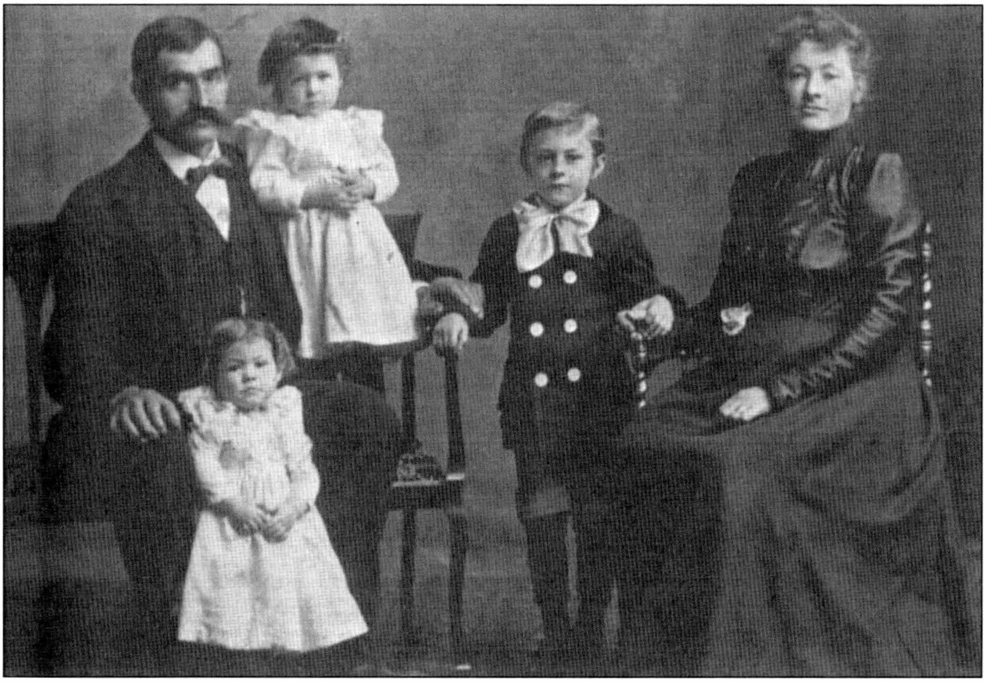

Photographed here about 1910, the William Oeller family owned a ranch southwest of the Lynwood Dairy. In 1912, a Pacific Electric Railway passenger train struck Oeller's fully-loaded hay wagon as he and his children were crossing the tracks near Long Beach Boulevard. Oeller, two sons, and two daughters were in the wagon. Tragically, Oeller and his daughters were killed, but his son somehow survived the accident.

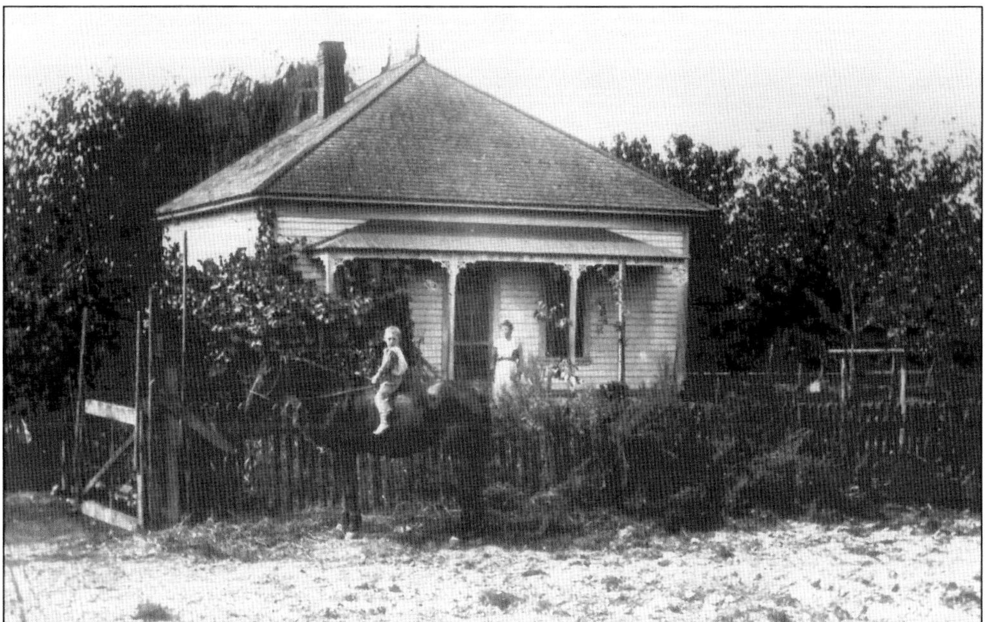

The Oeller home is photographed around 1912. The son is on a horse outside the front lawn as his mother watches from a close distance.

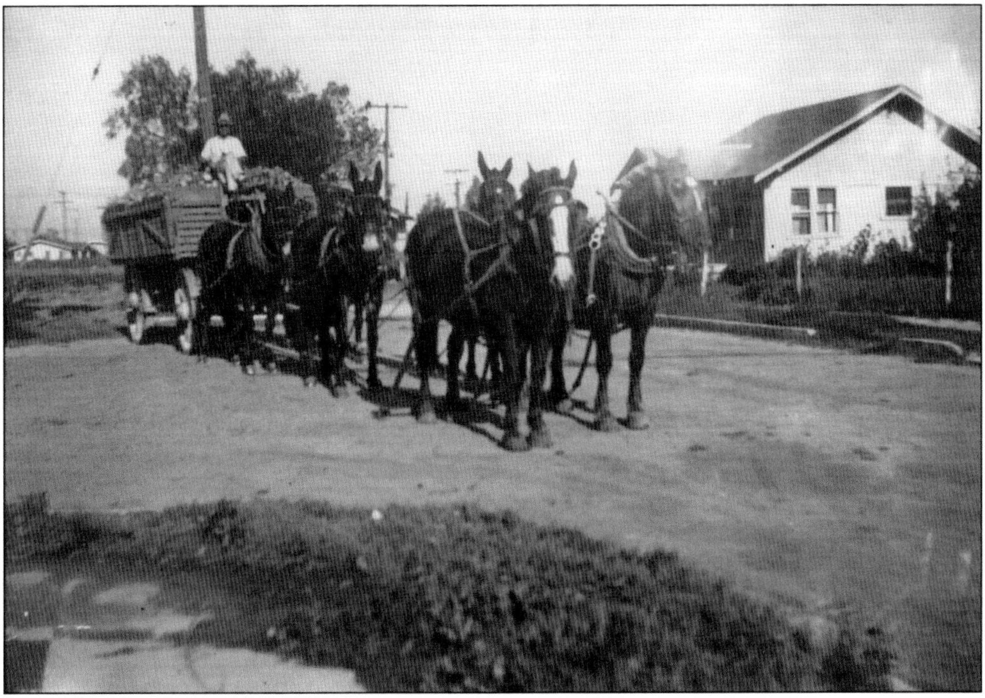

Early settlers harvested sugar beets, and this photograph shows a farmer transporting a full wagon to the beet dump by the railroad tracks. Another beet dump near Caress Street (now Harris Street) included a large, elevated platform with two long ramps that led to a scale. After the wagonload of sugar beets was weighed, the railroad freight line conveyed the yield to a sugar refinery in Santa Ana.

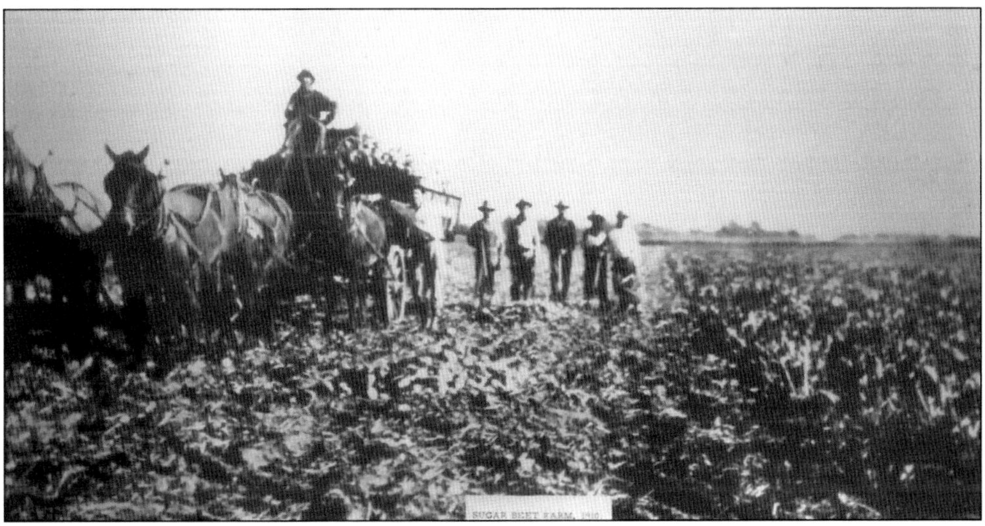

A sugar beet farm near the railroad along Fernwood Avenue is pictured in 1910. Jack Willard, a resident dating back to 1914, recalled, "When the farmers harvested the beets, they cut the tops off and threw them on the ground. After the harvest, they ran cattle in there, and the livestock fed on the beet tops. Lynwood school children who lived in the area had to go down the railroad tracks or else go through this beet field, swarming with cattle." Being afraid of cattle, they walked on the railroad tracks to school when cattle were feeding.

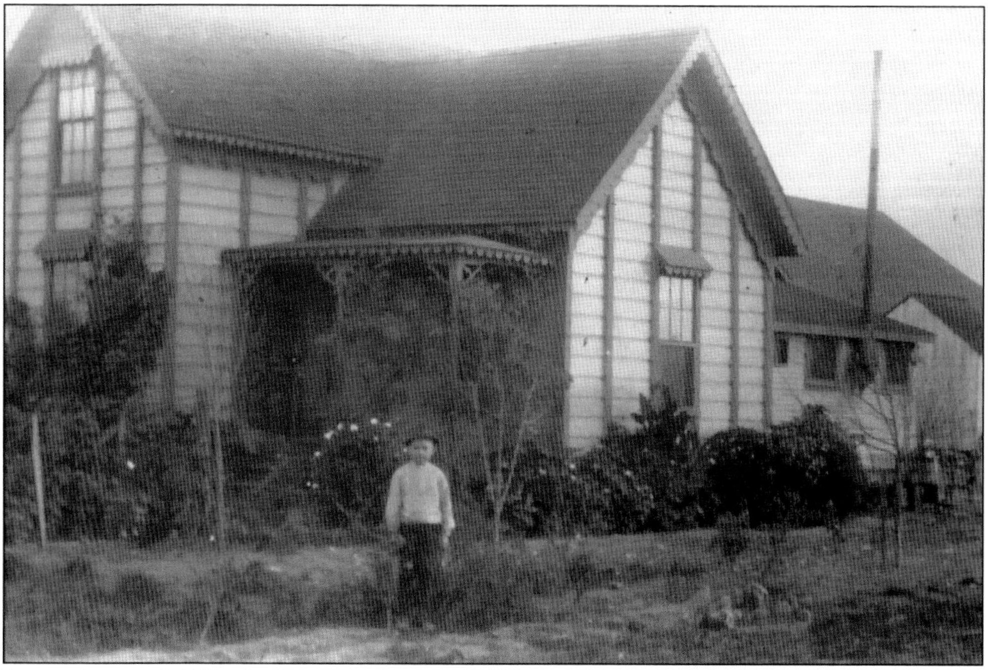

Pictured around 1910, this home is the original birthplace of Bertha Rickenback. The child in the picture is unidentified.

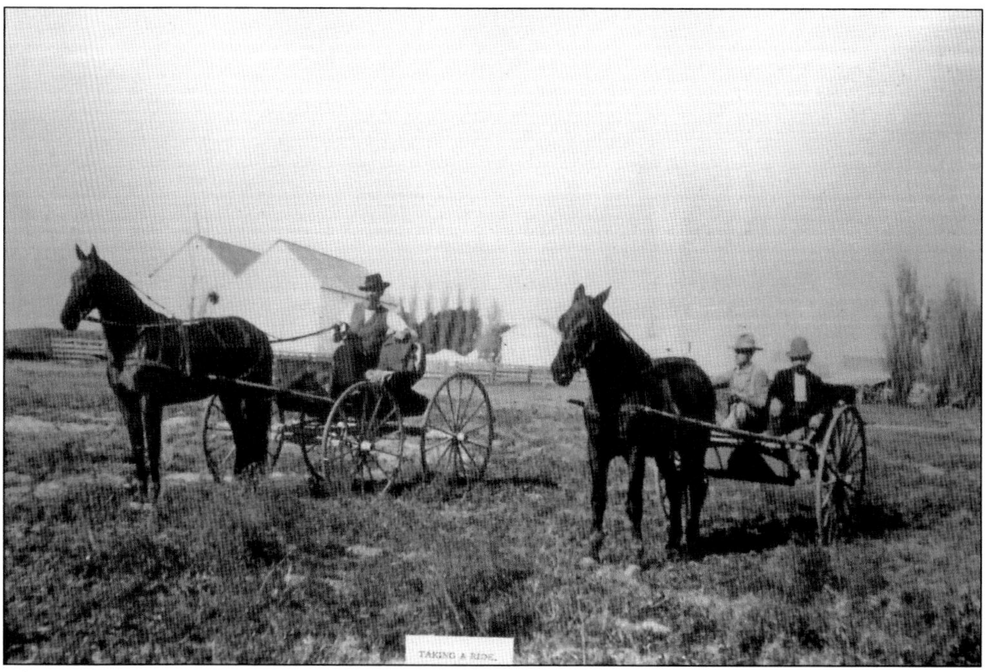

This c. 1900 photograph shows men on double-seat buggies riding through a farm on what looks to be a casual outing among friends. Because streets were not paved, travel across fields was common.

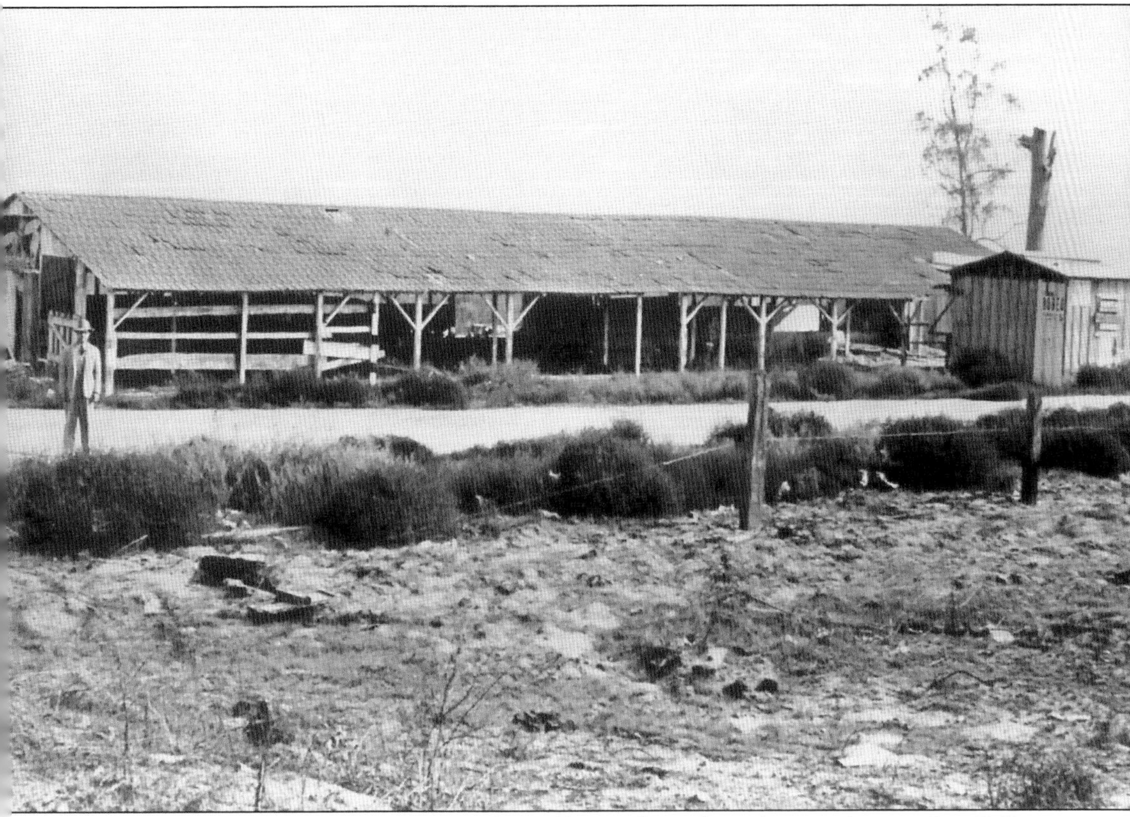

The Dolf family farm is shown about 1910. The Dolfs ran a large dairy that was destroyed in 1940. Today, the Western Gear Corporation, then Western Gear Works, is still standing on the same site at Alameda Street and Imperial Highway. The Dolf family dairy farm occupied a portion of the 400-acre farm and ranch land on what is now an industrial area that covers nearly all the west side of the city from Century Boulevard (now Martin Luther King Jr. Boulevard) to Euclid Street between Alameda Street and Santa Fe Street. Among industries now on the site are Pacer International, Jorgensen Steel Corporation, and the vacant Western Gear Corporation shown in the images on pages 48 and 49. The biggest change to present-day has been the construction of the 105 Freeway through the center of the city in the 1980s. By the end of the 1930s, the dairy industry was moving east to San Bernardino due to the housing boom in the Los Angeles area, which made way for new establishments.

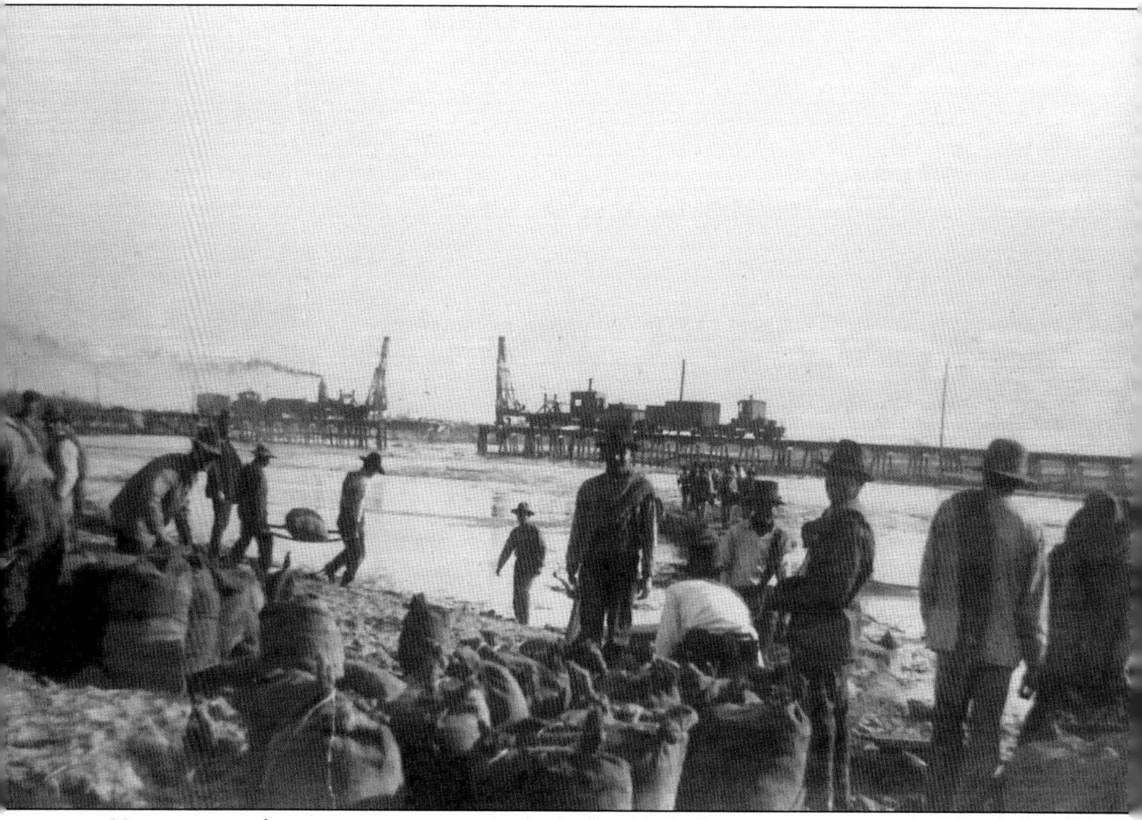

Here, a crew of men prepares to repair the bridge. Early day construction workers hauled sacks mixed with sand and concrete to projects. In 1917, a bond was issued to install earth levees to channel storm water to the Los Angeles River.

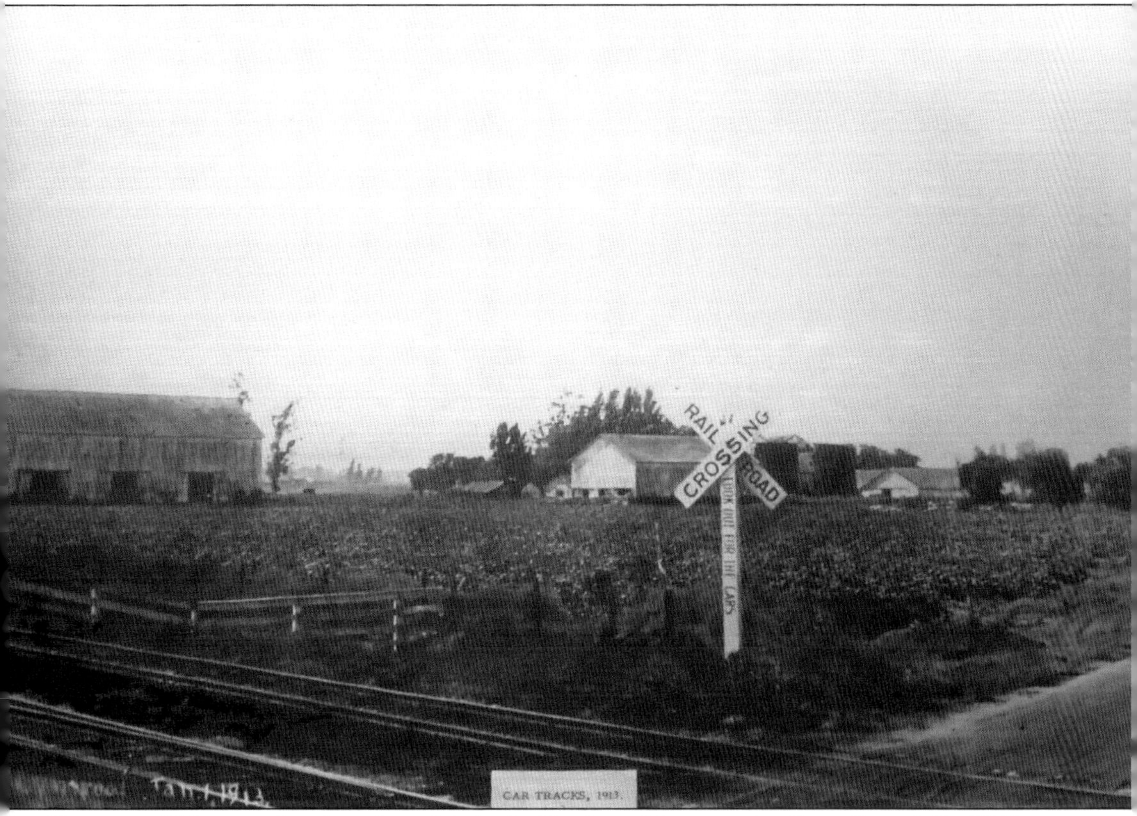

Shown in 1913 are railroad tracks at Modjeska Boulevard (present-day State Street). By 1925, it had become dangerous to cross these tracks. The area was more populated and people began commuting to work and shop. City council persuaded the railroad to install a wigwag alarm.

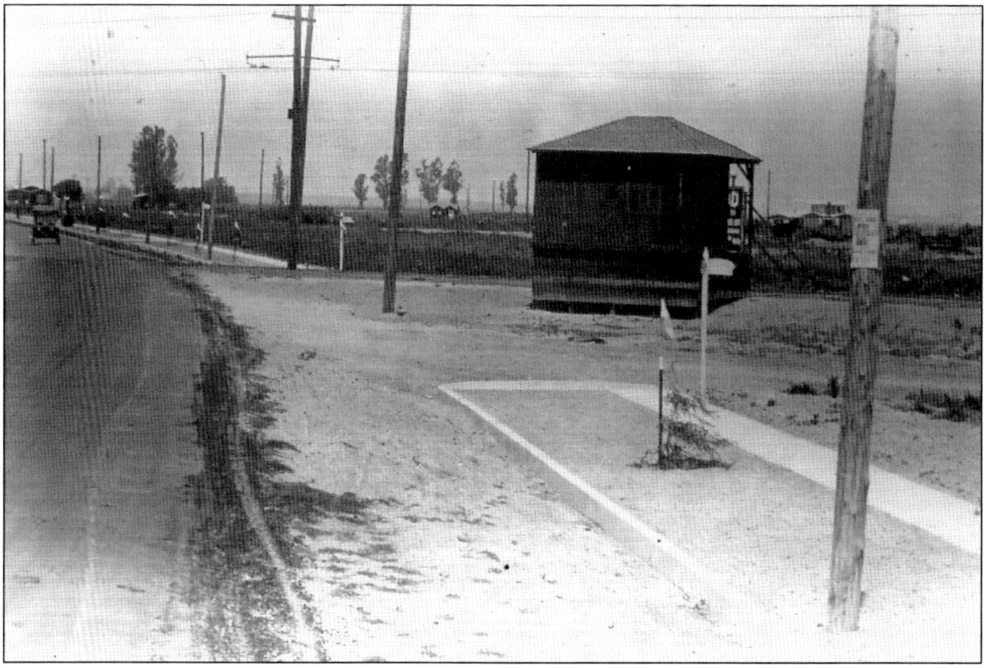

Here is a 1913 view of Long Beach Boulevard facing north toward Fernwood Avenue. In the 1920s, businesses arrived on Long Beach Boulevard from Fernwood Avenue to Imperial Highway.

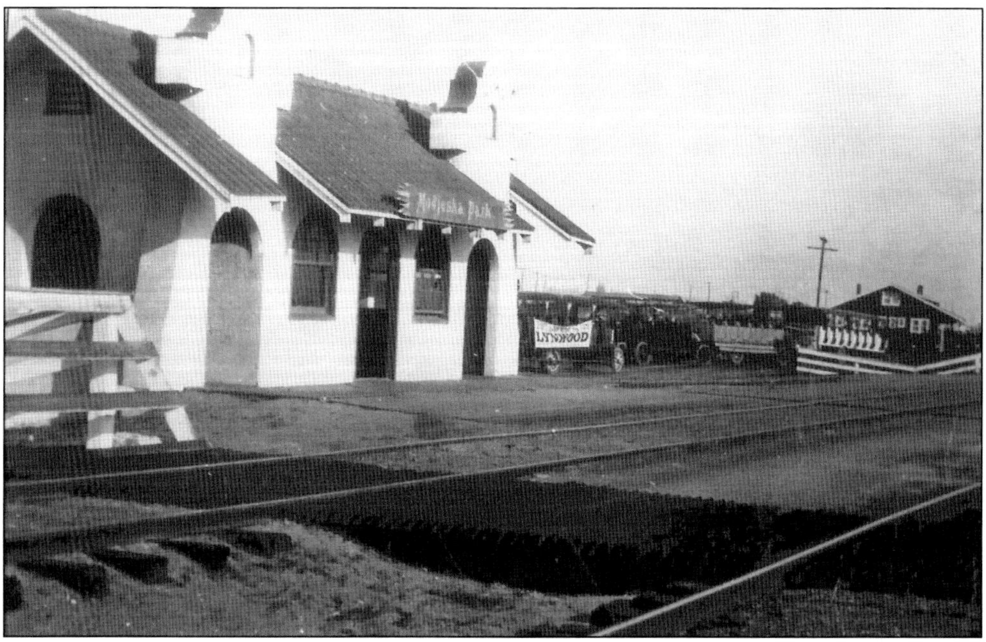

In 1905, the Pacific Electric Railway laid tracks connecting Los Angeles and Santa Ana, passing through what is now I-105 and the center of Lynwood. Lynwood's first train depot is pictured at the Modjeska Park Tract, which is now the site of Fernwood Avenue and State Street. The depot brought many visitors to the area but faltered without a right-of-way connection to neighboring cities. The Modjeska Park Tract was named after Shakespearean actress Helena Modjeska, who was very popular in Southern California during the 1880s and 1890s.

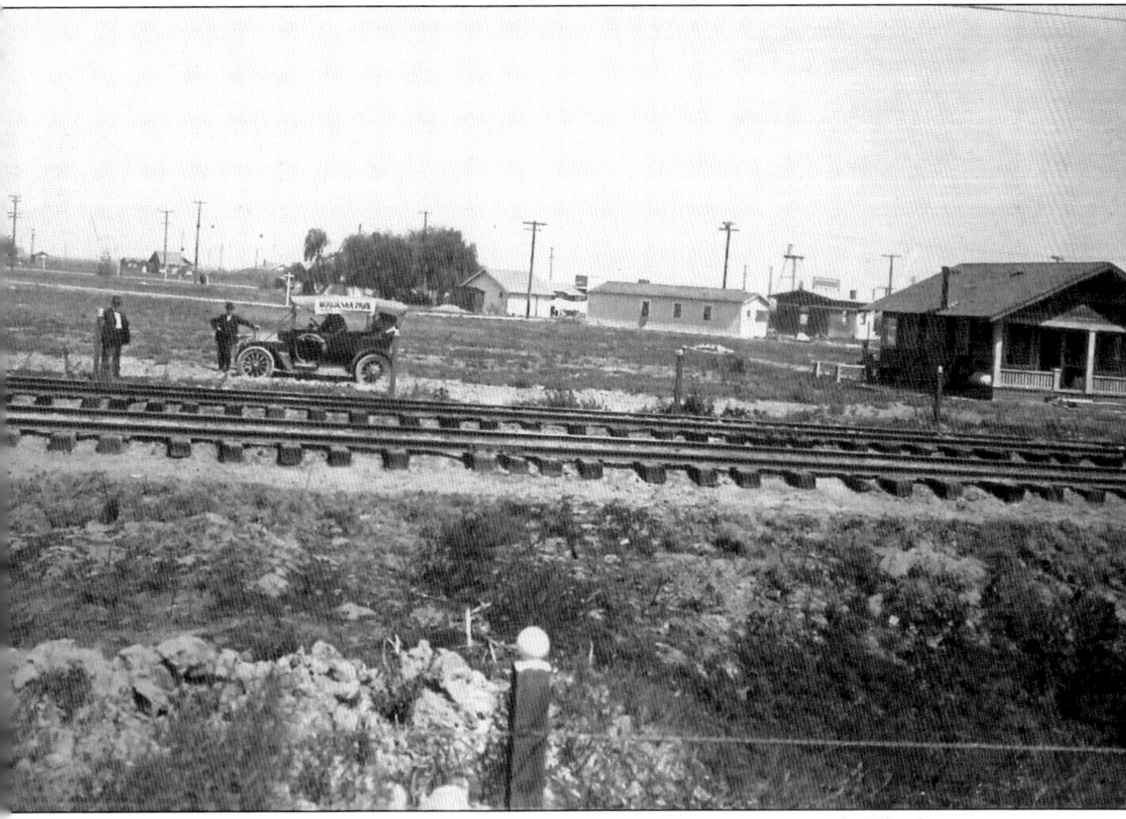

Two onlookers stand next to a 1915 automobile as they survey the train track. The banner on the car advertises "Modjeska Park," no doubt to promote the new subdivision to commuters and others.

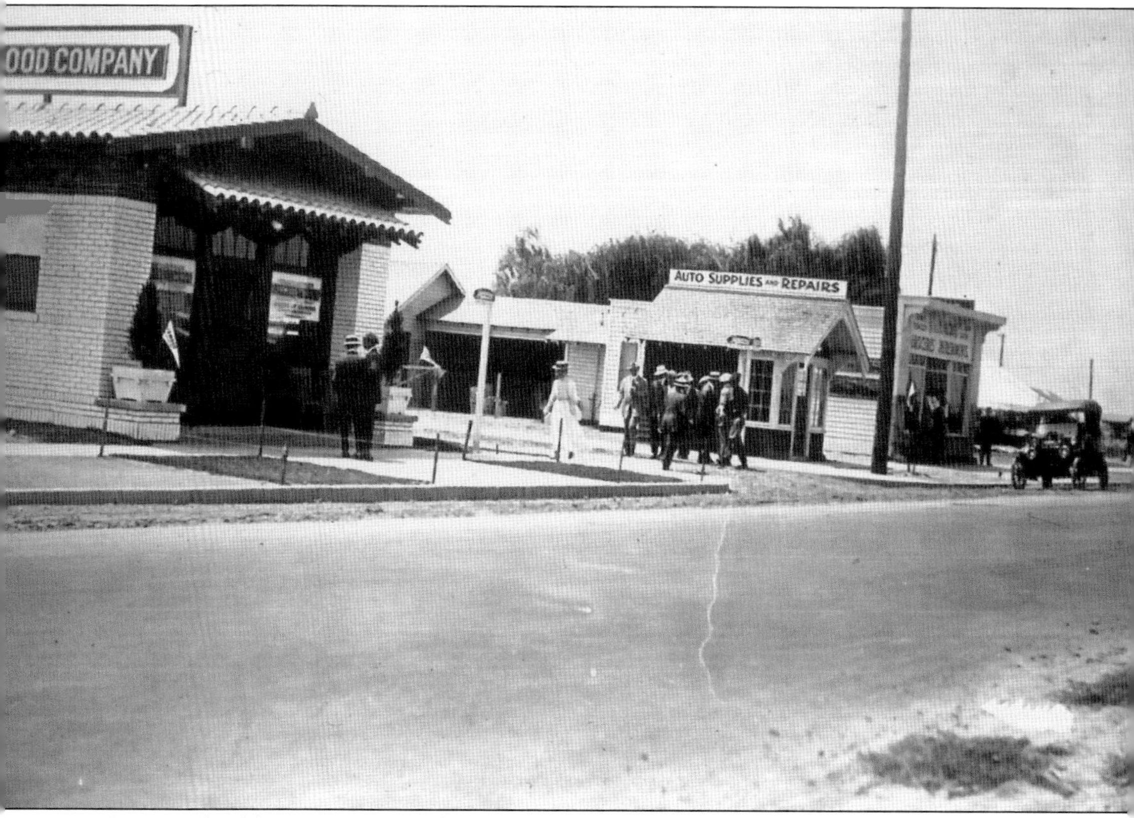

In 1906, land between present-day Long Beach Boulevard and Alameda Street was subdivided within the Modjeska Park Tract. The subdivision failed without a rail connection to adjacent towns. In 1913, it was absorbed into another subdivision developed by the Lynwood Company. From 1913 to 1921, land sales included free water, which became a problem that ultimately led to the incorporation of Lynwood. The Lynwood Company owned the brick structure shown at Mulford Avenue and Long Beach Boulevard; the far-right building was Earl Seeples's first grocery.

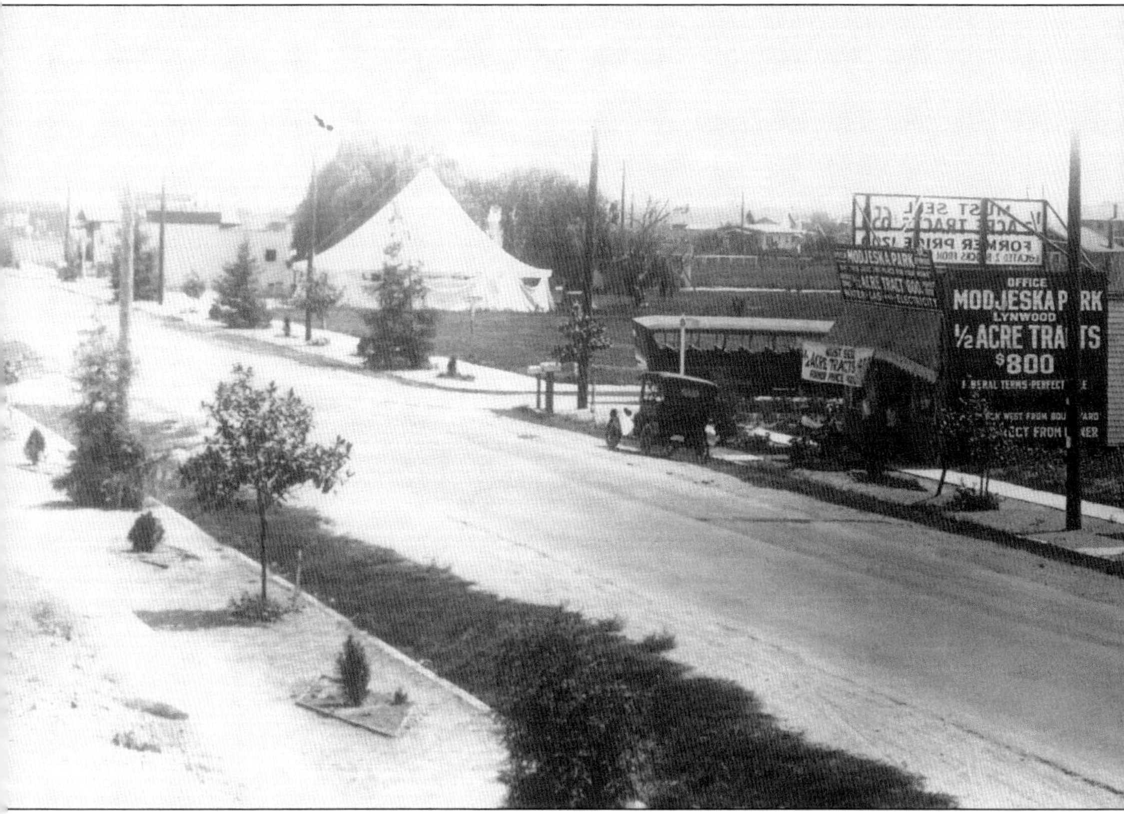

Lynwood Company sales staff served lunch to prospective buyers in the large tent shown. The billboard advertises half-acre tracts for $800. The tent was used to separate legitimate buyers from those more interested in the bus ride and free lunch.

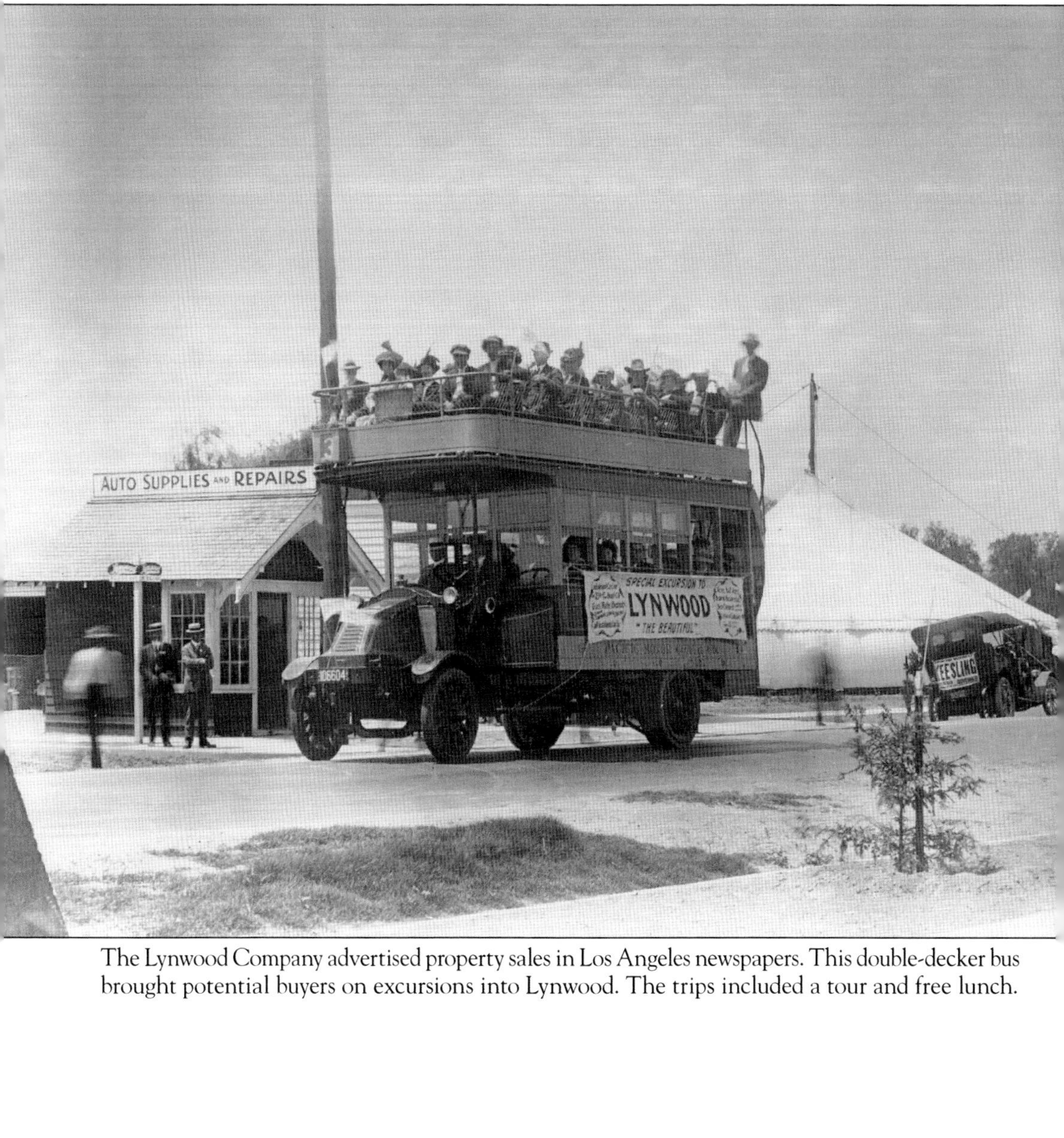

The Lynwood Company advertised property sales in Los Angeles newspapers. This double-decker bus brought potential buyers on excursions into Lynwood. The trips included a tour and free lunch.

Two

BUILDING A CITY

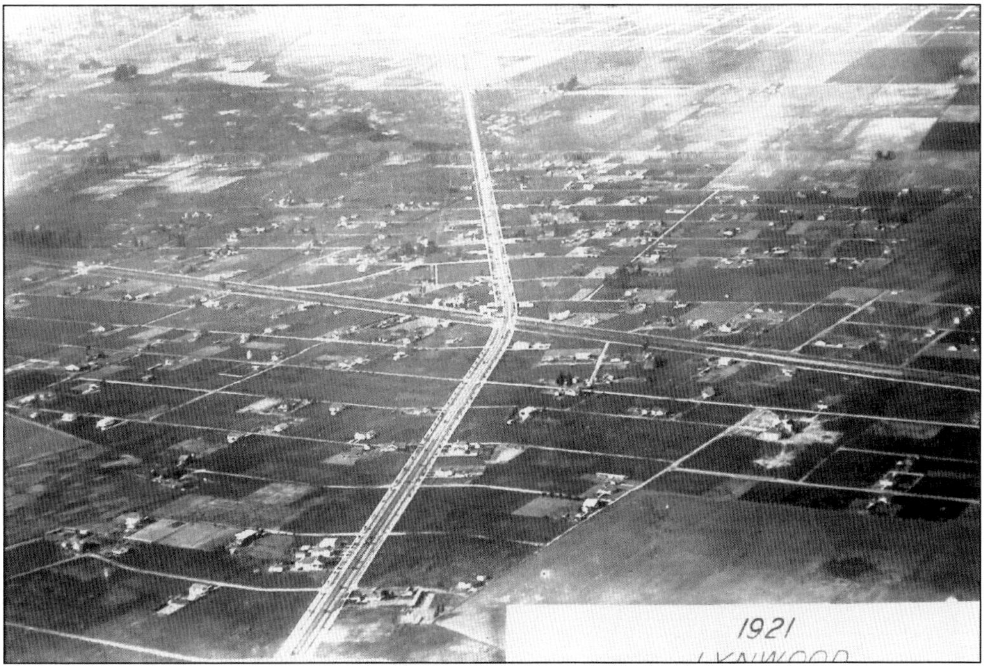

This 1921 aerial view of Lynwood faces north toward Long Beach Boulevard.

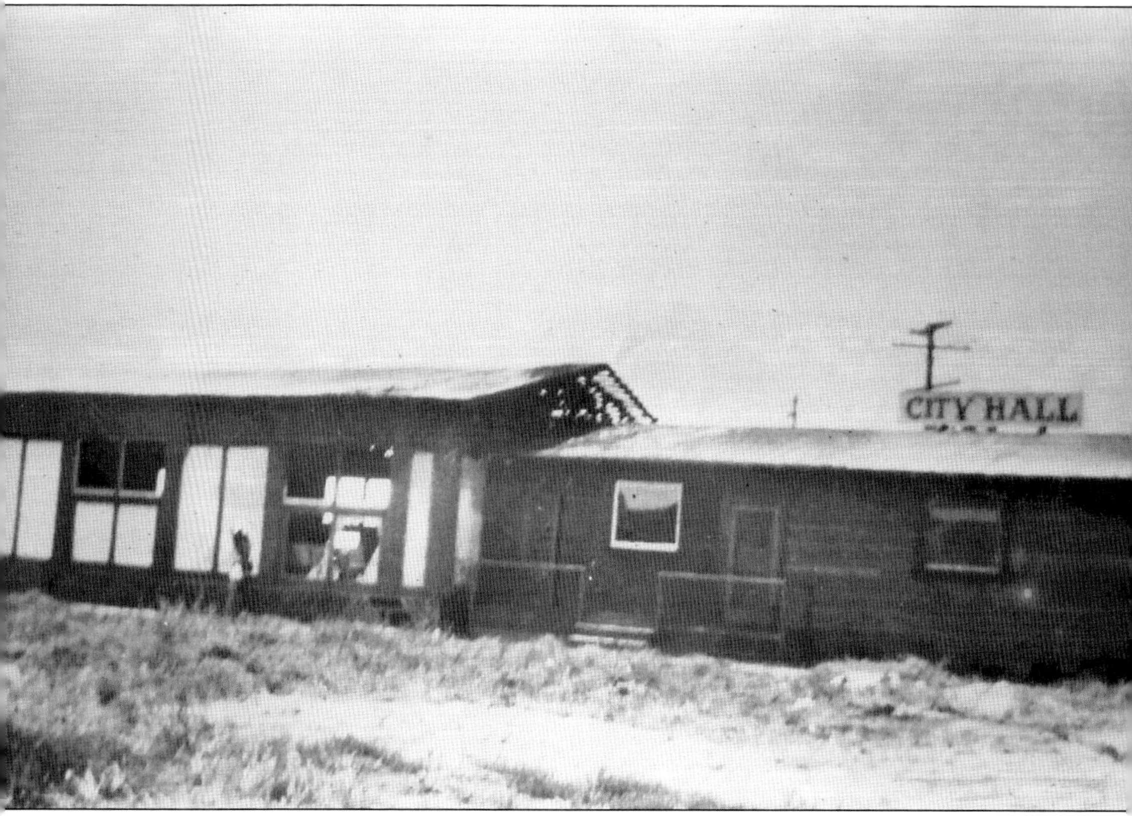

City hall is pictured here after the 1927 fire. The building was located at Plaza and Court Streets. It comprised city administration offices and the fire department. Fire chief C.W. Roberts attributed the fire to defective electrical wiring. City business was conducted from several places until the new building was completed a year after the fire.

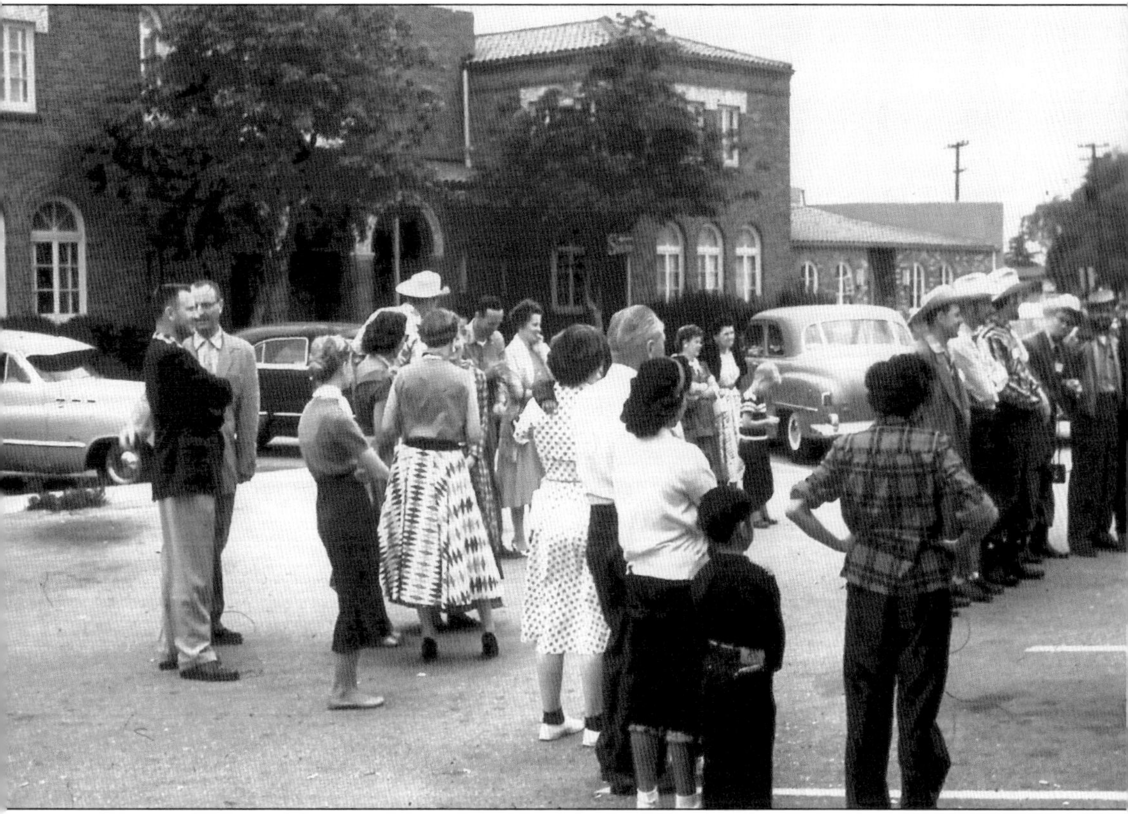

A good crowd turned for the Pioneer Days event, held in the parking lot of the new city hall, shown behind the trees. The 1928, two-story brick building contained all city offices and council chambers until 1956, when city administrators moved to the Bullis Road site. The first court in Lynwood was established in this building in 1930, and C.E. Day was the first judge. The court heard traffic and police cases only, not major criminal offenses.

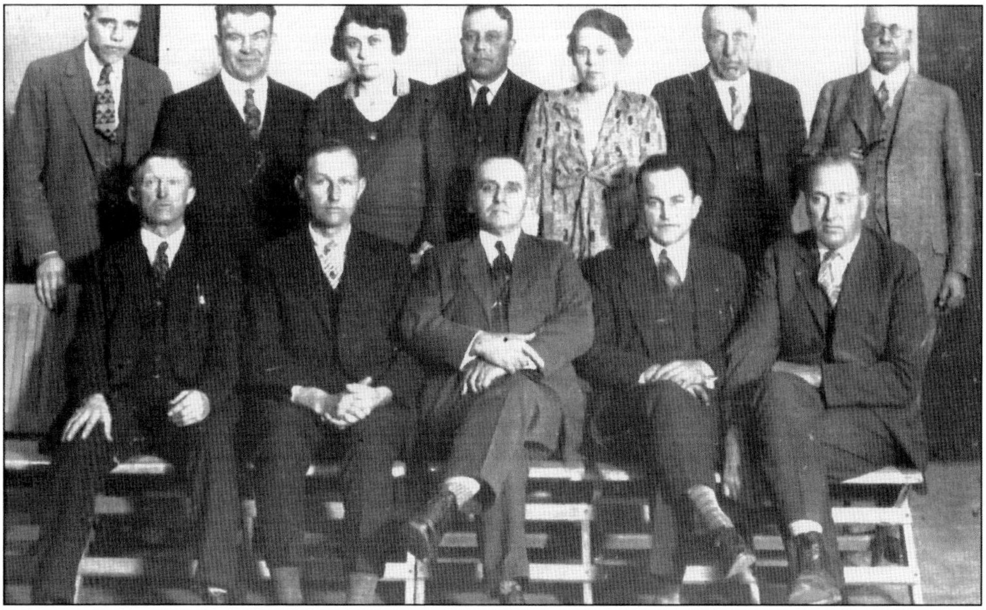

Shown is an early Lynwood City Council. Shown from left to right are (first row) Jackson Tweedy, Al Skelton, George Greenmeyer, Walter Rice, and Herbert Murray; (second row) deputy city clerk Reuben Anderson, city clerk Clarence Stoddard, city treasurer Alice Rutter, city engineer Robert Miller, water clerk Caroline Bryant, building inspector W.J. Beymer, and city attorney C.J. Haynes.

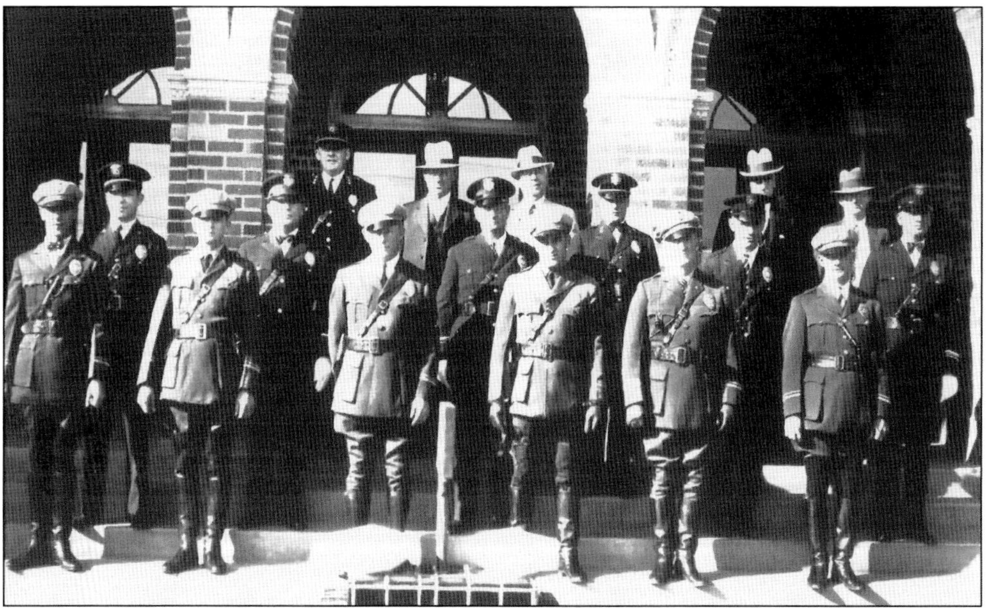

In 1921, Lynwood's closest local law enforcement office was the county sheriff in Compton. Here, from 1930, police, city staff, and elected officials are shown from left to right: (first row) R.J. Richards, C.R. Reed, Nels Anderson, Clair Diedrick, George Marts, and Charles J. Miller; (second row) John Bennett, S.J. Terwilliger, Bob Reynolds, C.R. Crumley, John Toohey, and an unidentified officer; (third row) chief of police Thomas Hogan, councilman Lars Anderson, Judge C.E. Day, councilman Forrest Snodgrass, and councilman Jackson Tweedy.

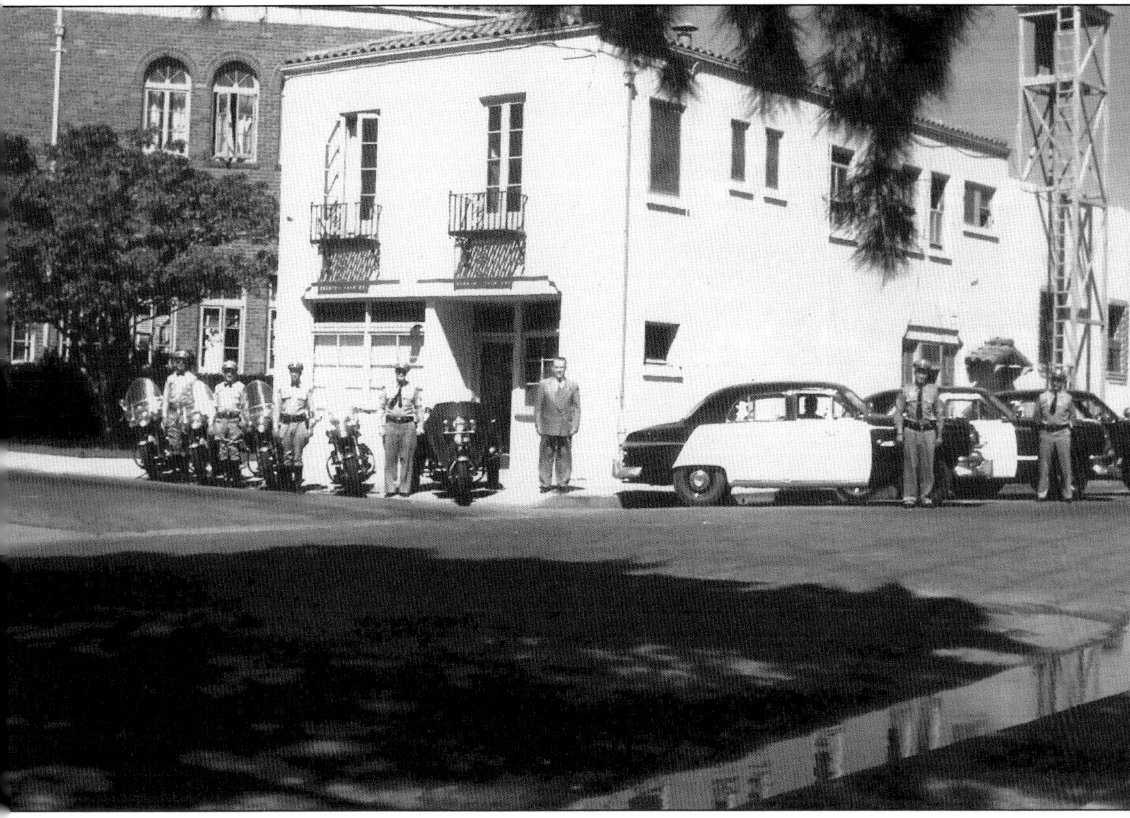

This is a c. 1950 photograph of Lynwood's old police station, which was located on Court Street, at the present-day location of the Plaza Mexico Shopping Center. City hall is visible in the background.

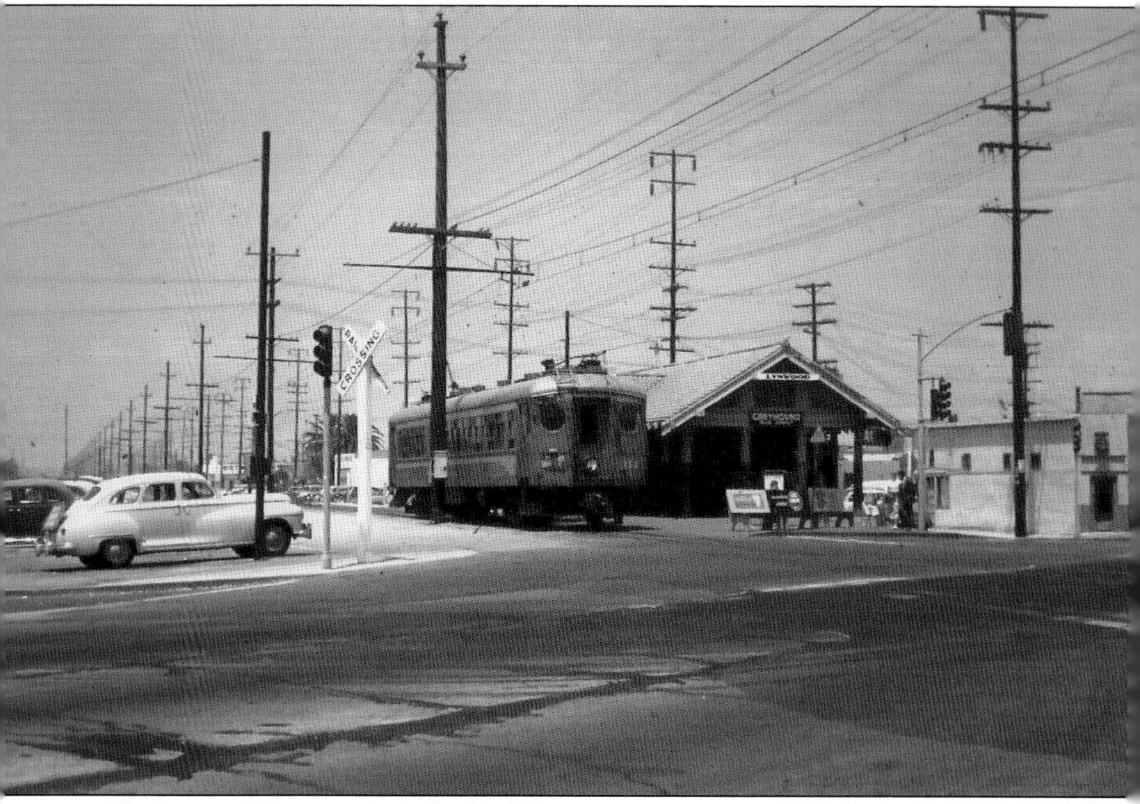

The Lynwood Company built this Red Car passenger station in 1917 for the Southern Pacific Railroad in return for improvements to the intersection by the railroad, which included landfilling, grading, installing drainage culverts, and relocating a new cattle yard. The Lynwood stop was originally a shed-type shelter and bench, adjacent to sugar beet fields. The Lynwood depot is the only remaining Red Car station, and it is in the National Register of Historic Places. The building now sits inside Lynwood City Park on Martin Luther King Jr. Boulevard and Bullis Road. The depot was recently refurbished and now home to the Greater Lynwood Chamber of Commerce.

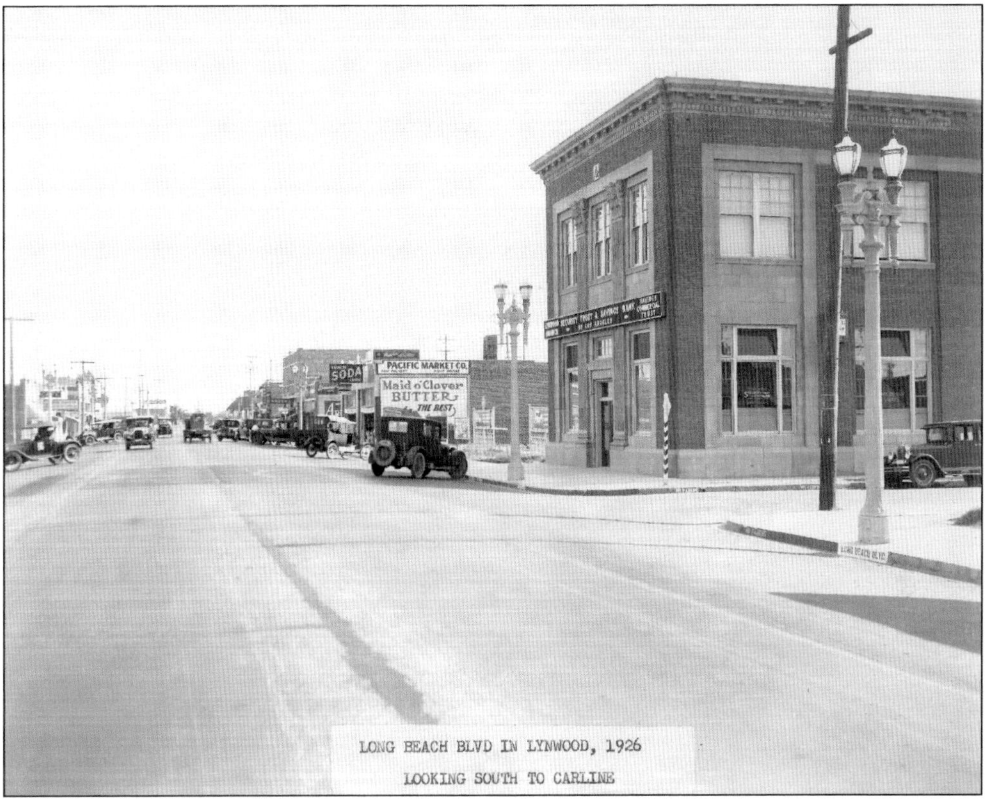

This 1926 photograph shows Long Beach Boulevard facing south toward Fernwood Avenue. The scene reveals extensive development downtown. The large, masonry two-story building on the right is Lynwood Branch Security and Savings Bank, the first bank to serve Lynwood.

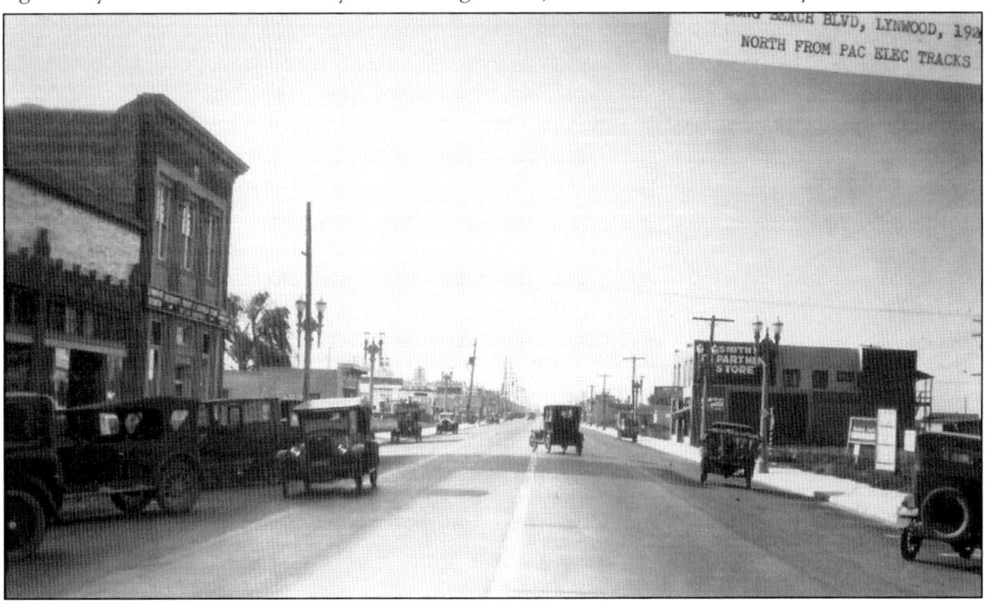

This undated northward view shows Long Beach Boulevard as seen from the Fernwood Avenue train depot.

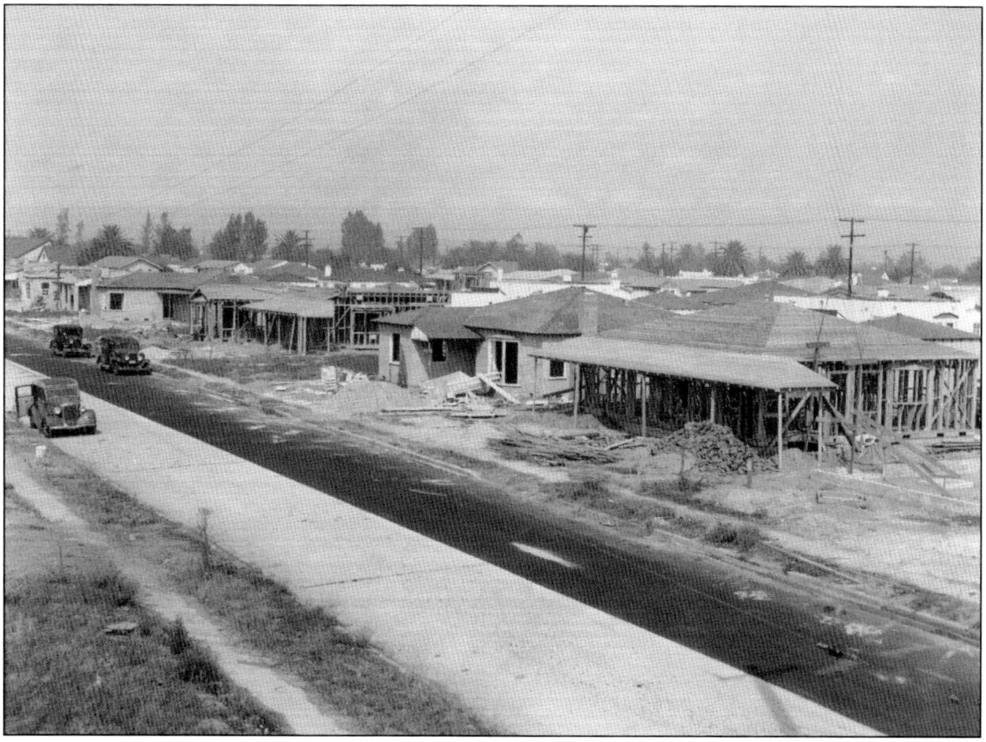

This photograph shows a new tract of homes being built in the early 1940s. The site is believed to be northwest Lynwood.

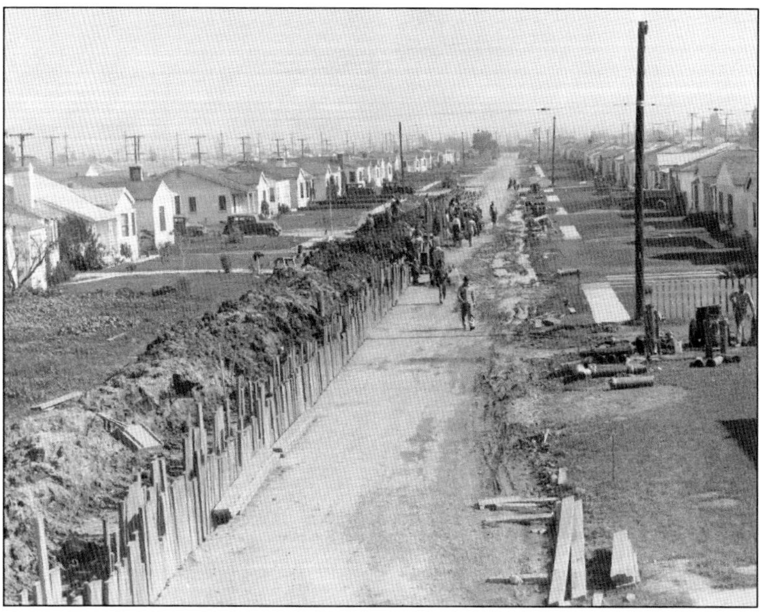

When Lynwood incorporated in 1921, there were no sewers. As homes developed, cesspools or septic tanks were used to dispose of waste. In 1923, the Los Angeles County Sanitation District was formed, with work to begin on the sewer system. Pictured here is a crew of workers installing the sewer lines under a Lynwood street in the mid-1930s.

Contractors are installing a sewer-line system in Lynwood in the mid-1930s.

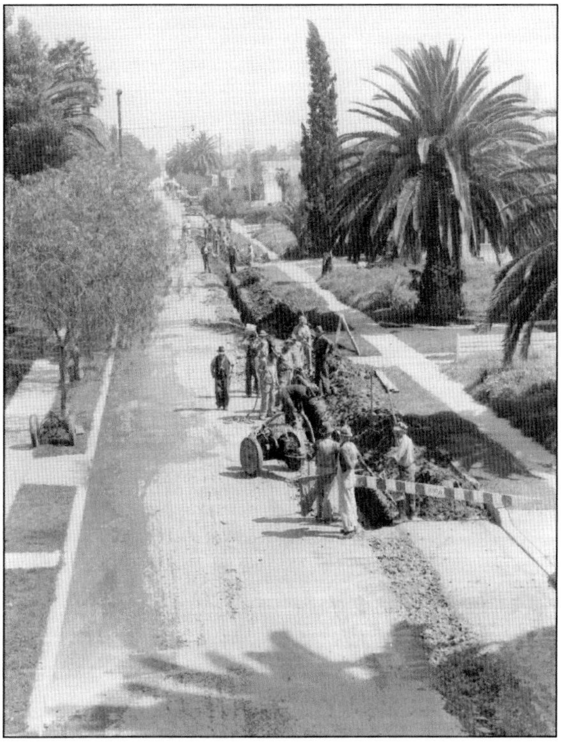

An unidentified street in Lynwood is shown in the mid-1930s during the installation of the sewer system.

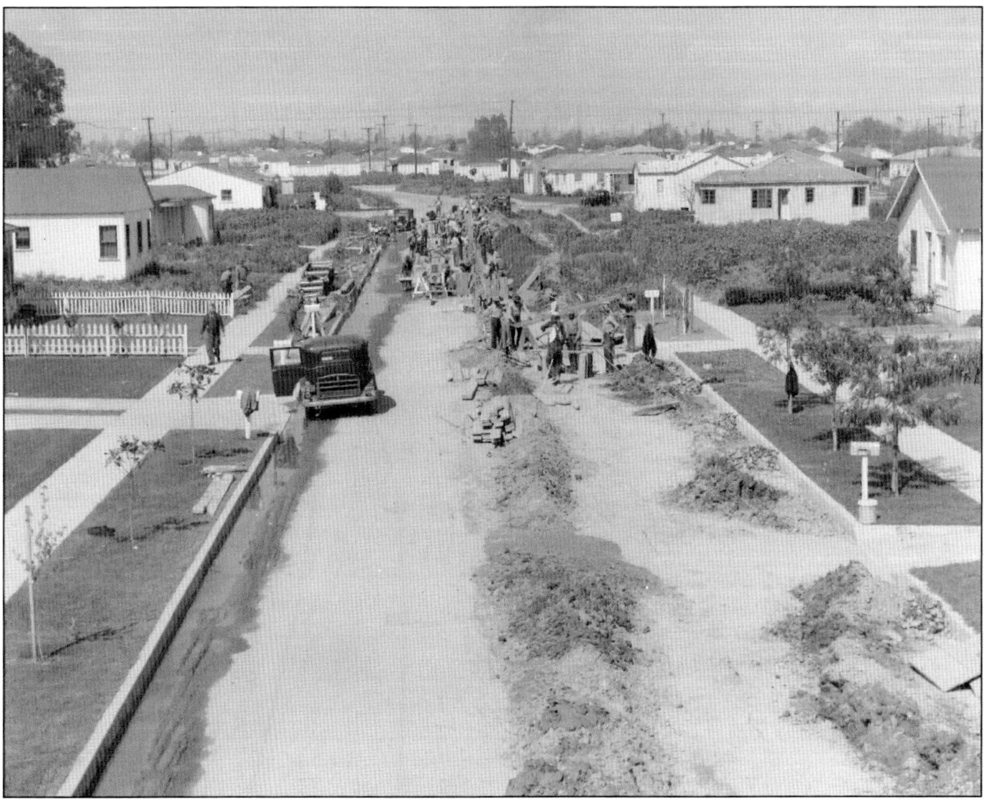

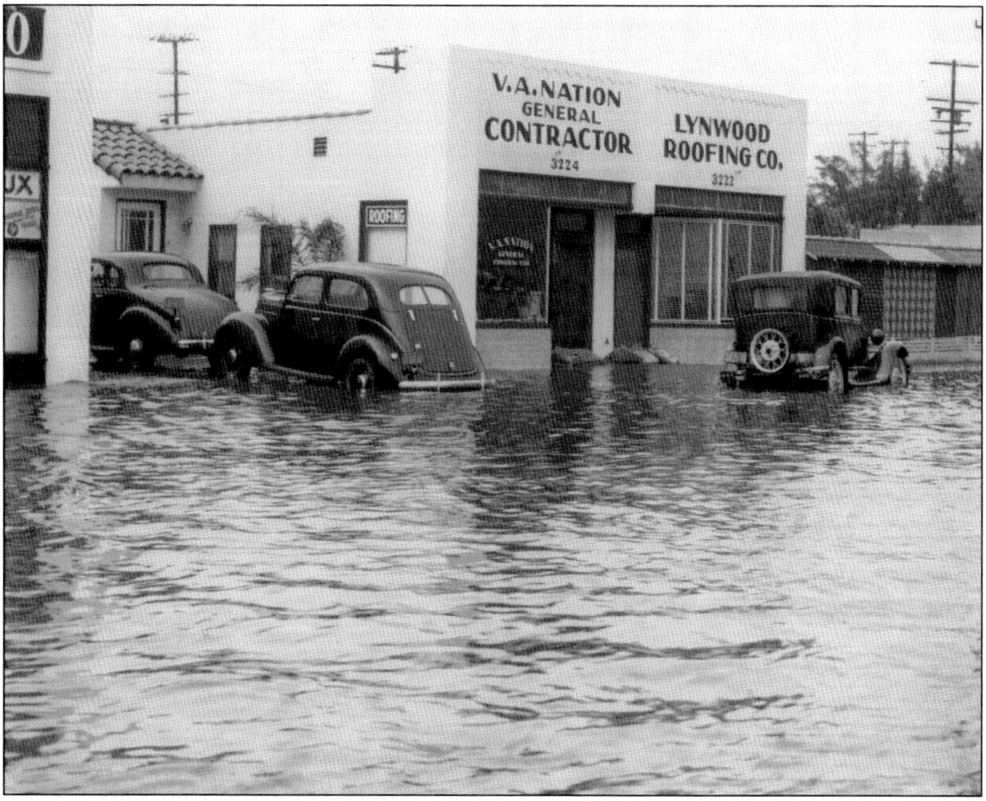

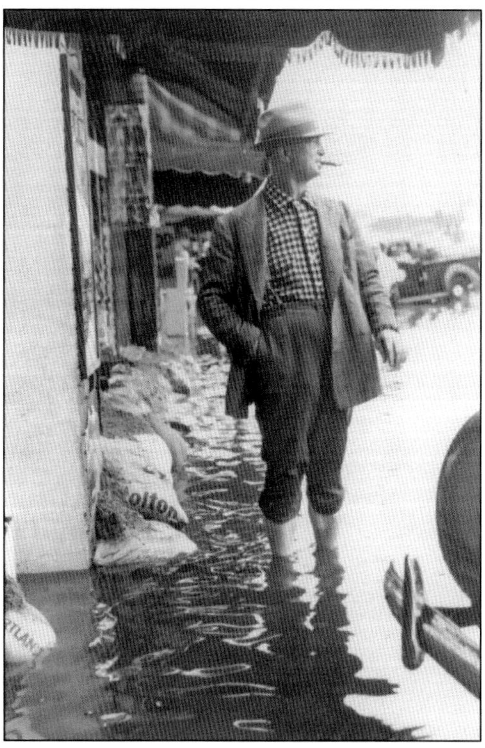

Floodwaters swamp V.A. Nation office and Lynwood Roofing on Imperial Highway east of Long Beach Boulevard in 1934. Long Beach Boulevard businesses were plagued by recurring floods. One source was the high grade of the rail bed in the middle of the road. Business doorways were much lower, so water pooled along the buildings and doors. The other floodwater came from pools that formed around Peach Street to the railroad. From there, water flowed eastward, straight down to Fernwood Avenue and Long Beach Boulevard.

City attorney Charles Ruby stands ankle-deep in water outside his office door on Long Beach Boulevard, enjoying a cigar.

Ed Fisherman takes a shoveling break and smiles after this mid-1930 flood on Long Beach Boulevard.

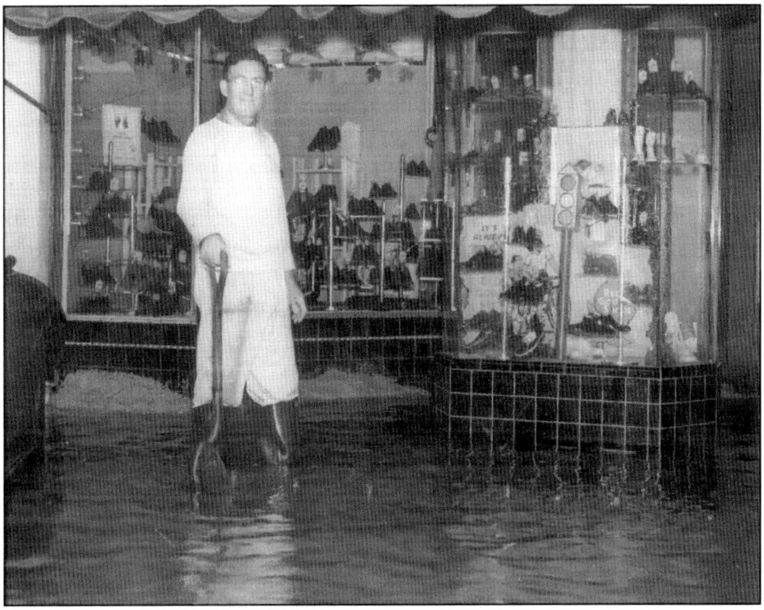

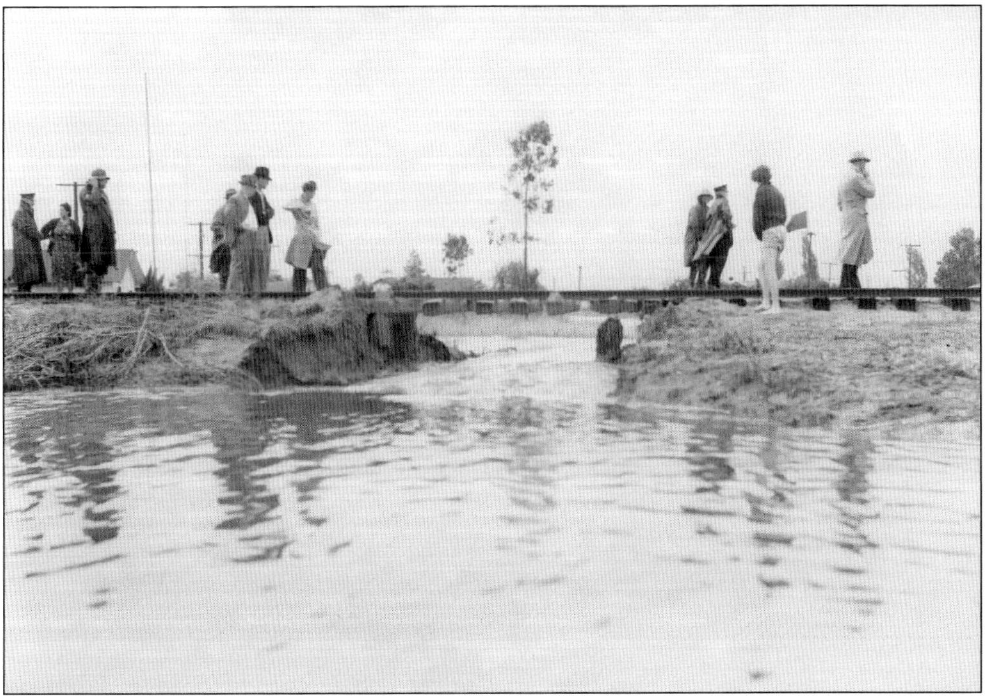

The business merchants on Long Beach Boulevard petitioned the city engineer for a solution to the drainage issue created by the train bed. In the late 1930s, the city was granted permission from Pacific Electric Railway to construct culverts beneath the tracks at Peach Street and California Avenue, but culverts did not solve the problem entirely. Water no longer flowed to Long Beach Boulevard but, instead, flooded homes along Peach Street. By 1936, floodwaters had evolved into one of Lynwood's most contentious problems. After a study by Los Angeles County Flood Control officials, the Los Angeles River bed was lined with concrete and a new railroad bridge was implemented.

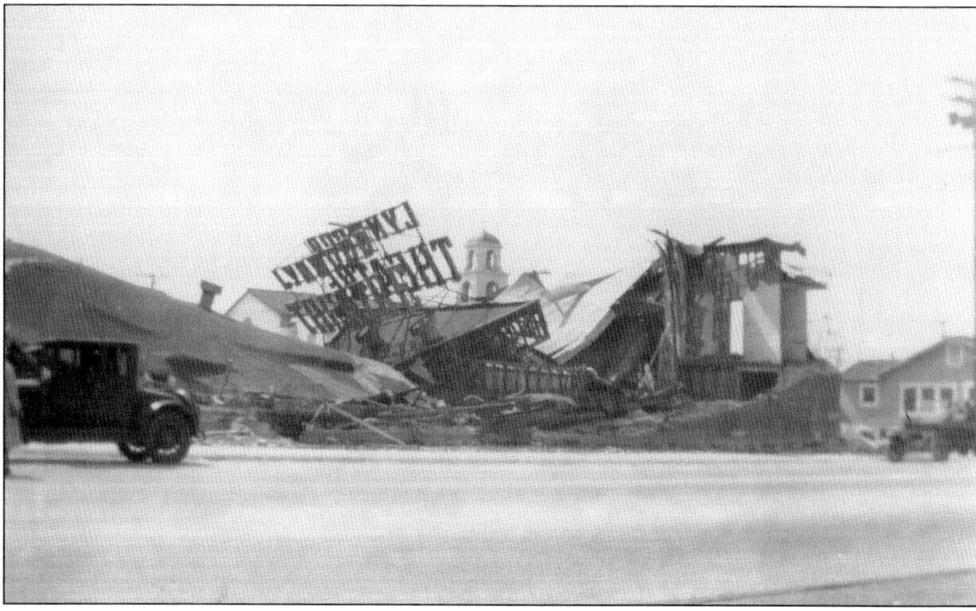

The Lynwood Theater, located on the corner of Imperial Highway and Long Beach Boulevard, was among the structures leveled by the 1933 earthquake. The earthquake eliminated all doubt regarding the need for earthquake-resistant structures in California.

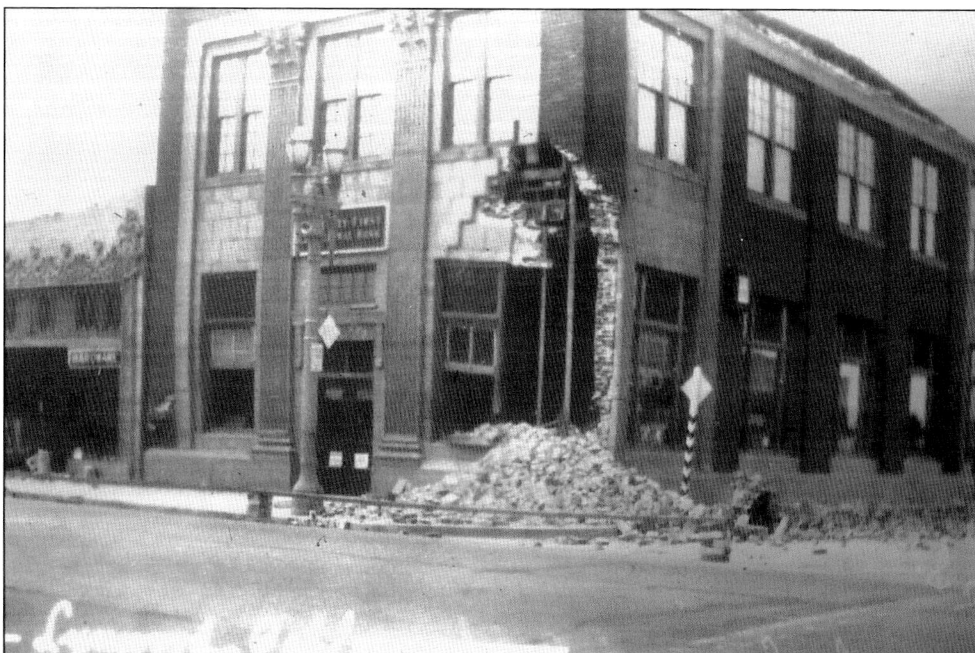

The 1933 earthquake lasted for 15 seconds, but scores of unreinforced masonry buildings collapsed in that short time. This disaster led to changes in California's building codes. The Lynwood Security First National Bank on the corner of Mulford Avenue and Long Beach Boulevard is pictured after the earthquake.

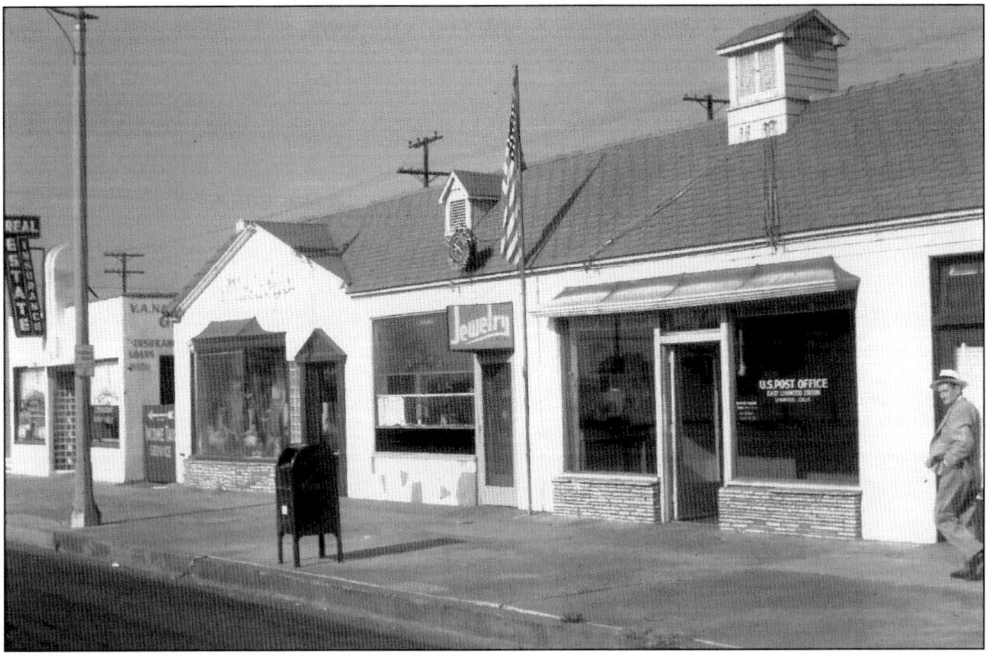

In July 1938, this post office substation on Atlantic Avenue operated window-service only since no home mail delivery service was available to the eastern part of town. Residents had to go to the post office to get their mail. By 1965, a new post office was built at the present site on Atlantic Avenue. Charles Parker was the postmaster at the time. He had lived in the area for 33 years.

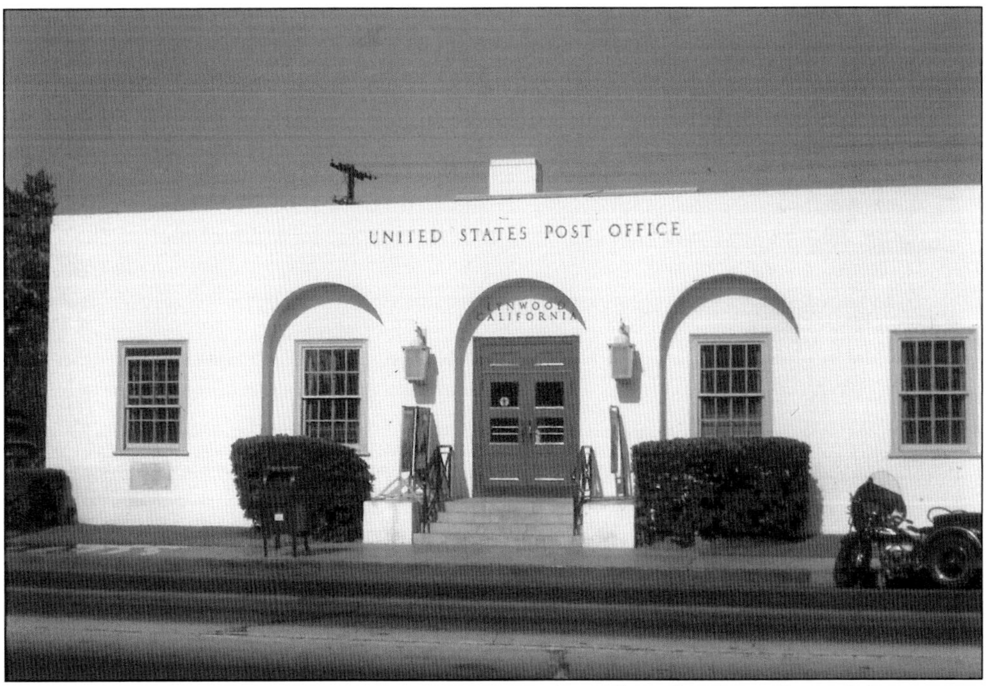

The Lynwood post office on the corner of Long Beach Boulevard and Beechwood Avenue was the first federal building in Lynwood, opening on July 1, 1940. It cost $75,000 and is still in use today. The entrance has been modified slightly.

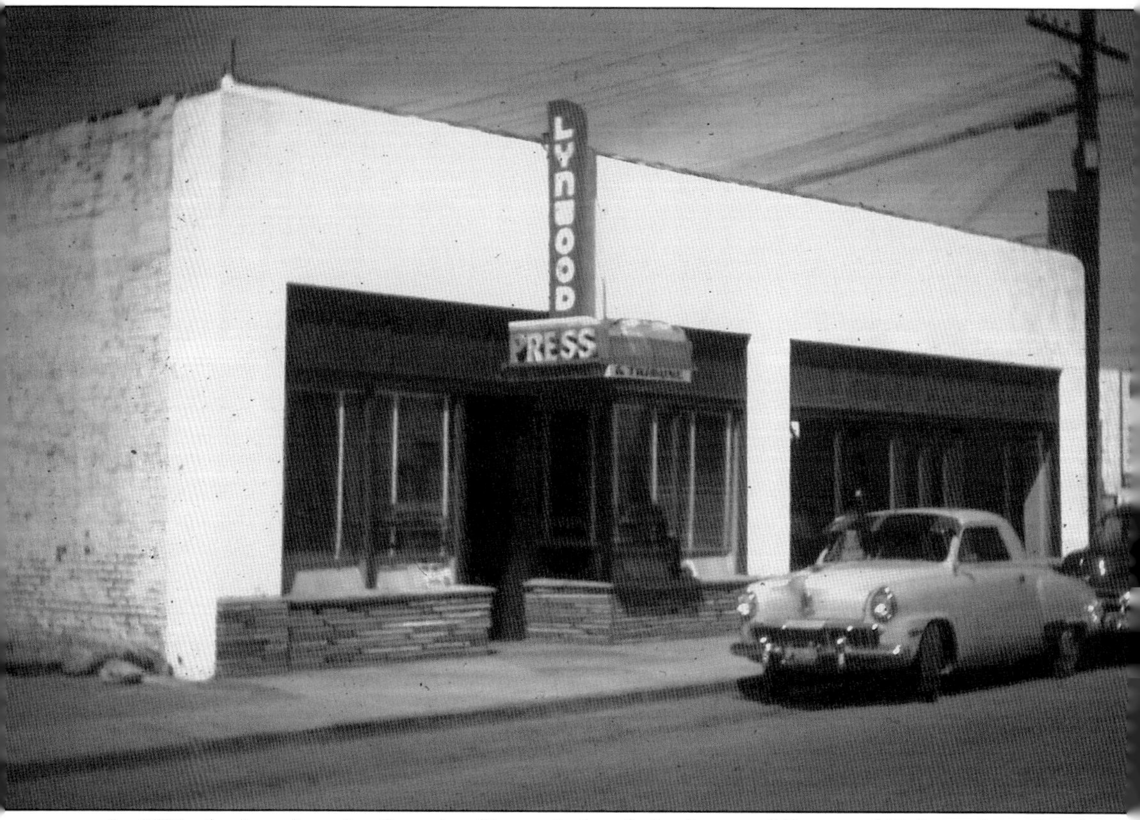

In 1931, the Los Angeles Superior Court declared the *Lynwood Press and Tribune* the official publication of Lynwood. The newspaper office pictured here was on Mulford Avenue just across from the old city hall on Plaza Street. The publication was originally named the *Lynwood Tribune,* when owned by "Pop" Whitaker, who was also editor and publisher of the newspaper.

It became very popular to sell and buy war bonds during World War II. The Lynwood Victory House stood on Mulford Avenue on a vacant corner lot. City officials and Victory House committee members were on site for the grand opening on April 16, 1943.

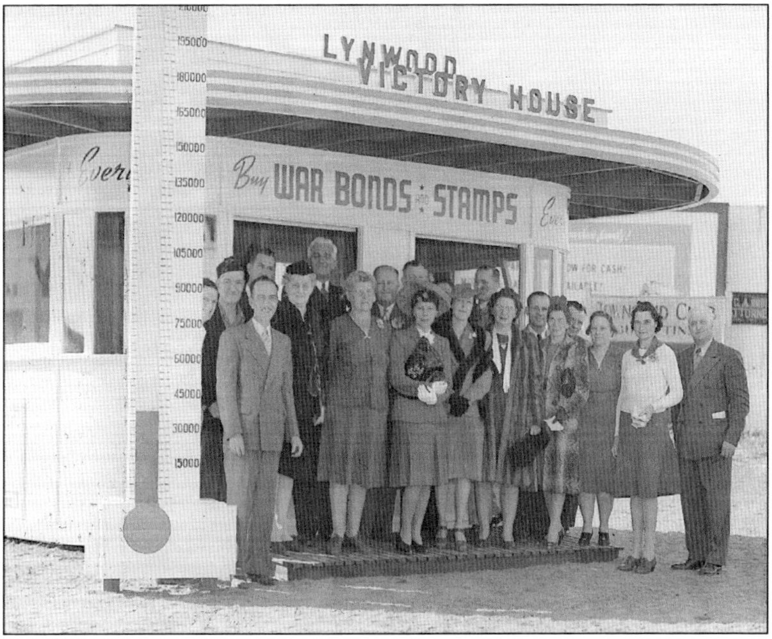

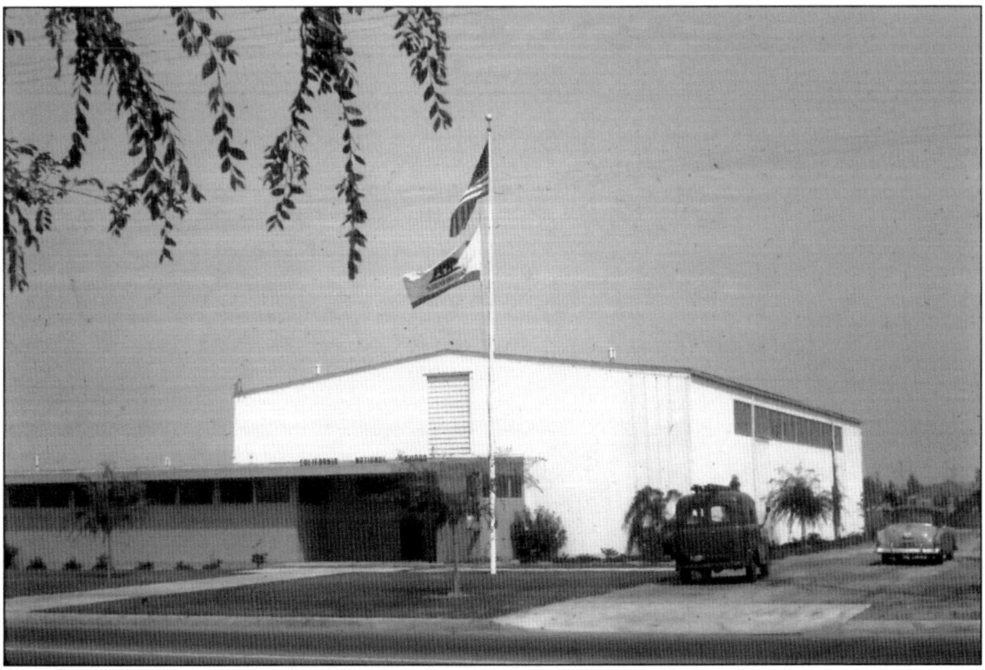

This photograph shows the old National Guard building located on Bullis Road, constructed in the 1940s. The building is no longer occupied.

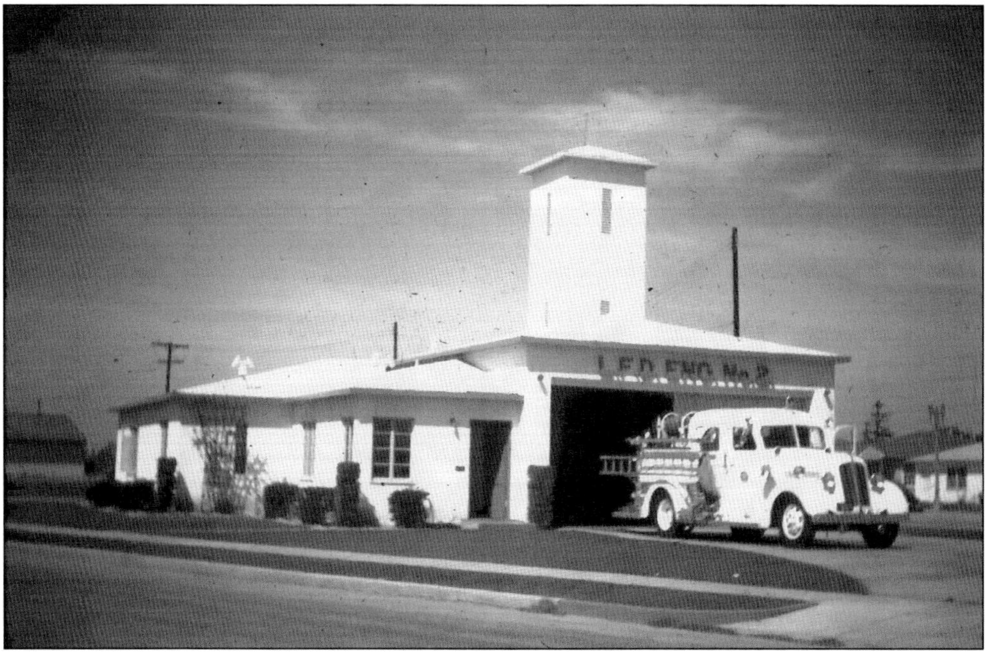

The first firehouse was built on the west end of the old city hall building on Mulford Avenue. Fire Station No. 2, on Martin Luther King Jr. Boulevard, was constructed in 1948. The fire truck shown here was purchased in 1948. Firemen at the time were delighted with the new model, which was better equipped and pumped water faster than the old truck.

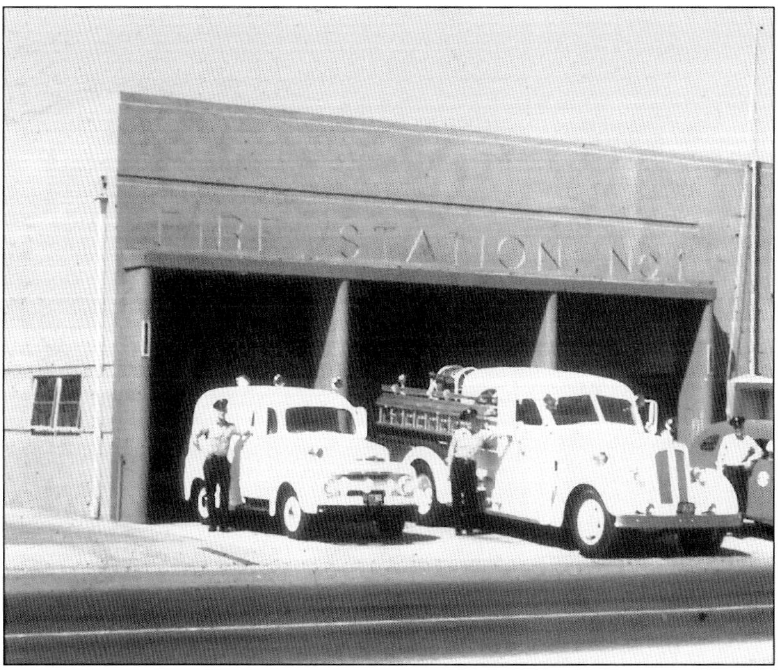

Pictured here in the 1940s is Lynwood Fire Station No. 1, located on Imperial Highway. The fire truck and ambulance are showcased, and the station is still in use today.

Three

Industry and Civic Development

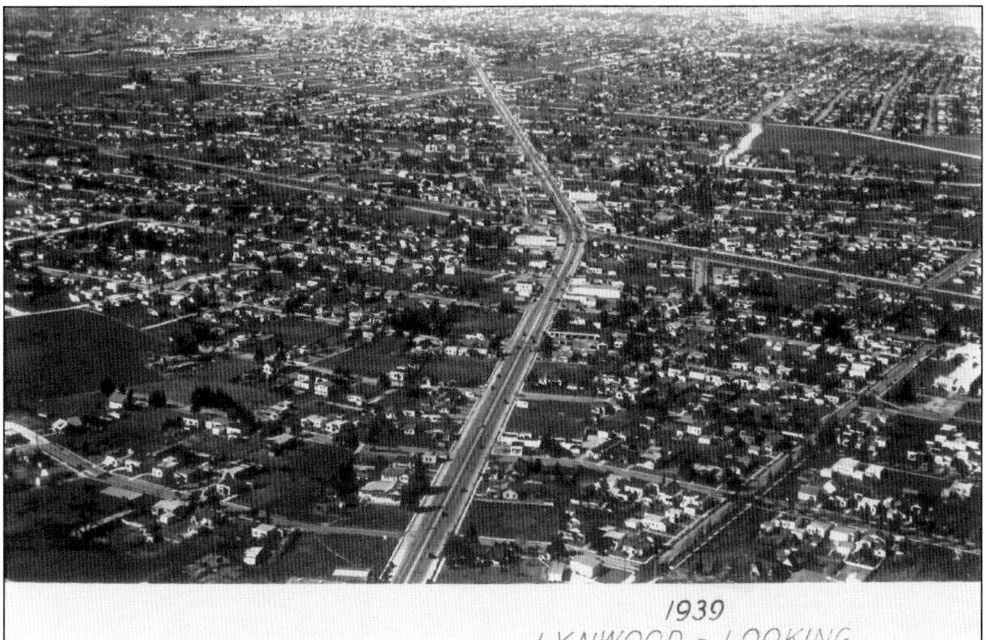

This 1939 aerial photograph of Lynwood faces north.

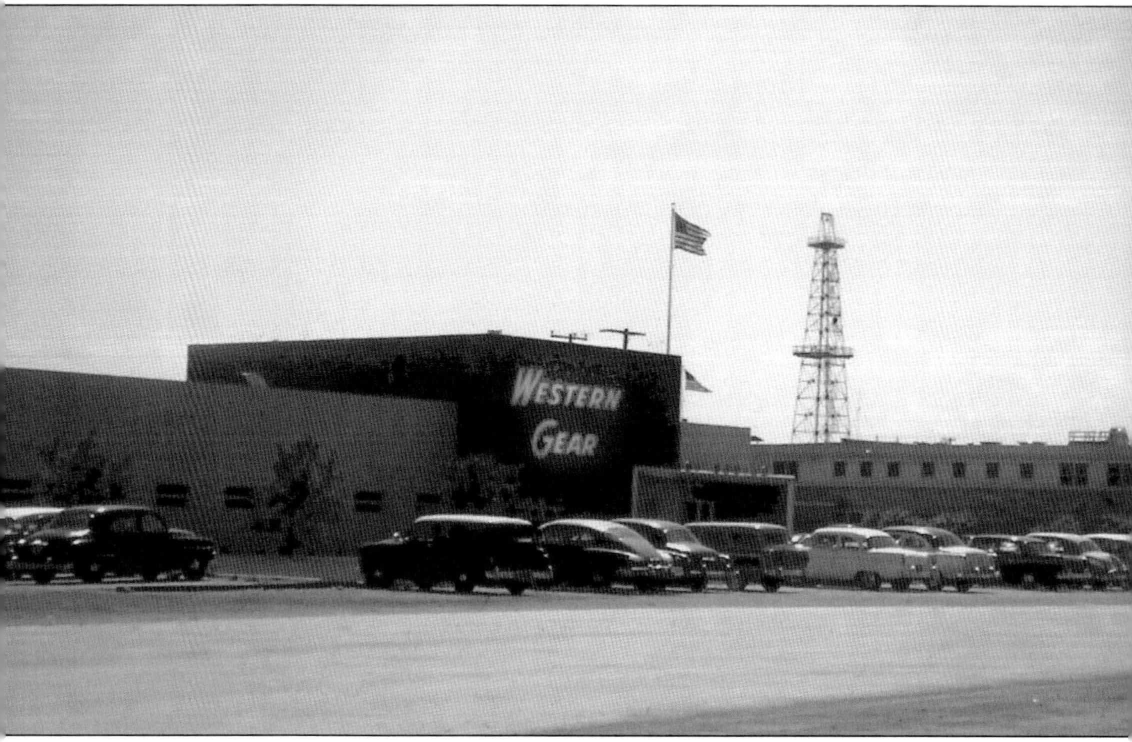

In 1941, Western Gear Works built a large manufacturing plant on the site originally owned by the Dolf family, who ran a sizeable dairy on the corner of Imperial Highway and Alameda Street. The name Western Gear Works was formally changed to Western Gear Corporation in 1955. The new plant pictured here became one of the largest firms in the Los Angeles area, and over the years the firm expanded to cover five main areas of industry: marine, aerospace, engineered construction, airport systems, and industrial. Western Gear Corporation was known for producing gears and other products for the US military during World War II. By 1971, the company served a variety of industries, employing nearly 900 people and occupying approximately 21 acres of property.

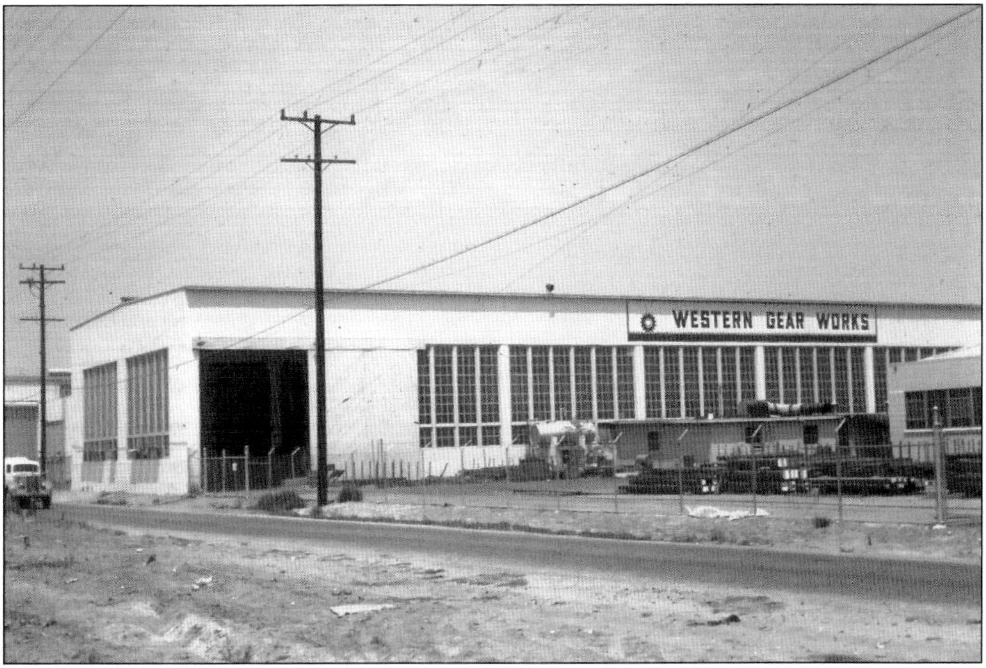

Pictured here in the 1940s is another view of Western Gear Works, later renamed Western Gear Corporation. One of the first original buildings to be constructed in the 1940s, it still remains standing on the same site on Alameda Street.

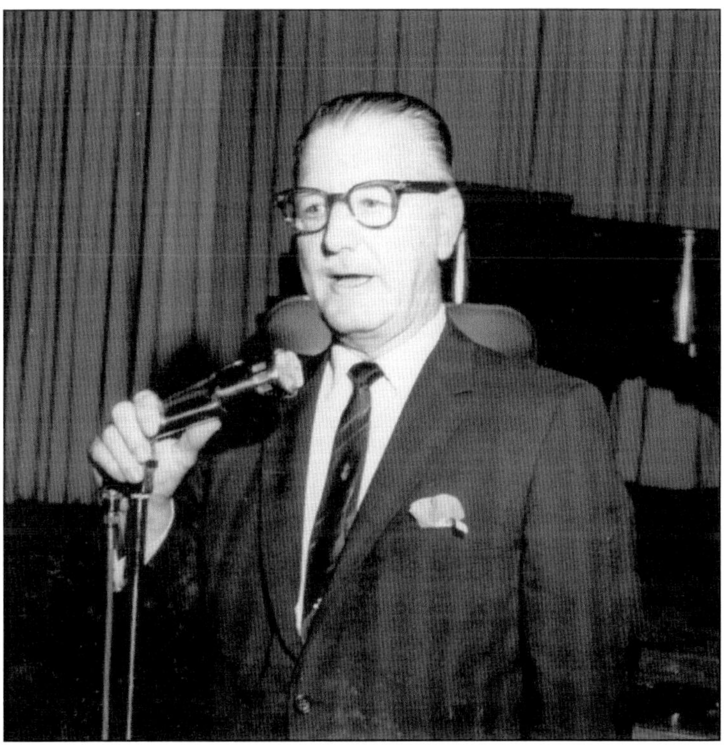

Joseph McMillan was a member of the Lynwood City Council and was mayor in the mid-1960s. He was also the public relations director for Robertshaw Controls.

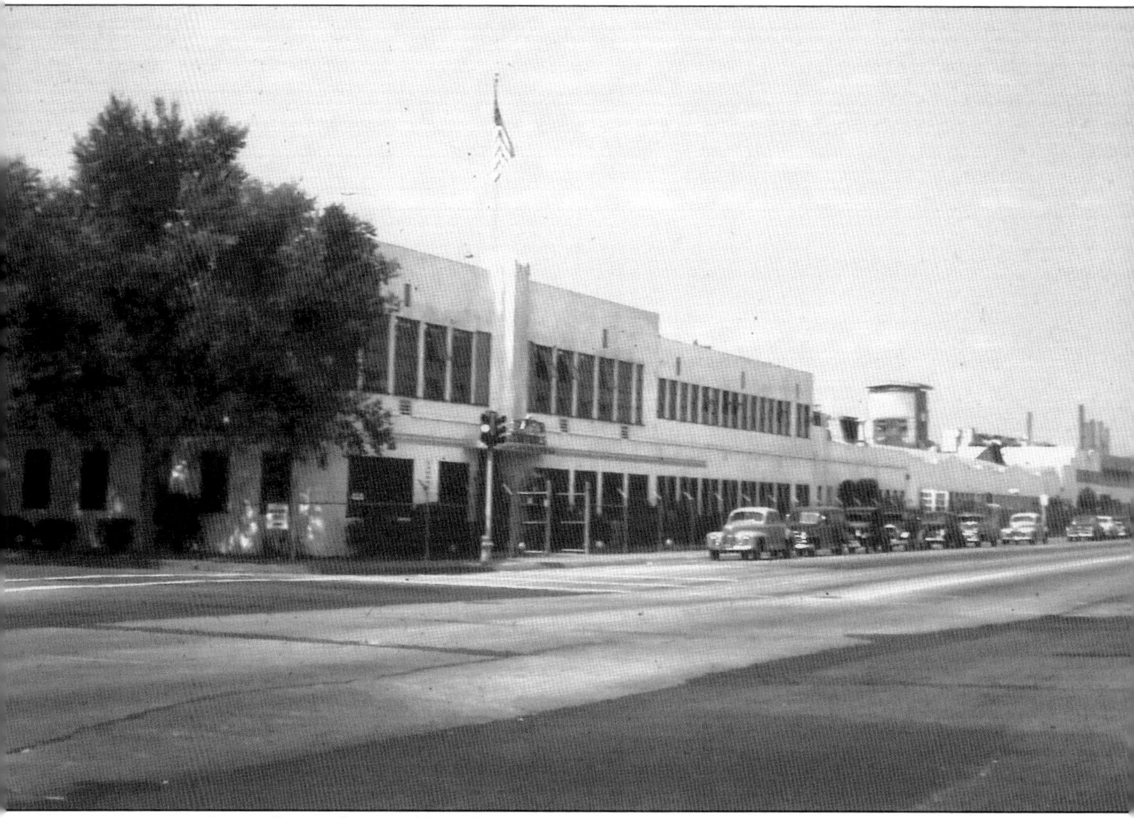

Grayson Controls was founded by John H. Grayson in 1927, when he invented a thermostatic heat control for gas heaters. Grayson first made the controls at home in his garage on Cornish Avenue. He received so many orders that he needed more space. Photographed here is the building where Grayson relocated in the early 1950s. The large building was diagonal, and it extended across the street to the southwest corner on Imperial Highway and State Street. By 1955, the company moved again, and other large companies occupied the site until 2000, when the building was demolished. Currently, the site is used for parking.

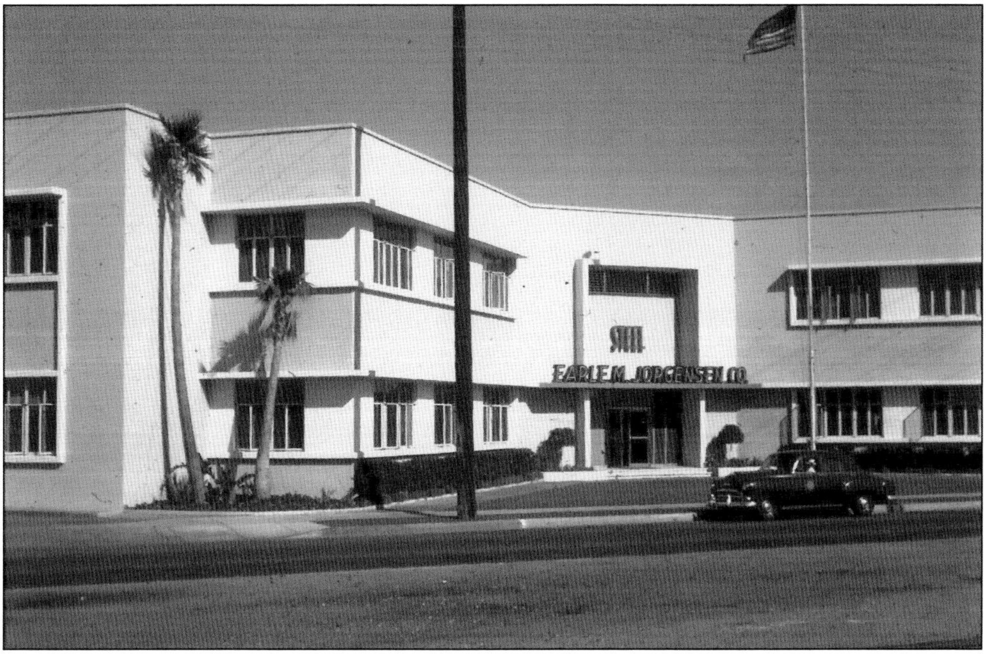

Jorgensen Steel Company provided crucial jobs in Lynwood's early growth period and is an important community fixture to this day.

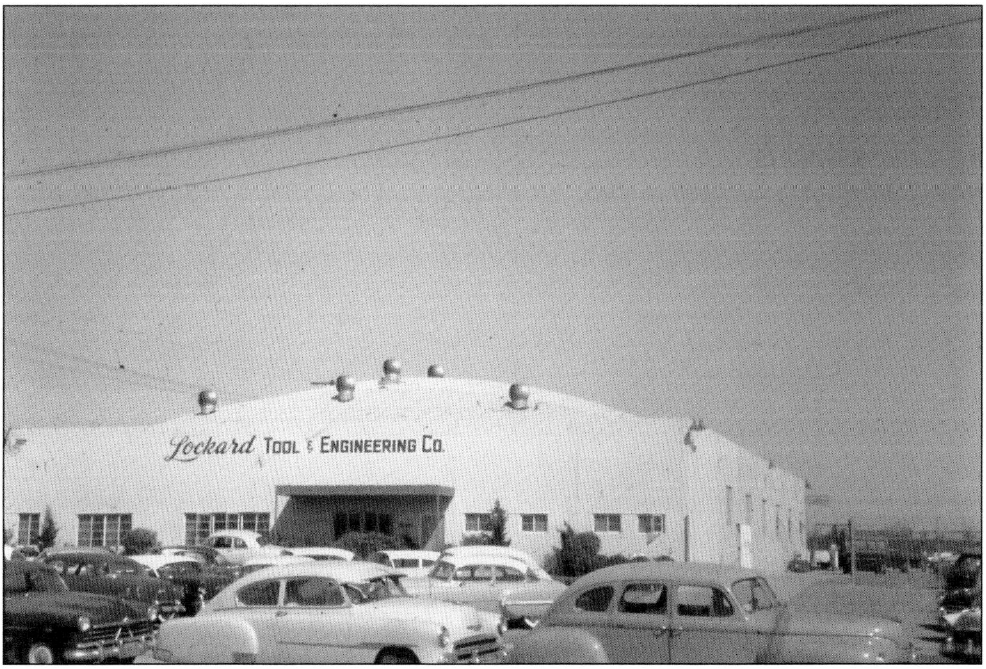

Lockard Tool and Engineering Company was one of the many companies located in the industrial area along Wright Road.

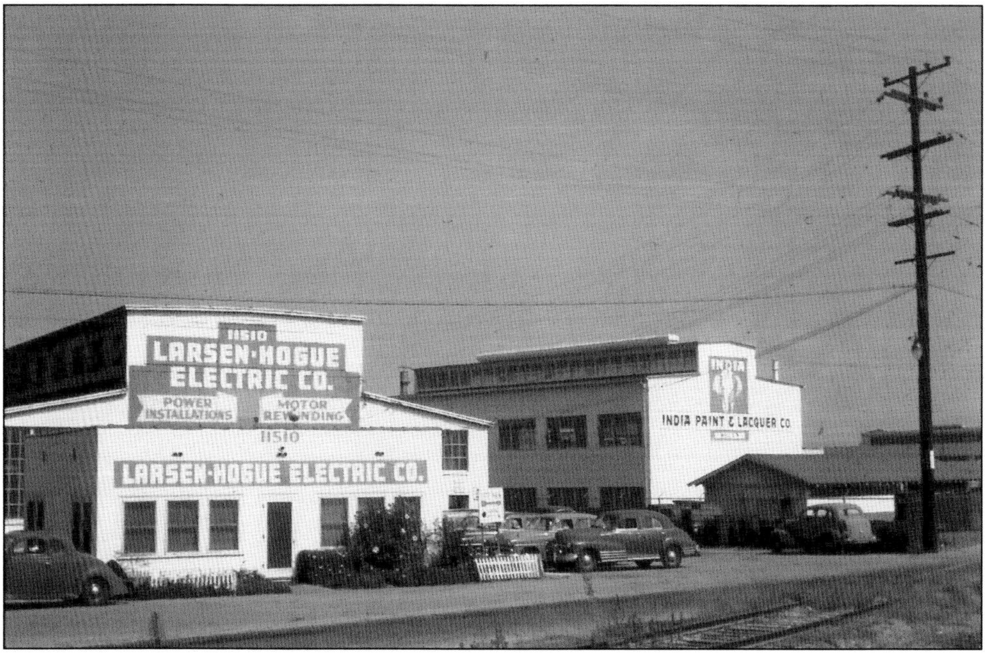

The Larsen-Hogue Electric Company and India Paint and Lacquer Company were part of the industrial community located in Lynwood in the 1940s. A new stucco structure replaced the Larsen-Hogue Electric Company, and the India Paint and Lacquer Company building is still in use, now by Legends Manufacture. Both buildings remain on the same site at the southeast corner of South Alameda Street and Imperial Highway.

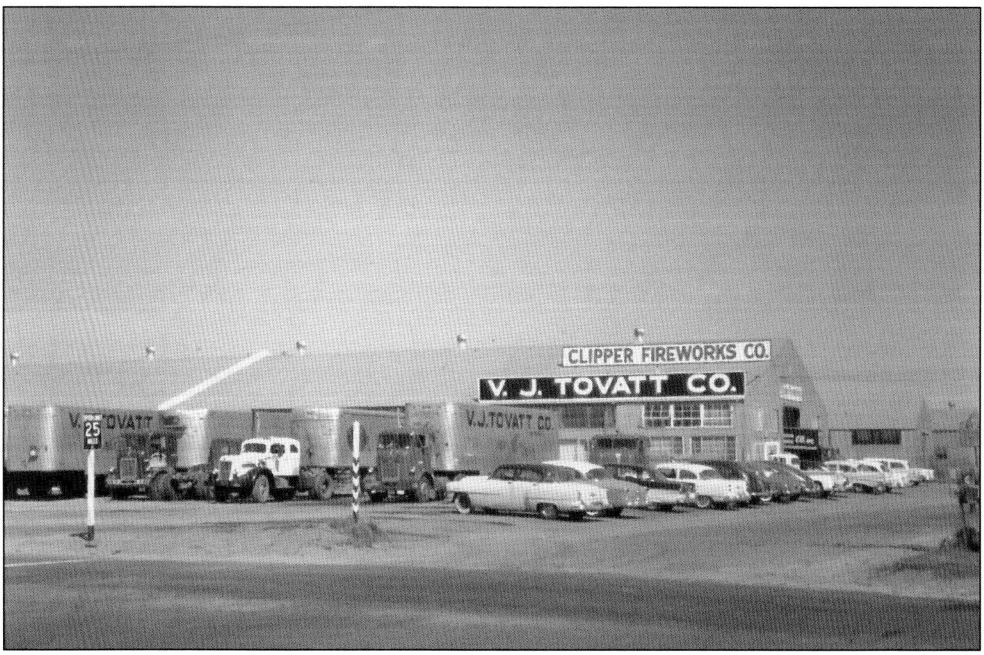

Shown here is the Clipper Fireworks Company, owners of the famous "Block Party" fireworks trademark. The company was located on the corner of Wright Road and Martin Luther King Jr. Boulevard.

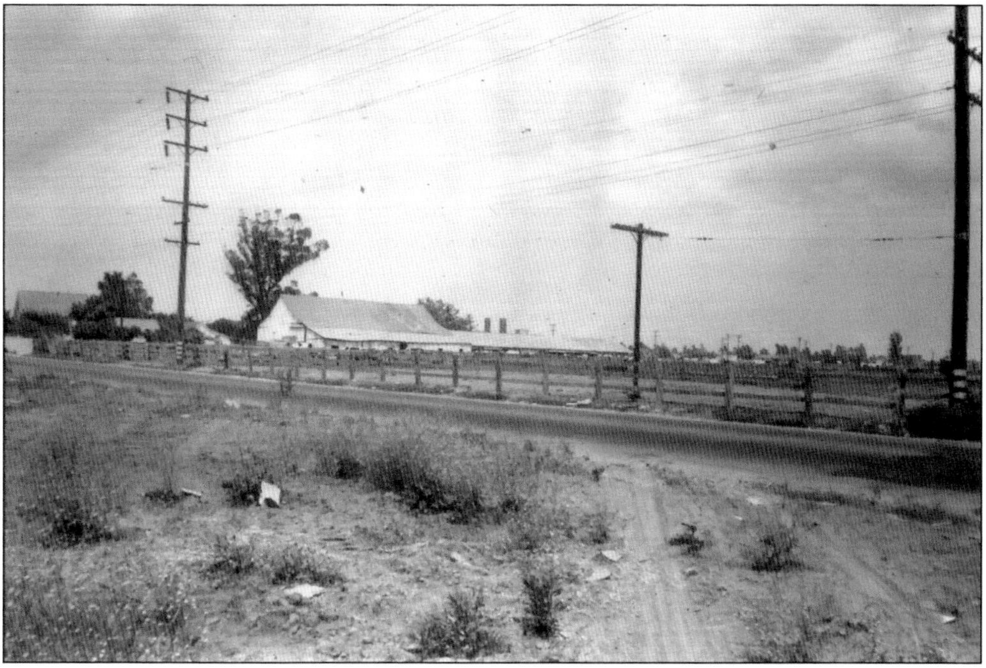

Pictured is the future home of the Willard Concrete and Machinery Company on Wright Road.

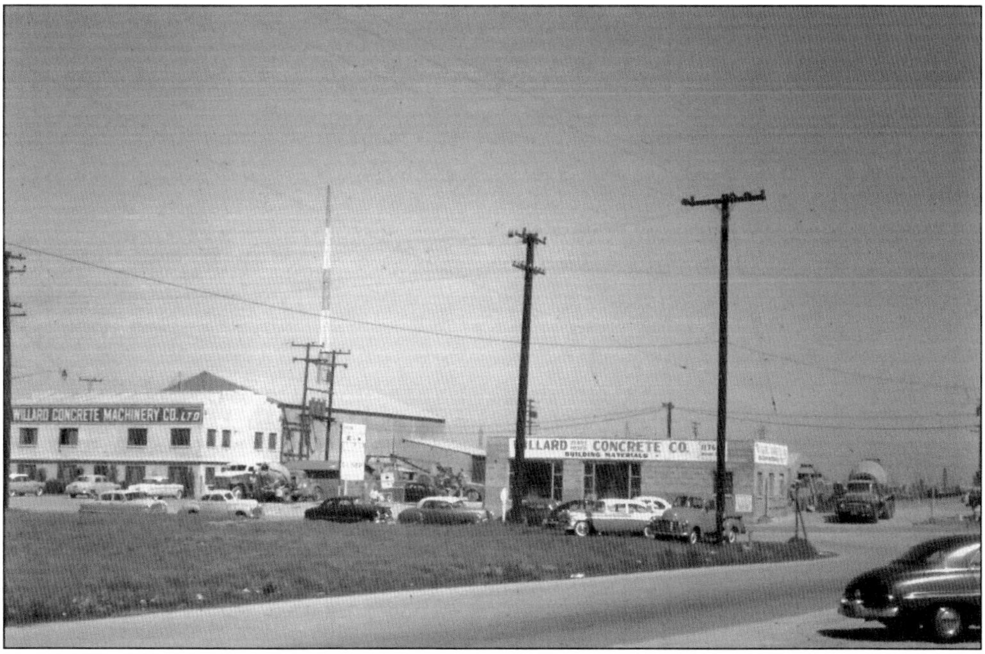

This photograph shows the site of the Willard Concrete and Machinery Company at 11700 Wright Road at Fernwood Avenue. The company was founded by Carl Willard and his son Jack. It started at the corner of Imperial Highway and Fernwood Avenue, near Alameda Street, and operated there for years before moving in the 1950s to the site shown here.

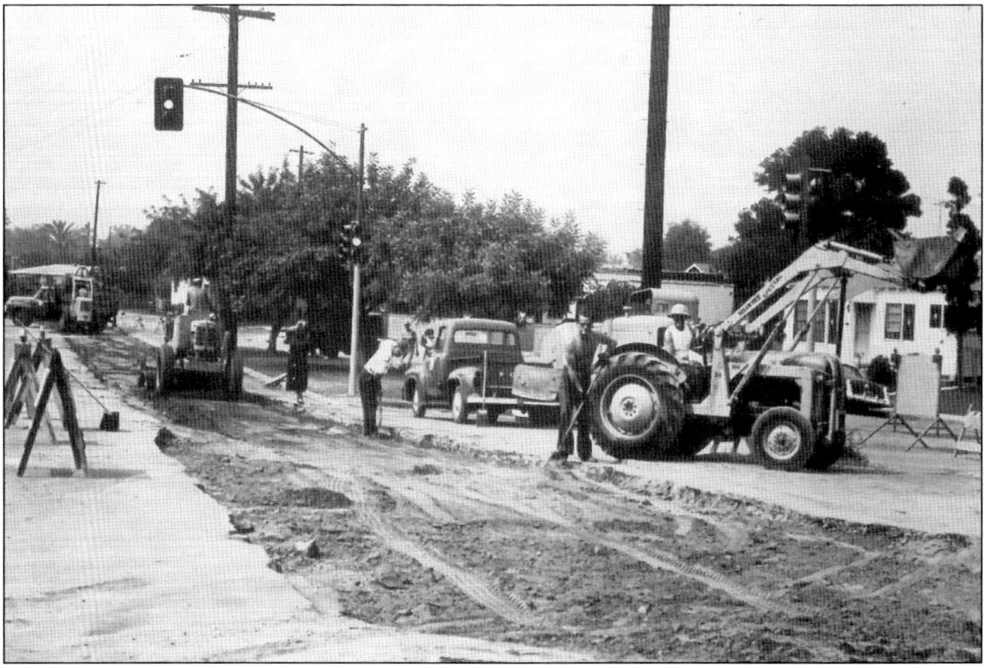

City employees are shown installing storm drain trunks on Bullis Road around 1958. The work is being done south of Fernwood Avenue on Bullis Road. From left to right, the workers are Mike Williams (driving tractor), Larry Nolan (with shovel, looking downward), Maurice E. Wood (without shirt), and Cliff Nelson (sitting on tractor).

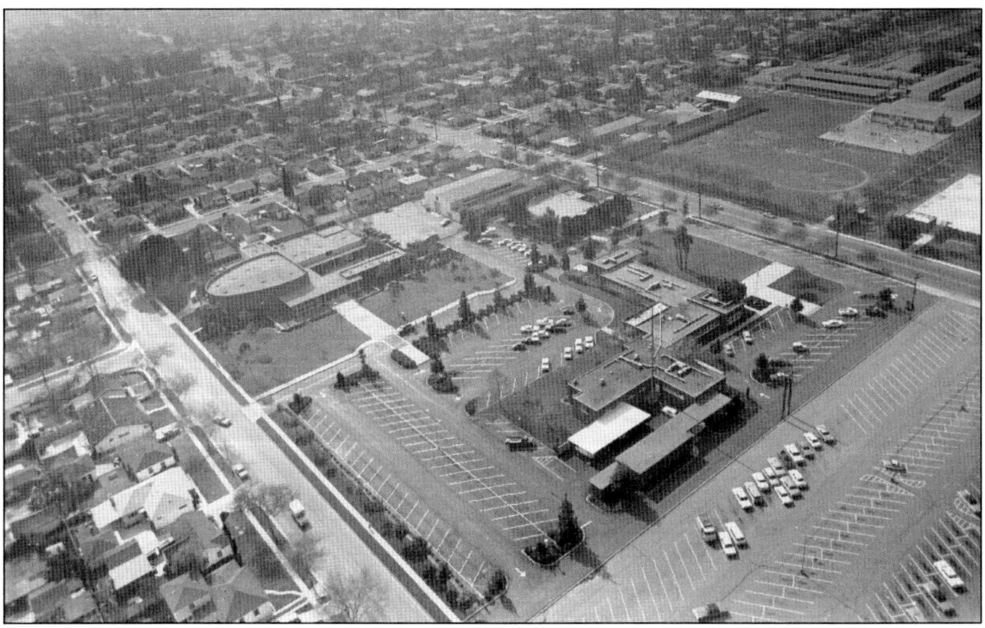

This is an aerial view of the civic center complex, facing southwest. It is bordered on the west by Bullis Road and on the east by Ernestine Avenue.

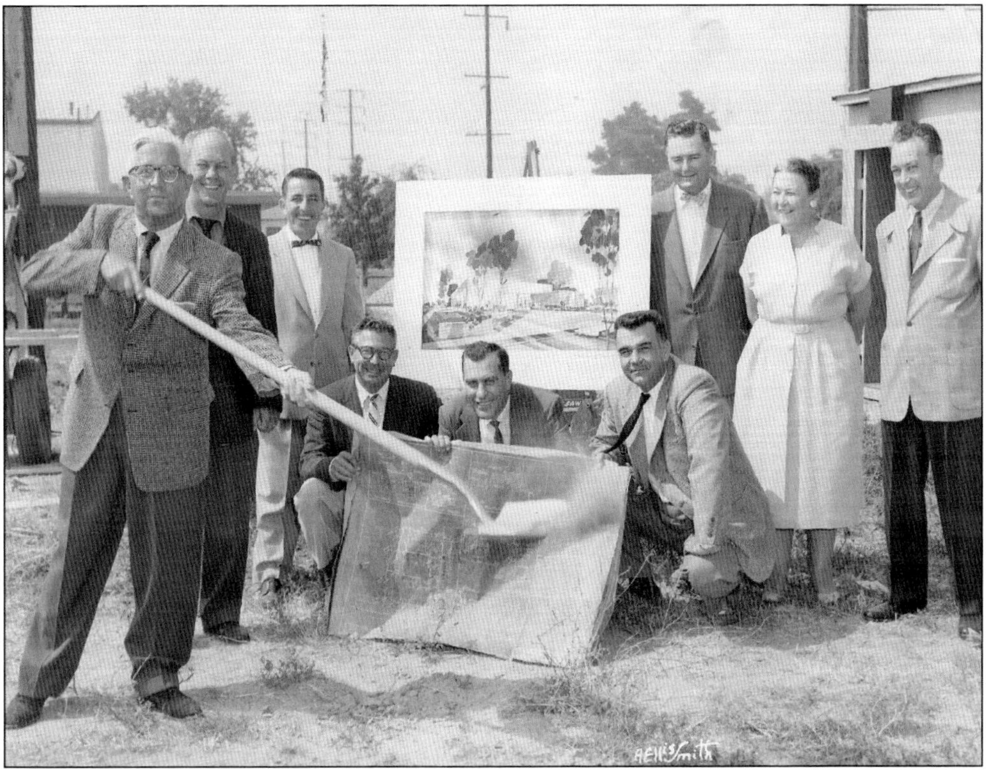

Pictured at the 1956 ground-breaking ceremony for the original library are, from left to right, Los Angeles County supervisor Burton Chace (with shovel), Lynwood councilman Peter Bruner, Tom Pender, architect Mr. Frolick, city manager Al Bateman, builder Jim Rowe, Jack Willard, Ruth Ann McMeekin, and Bud Pearson. The site also became the home of the Lynwood Public Works Department after the new library was built one block north of this site.

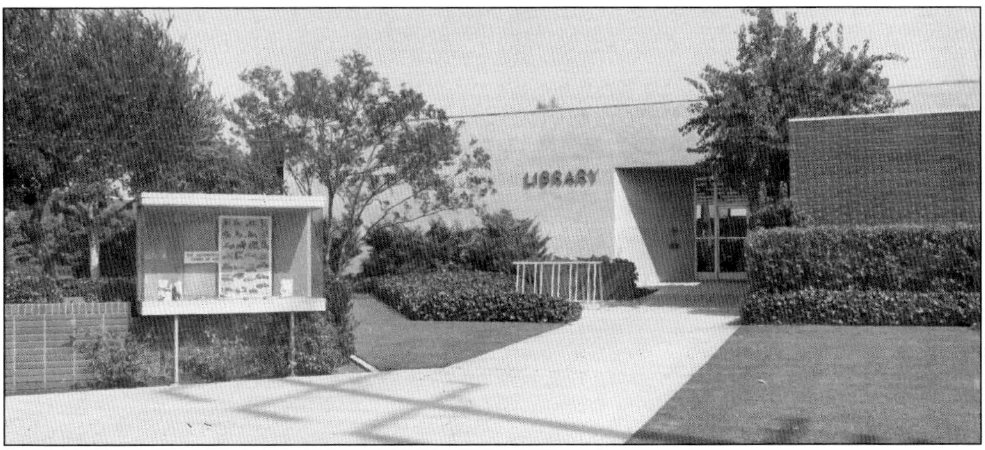

The original Lynwood branch of the Los Angeles County Library system opened in 1956 and later moved to a new site 100 yards north of the original site. The building pictured here later became the Lynwood City Hall annex with offices for the Public Works Department and Code Enforcement Division. The building was demolished in July 2011 to make way for a modern complex that will house a new city council chambers and several city departments. Construction is underway and is expected to be completed in 2013.

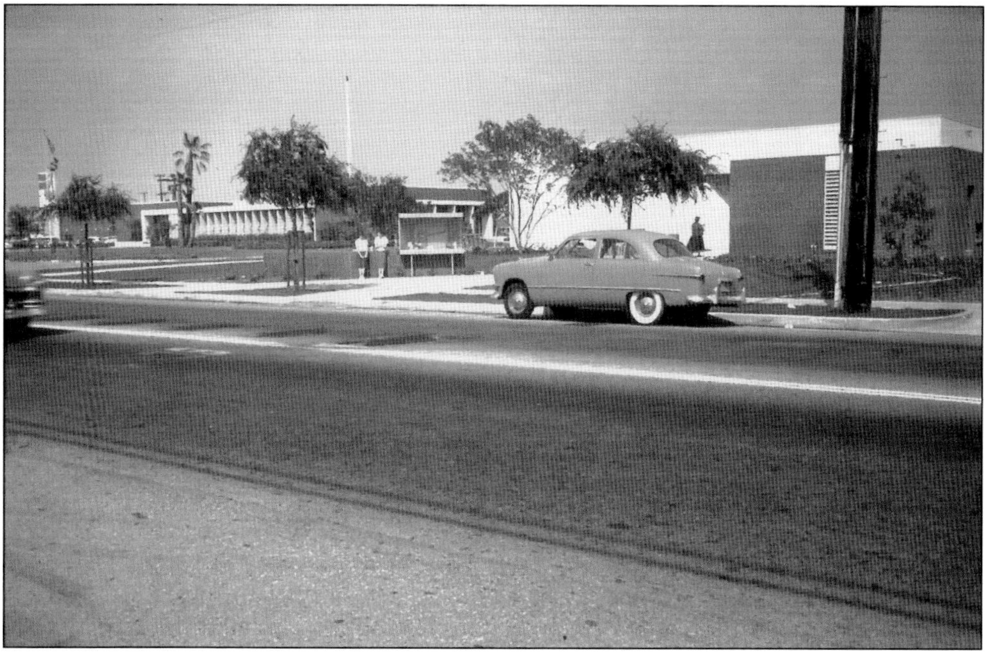

Bullis Road, facing northeast, is shown in the 1960s. This section was remodeled in the 1990s with a decorative median island and a crossing path.

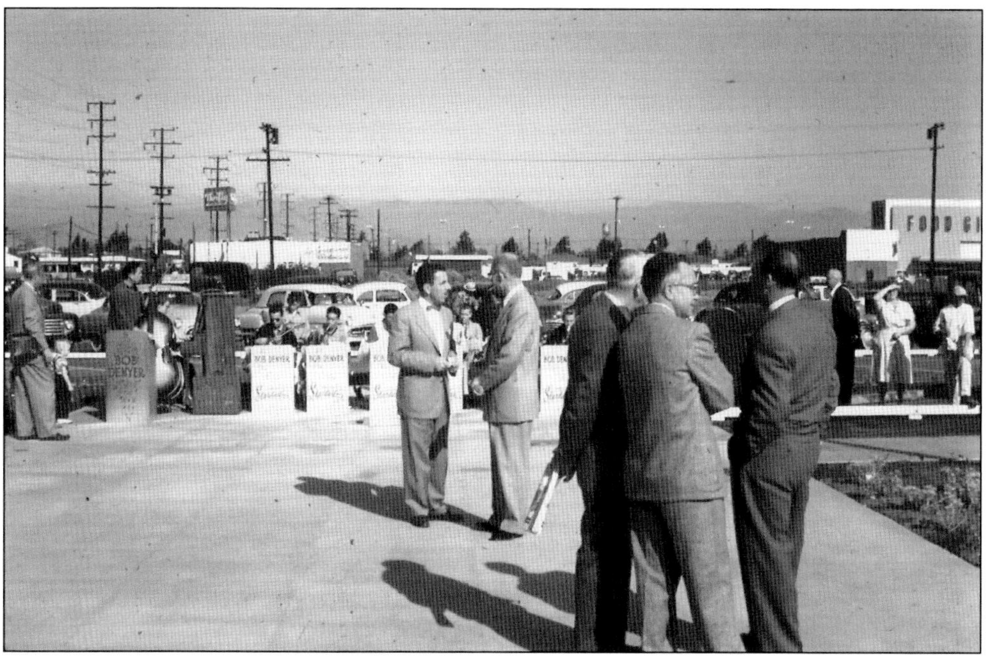

Pictured here is the dedication ceremony for the new city hall on Bullis Road in 1963. Local officials turned out for the traditional celebratory activities, including music and formal presentations.

Shown here is an aerial view of the Bateman Hall parking lot, taken in the 1960s, from Ernestine Avenue facing southeast. The Lynwood Senior Center, which opened in 2007, is now located on the site.

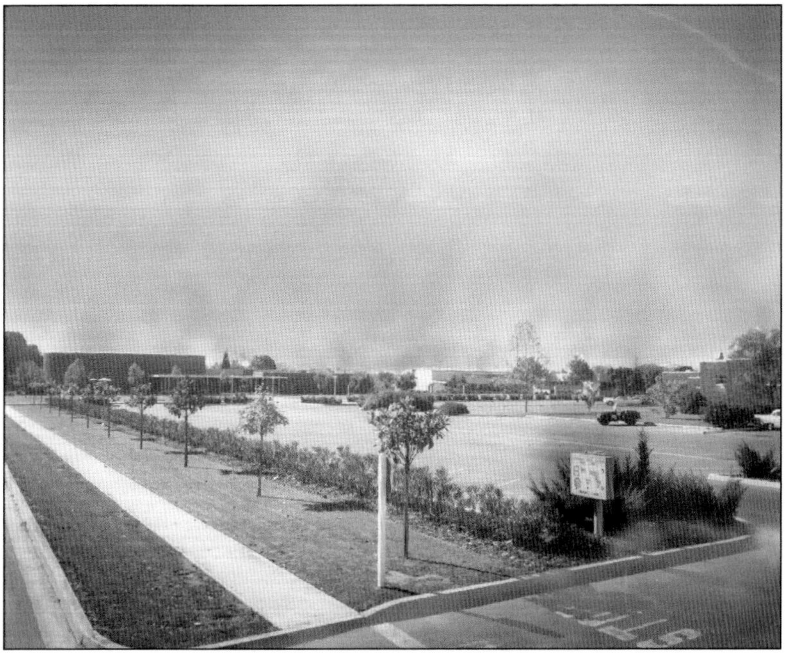

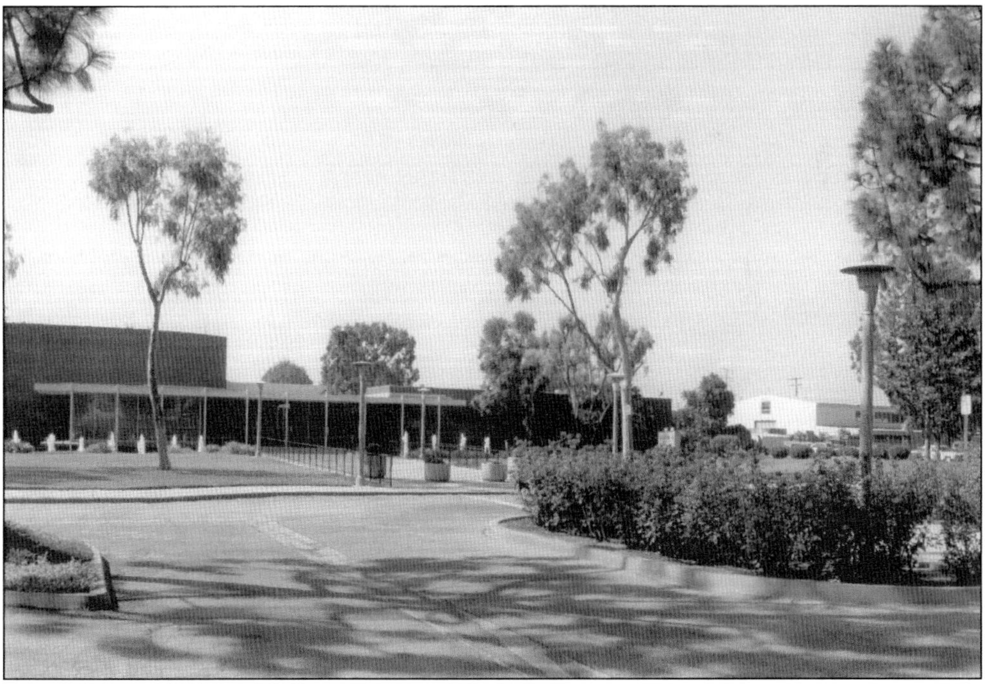

Pictured here is Bateman Hall in the 1970s. Before it was named Bateman Hall, the building was simply known as the civic center. Bateman Hall has been the venue for more than 15,000 events over the years, hosting more than 500 public and private events per year. This northeast view is taken from the site that is currently the Lynwood Senior Center.

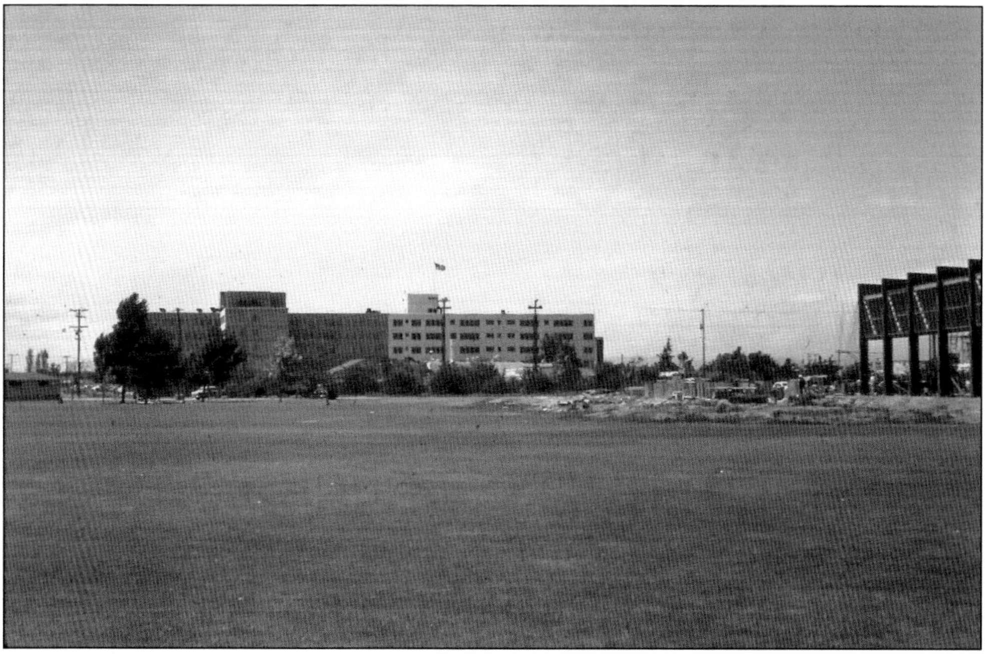

This 1956 image shows construction of the municipal natatorium. The open foreground is now the site of Lynwood's city park athletic fields, picnic areas, and the historical train depot.

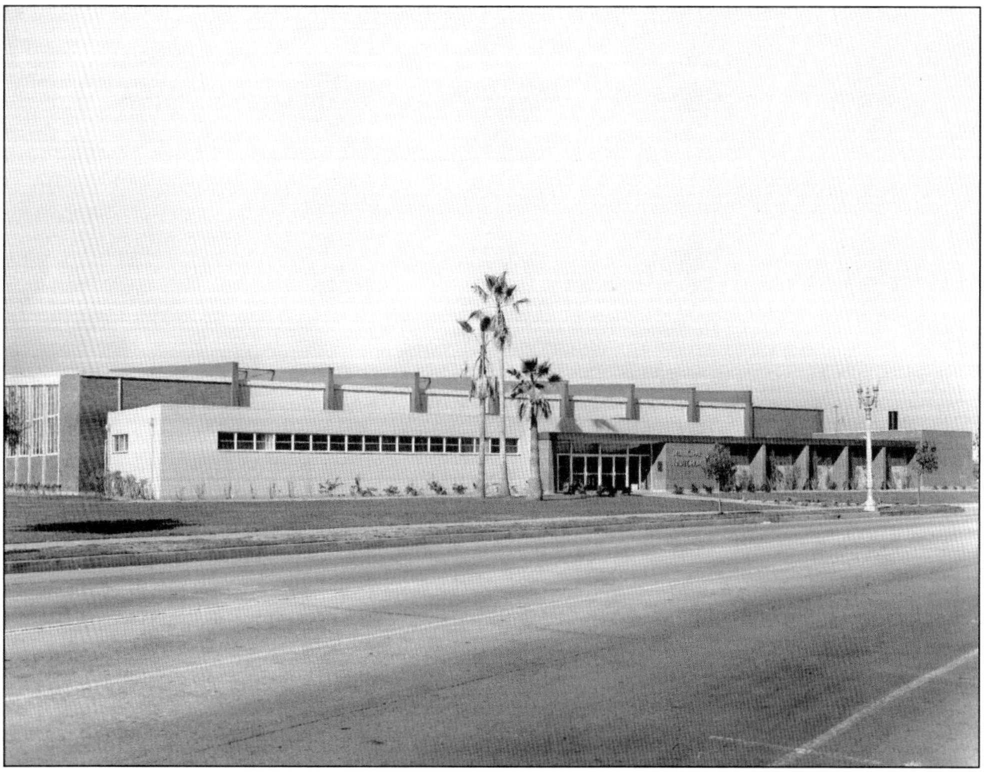

Photographed here in the 1960s, the natatorium underwent extensive renovation in the late 1990s and mid-2000s. It is still the largest indoor pool in operation in southeast Los Angeles.

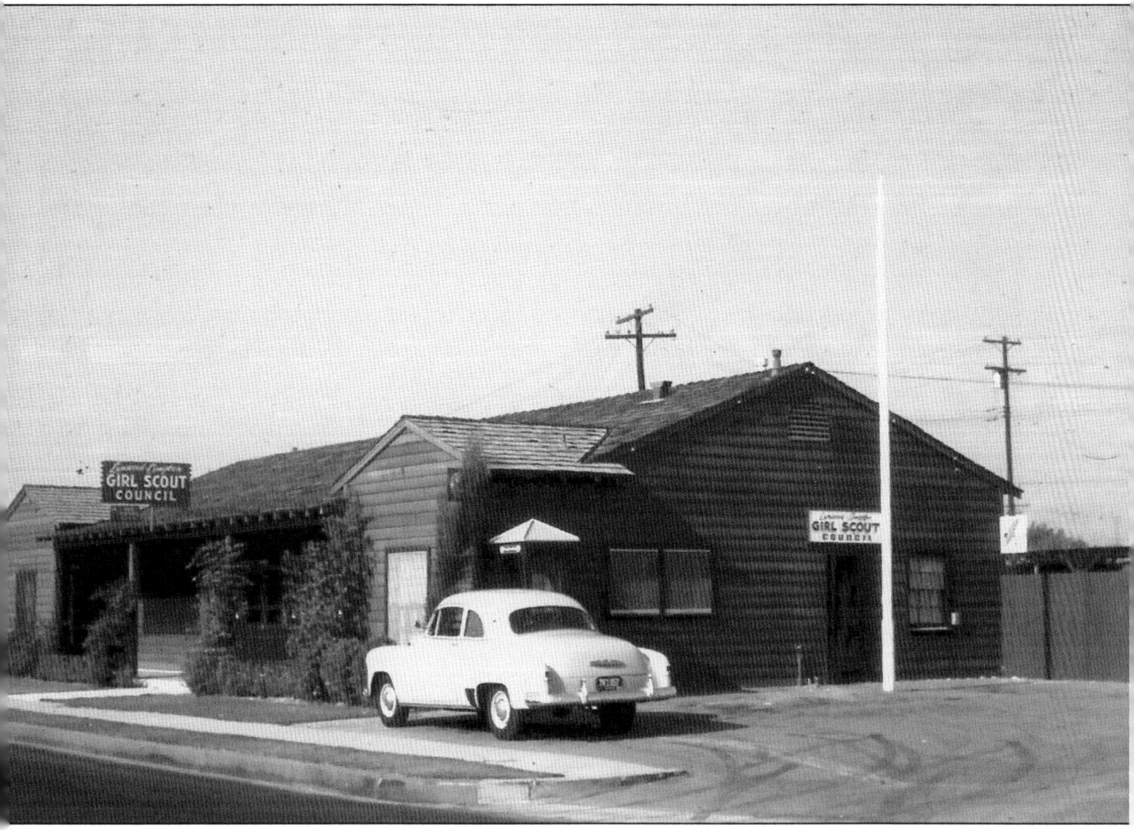

The Girl Scout building is shown here from the 1950s on Birch Street. The structure later served as a community teen center until it was demolished in the 1990s and replaced by the new, state-of-the-art youth center facility.

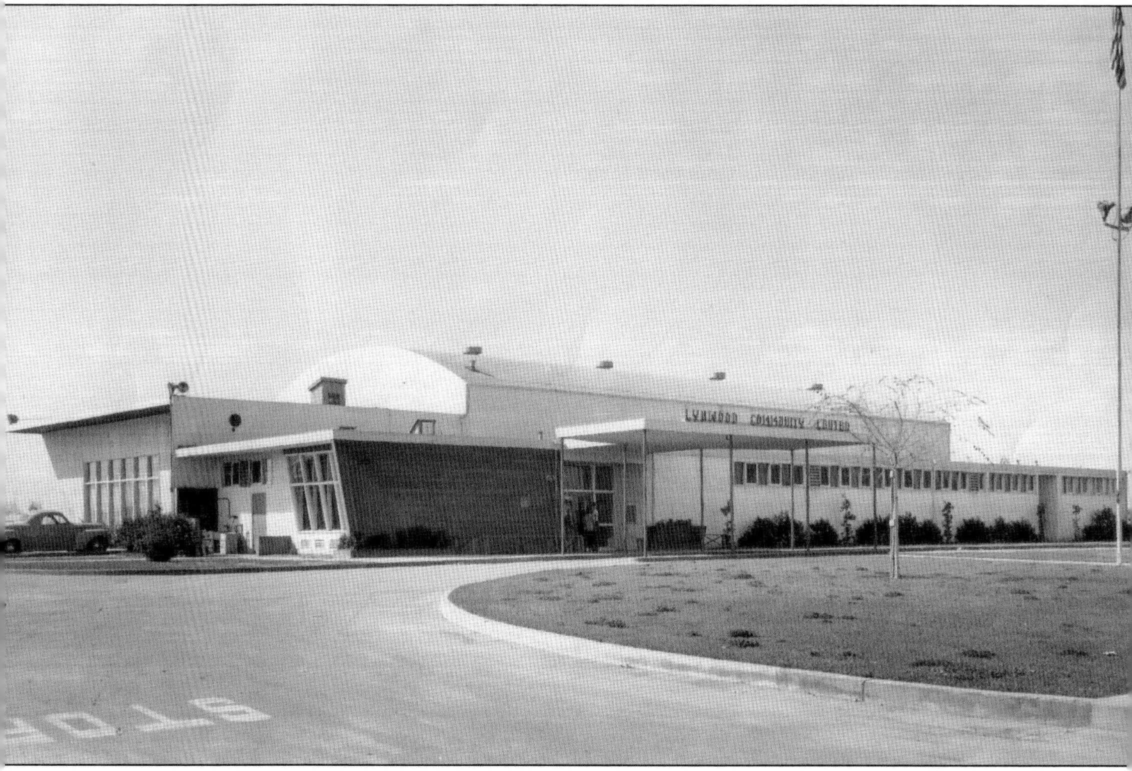

This building was the Lynwood Community Center, photographed here in the 1950s. It was first opened in March 1948 at a cost of $100,000 and featured an auditorium, activity rooms, a lounge, offices, a gymnasium, and spaces for different types of recreational activities. City records show the facility had been actively lobbied by residents since 1936.

Four

Shopping, Dining, and Entertainment

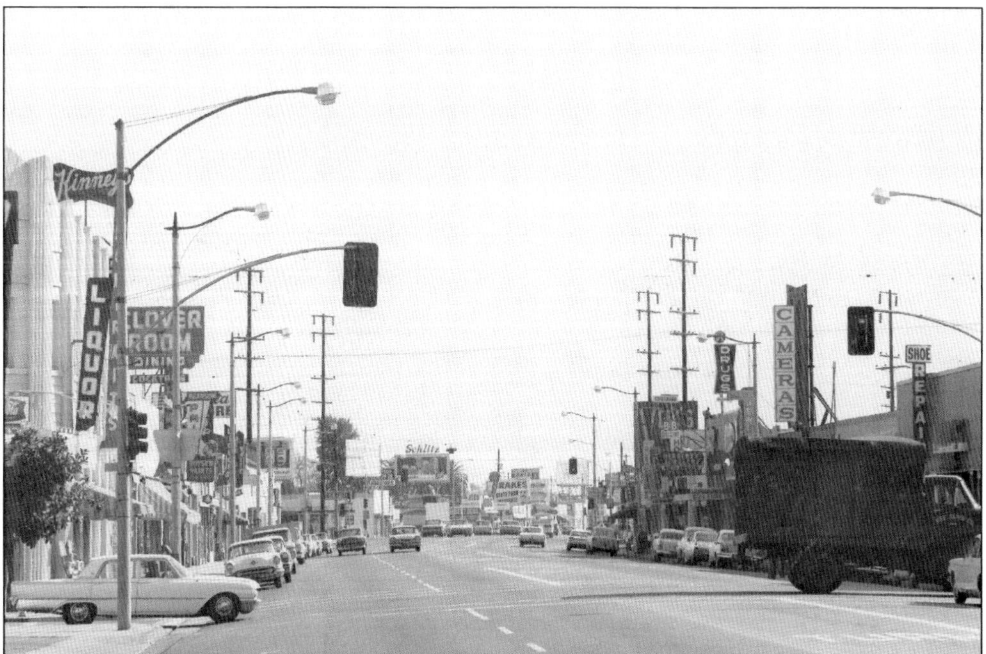

This 1950s photograph of Long Beach Boulevard reflects a period of commercial growth in the area.

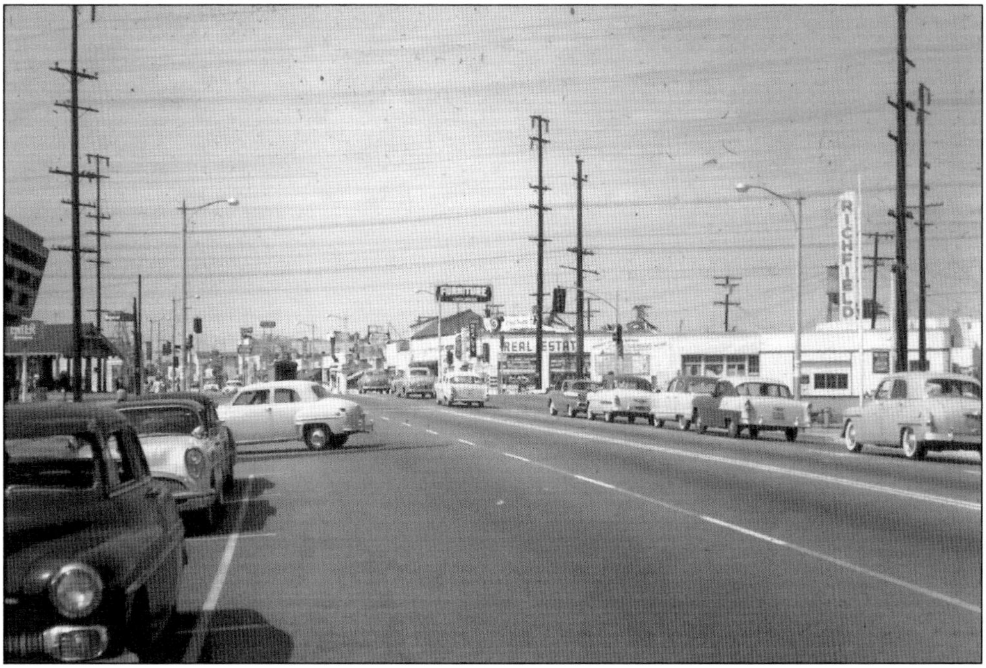

This 1950s image shows Long Beach Boulevard facing south toward the Pacific Electric station.

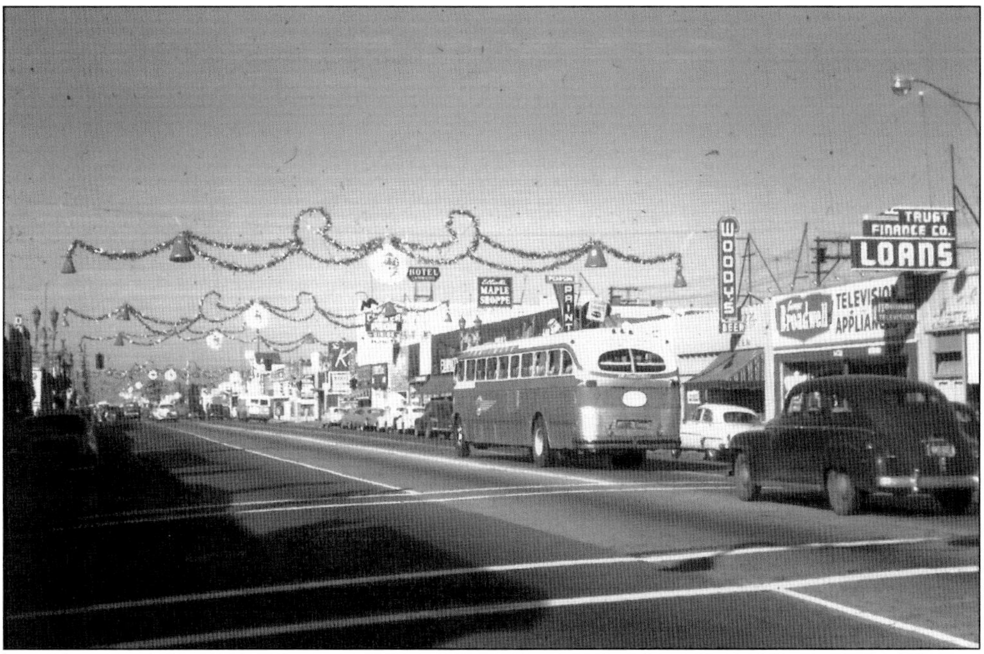

This section of Long Beach Boulevard, from Mulford Avenue, is still the heart of downtown Lynwood. Today, this area is home to Lynwood's main post office, the Plaza Mexico Shopping Center, and dozens of small and large businesses.

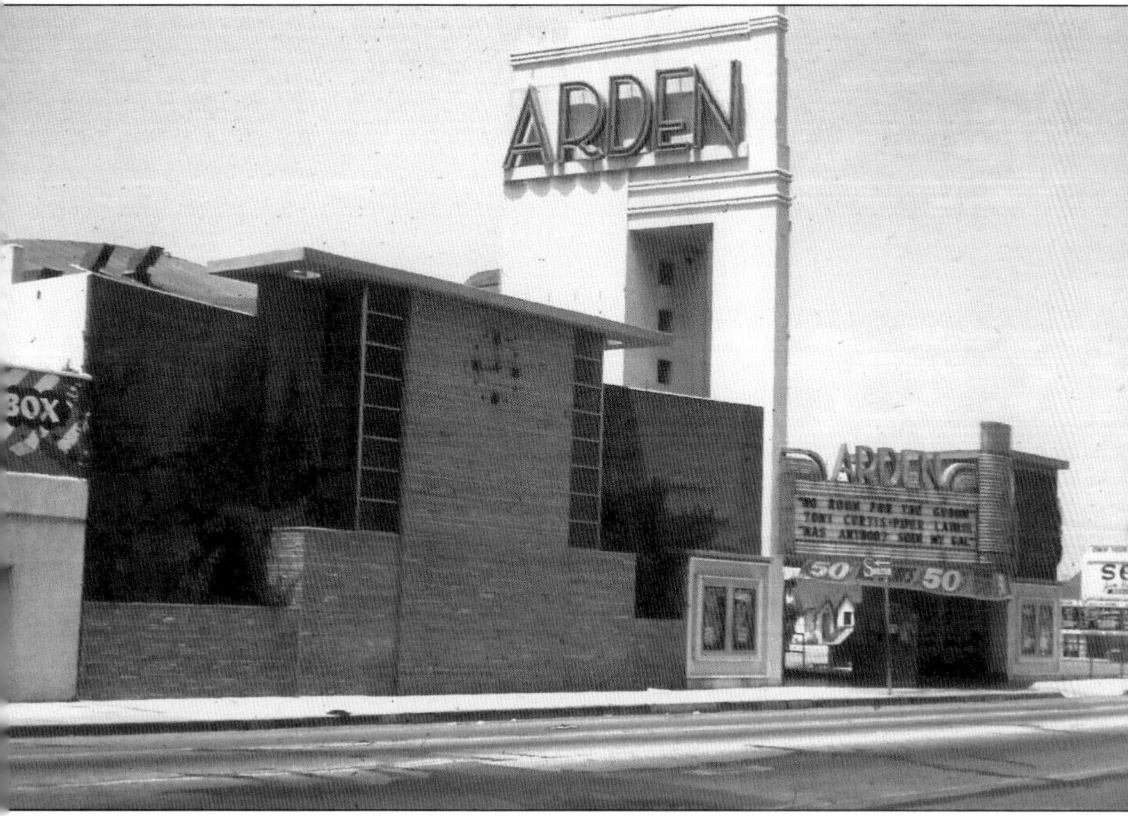

The Arden Theatre, designed by acclaimed architect Charles Lee, opened in 1942 on Long Beach Boulevard. The venue had a classic 1920s Art Deco look and was a prominent Lynwood attraction from the 1940s through the 1960s. A fire in 1988 destroyed the Arden, and it was never rebuilt. Charles Lee was known for designing some of the most historic theaters on the West Coast, including the Fox Theatres in Bakersfield, Beverly Hills, Westwood, and countless others.

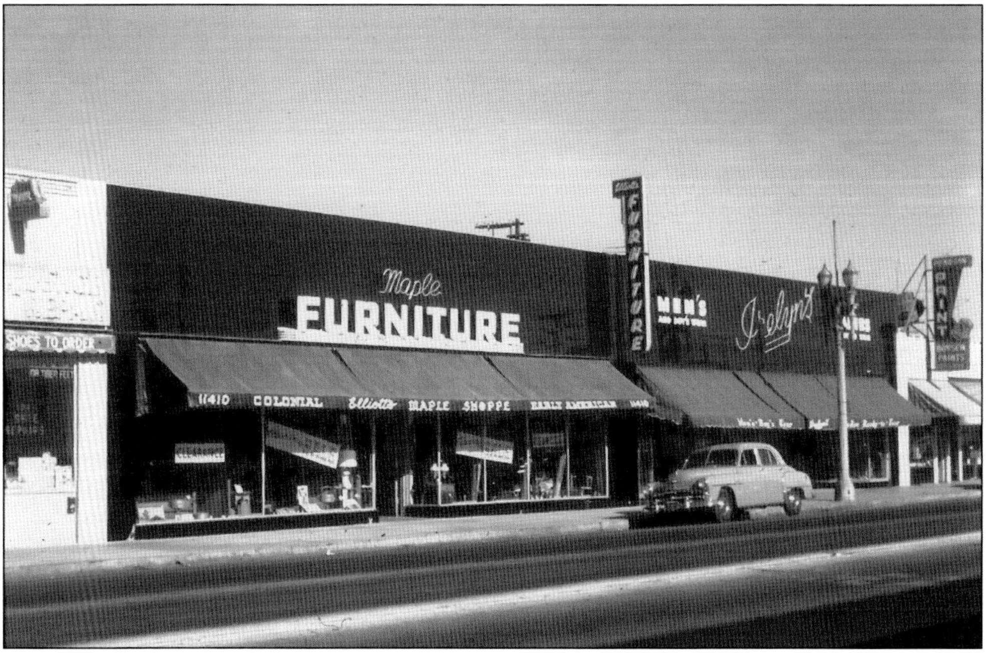

These downtown Lynwood storefronts were photographed in the 1940s. Furniture stores are still prominent commercial fixtures in the area.

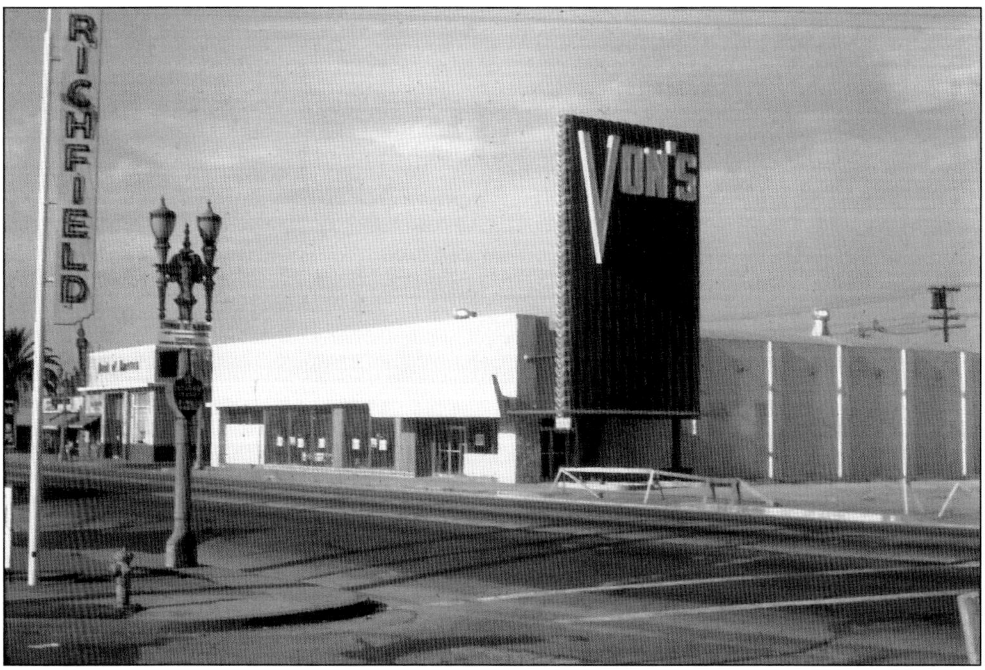

Von's Grocery Store on Long Beach Boulevard is pictured in the 1950s. Bank of America is seen to the left.

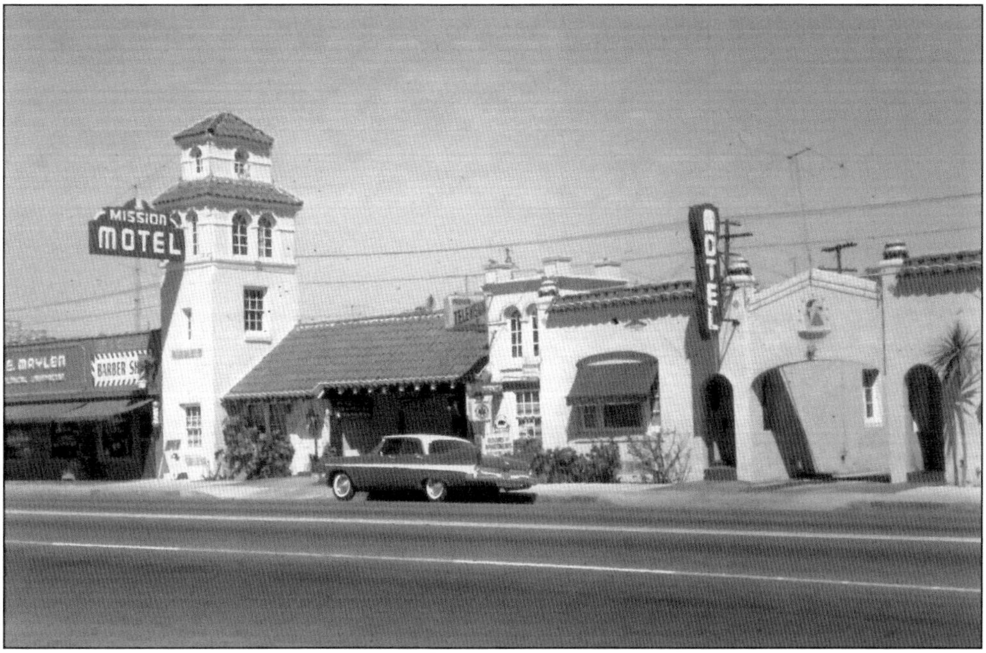

The Mission Motel on Long Beach Boulevard was designed to resemble a historic Spanish mission. The owners were community benefactors who donated to several local causes each year.

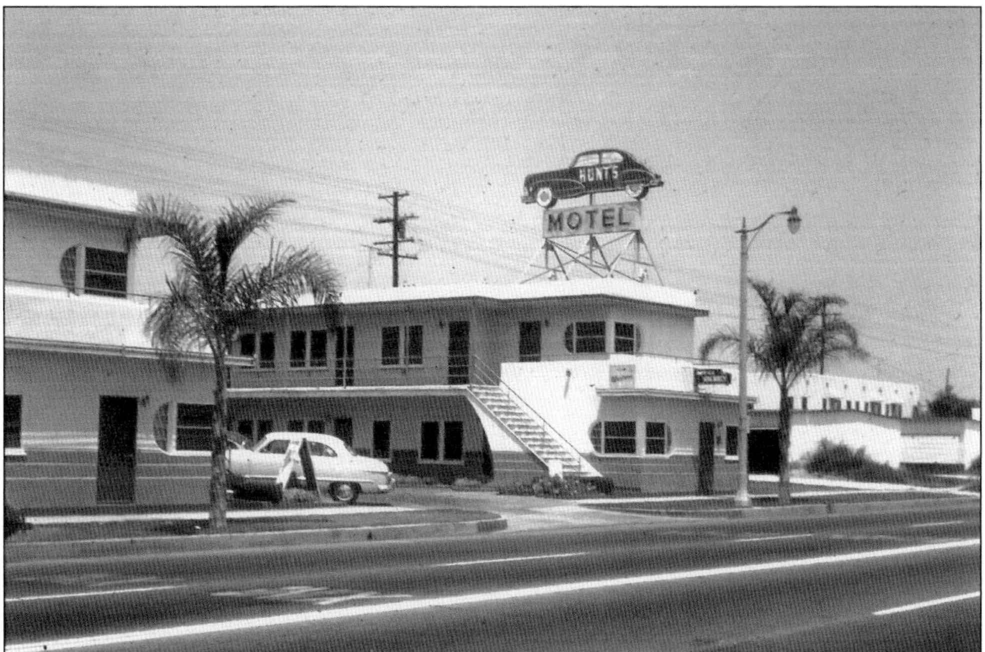

The Hunts Motel was located on Atlantic Avenue during the 1950s and 1960s, and the original neon sign is currently showcased in Las Vegas at the Fremont Street Neonopolis. The building shown here is now an Economy Inn.

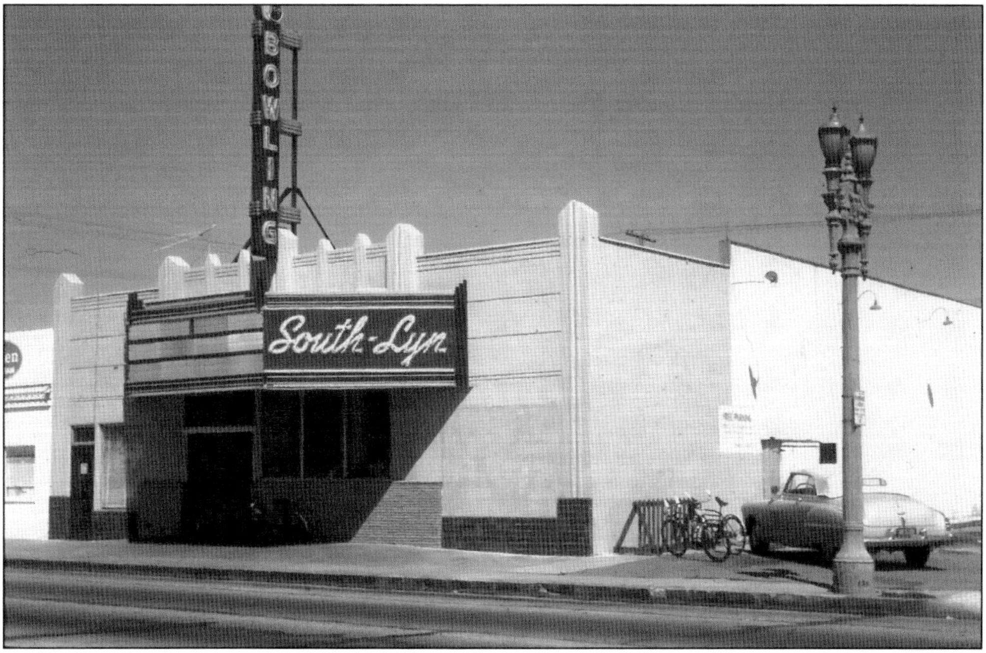

The South-Lyn Bowling Alley was located on Long Beach Boulevard and Lynwood Road across the street from the Arden Theatre. It had very unique outside design features. The front sign looked like a movie theater marquee, an homage to Lynwood's notable theater history. It is unknown if this building once housed a theater.

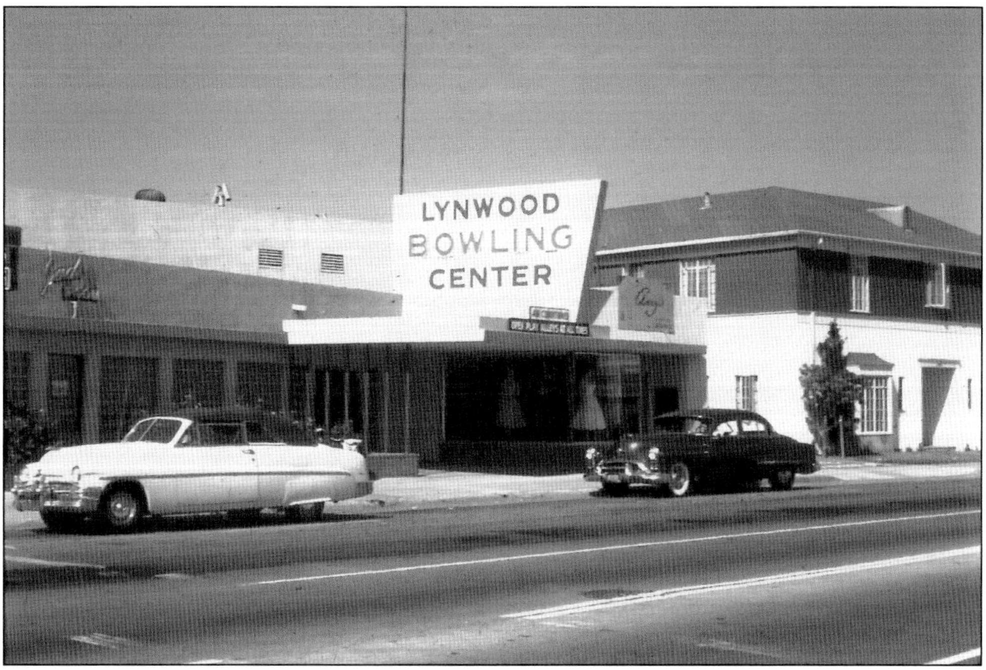

The Lynwood Bowling Center was located on Imperial Highway next to what was then the Harrison-Ross Mortuary. Bowling was very popular, and Lynwood once had four bowling venues. This building is currently vacant.

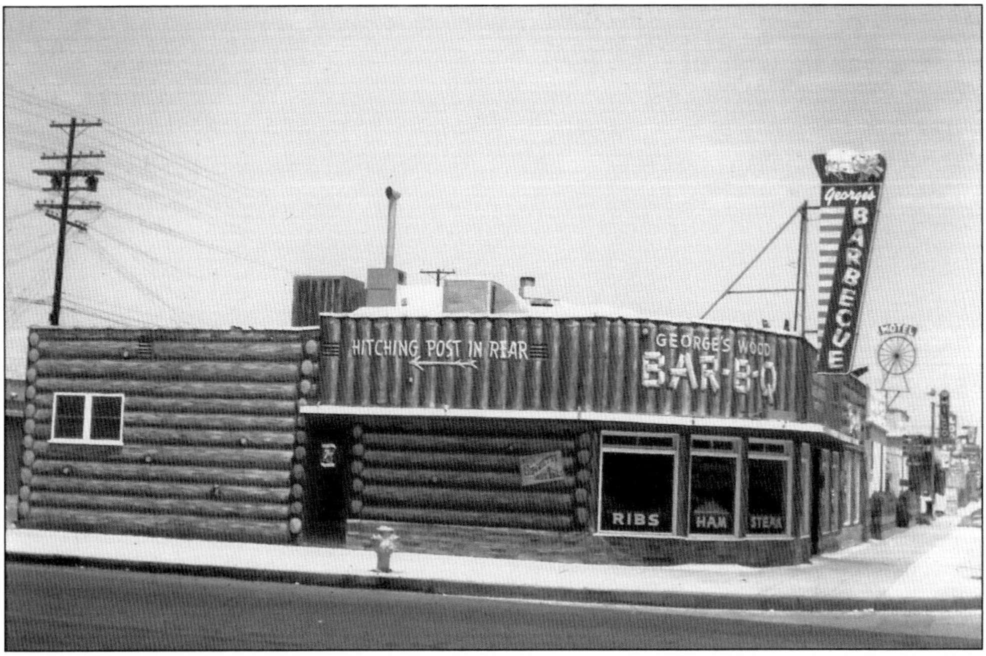

George's Wood BBQ was a popular Atlantic Avenue eatery in the 1950s, known for the best ribs and steaks in town. Lynwood locals frequented Wood's because of its fair prices and large servings. Lynwood was also the birthplace to the first Chris' & Pitt's Barbecue Restaurant chain, started in 1949.

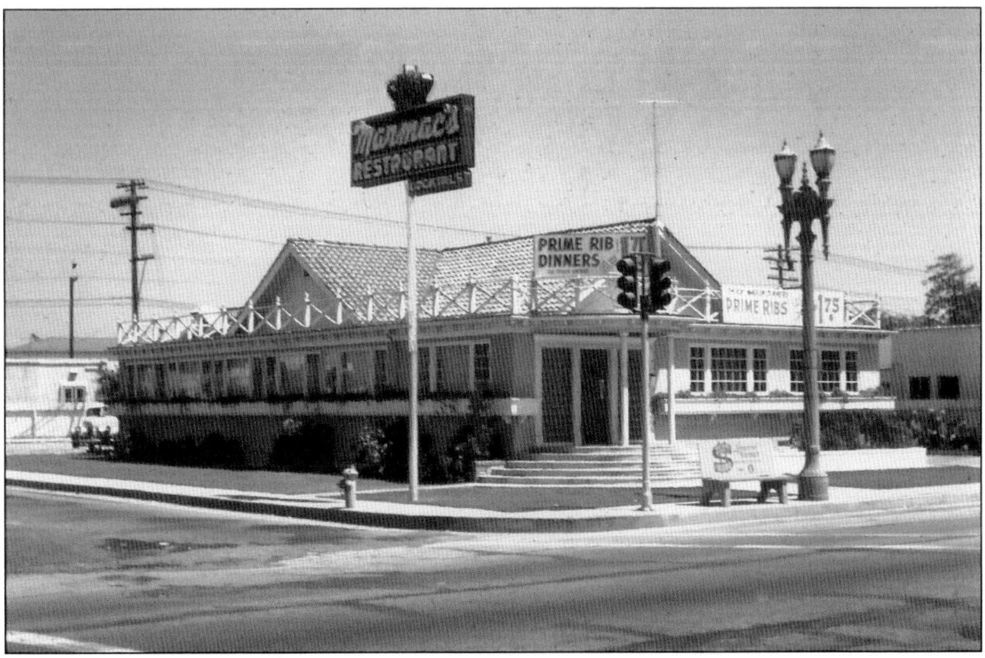

Offering a family-dining atmosphere, Marmac's Restaurant was a prime rib and steak eatery established in the 1950s on Long Beach Boulevard and Cedar Avenue. Presently, King Taco Restaurant is located on the site.

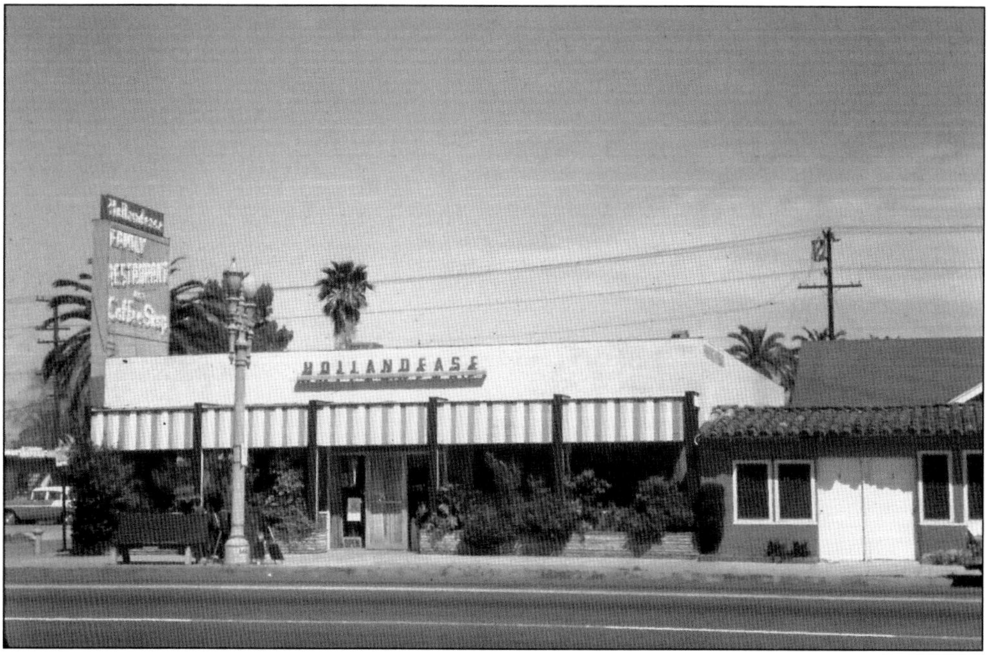

This Hollandease Restaurant, owned by Roy Craft, was located on the corner of Agnes Avenue and Long Beach Boulevard. At one point, the restaurant was host to the Toasters Club. Much of Long Beach has evolved and grown over the years; gone are the mom-and-pop restaurants, businesses, movie theaters, and bowling alleys. In recent years, Long Beach Boulevard supports larger retailers, furniture stores, and automobile dealerships.

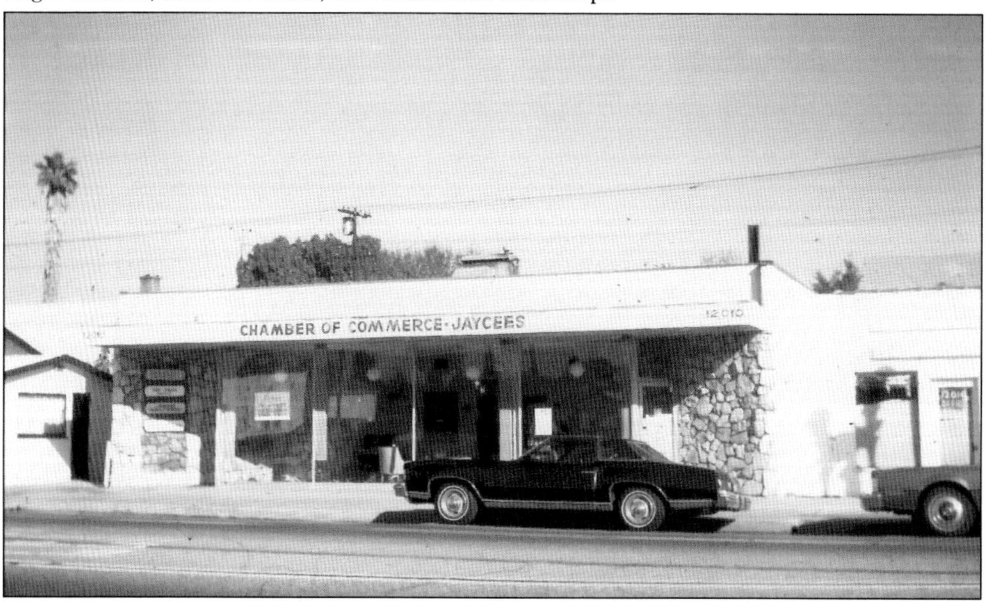

This c. 1969 photograph shows the early Lynwood Chamber of Commerce on Atlantic Boulevard. The Lynwood Chamber of Commerce was a regular participant in the Los Angeles County Fair. The chamber produced exemplary exhibits that publicized the community's many amenities. In 1969, the City of Lynwood won first prize for its display. Today, the new home of the chamber is at the historical Pacific Electric depot located at the entrance of Lynwood City Park.

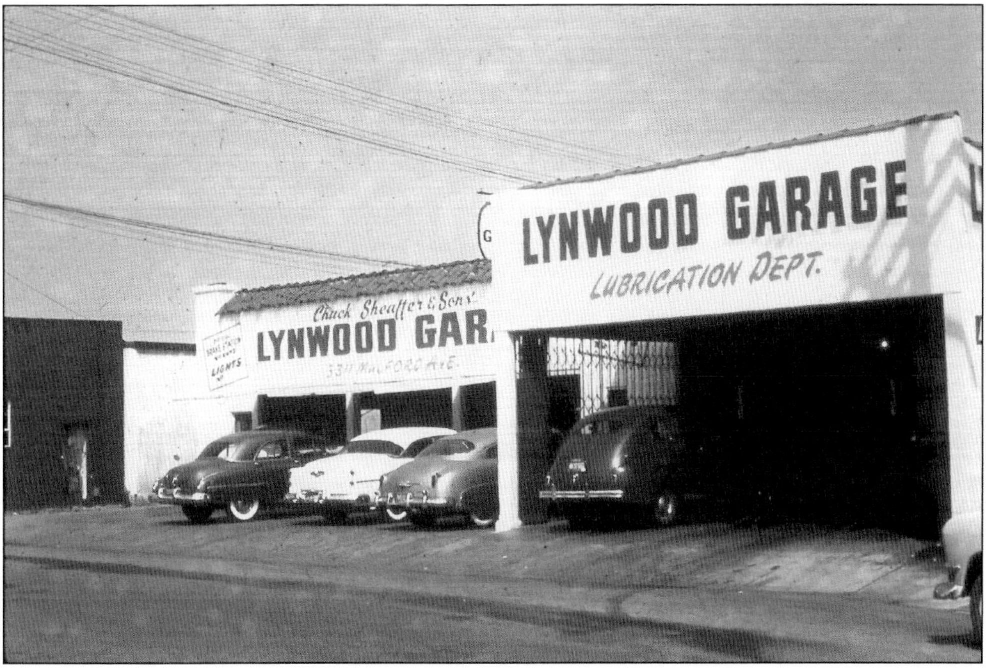

Chuck Sheaffer & Sons' Lynwood Garage was located on Mulford Avenue, off Long Beach Boulevard. The garage was also known by its shorter name, the Lynwood Garage. The building is a body shop today but looks much the same, with different paint.

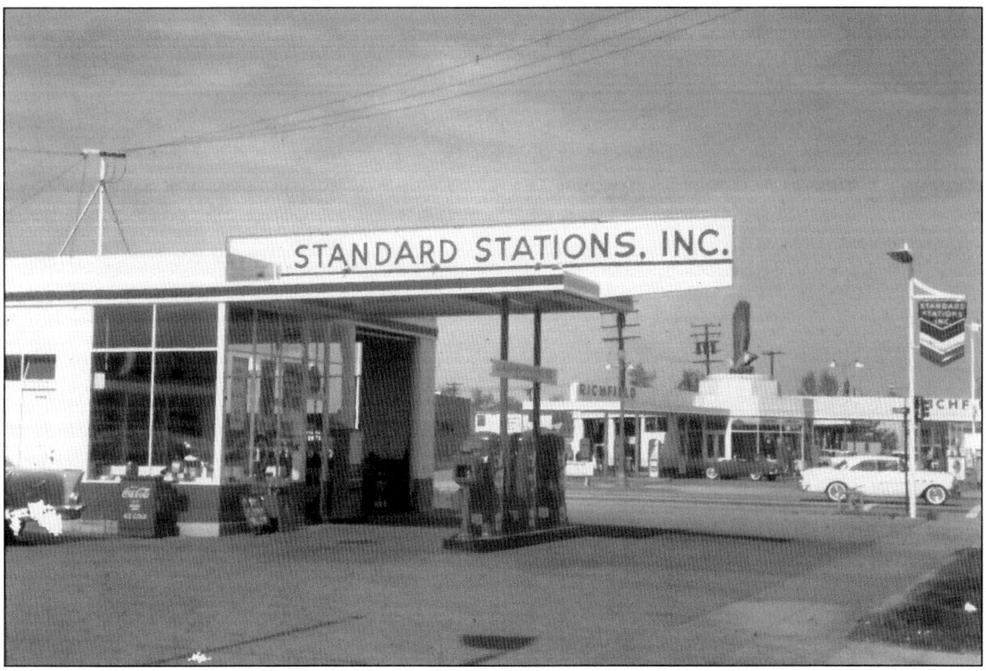

Standard Stations Gas Station on Long Beach Boulevard is shown in the 1960s near the intersection of Lynwood Road.

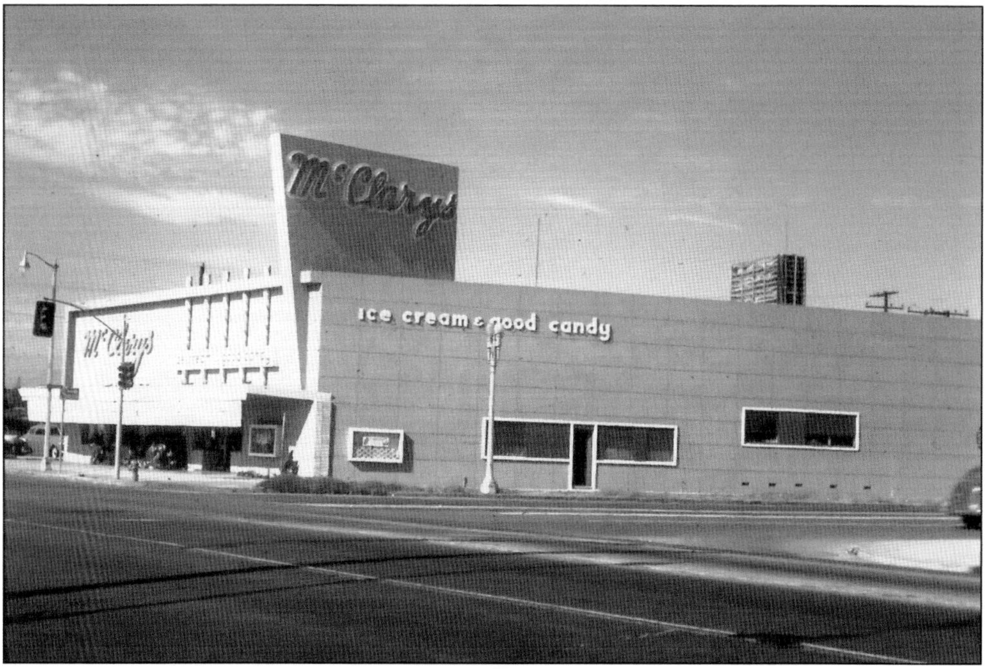

McClary's Ice Cream and Candy Shop on Long Beach Boulevard, shown here, is now the home of Helen Grace Chocolates, one of the largest family-owned-and-operated confectioneries and fundraisers in the West.

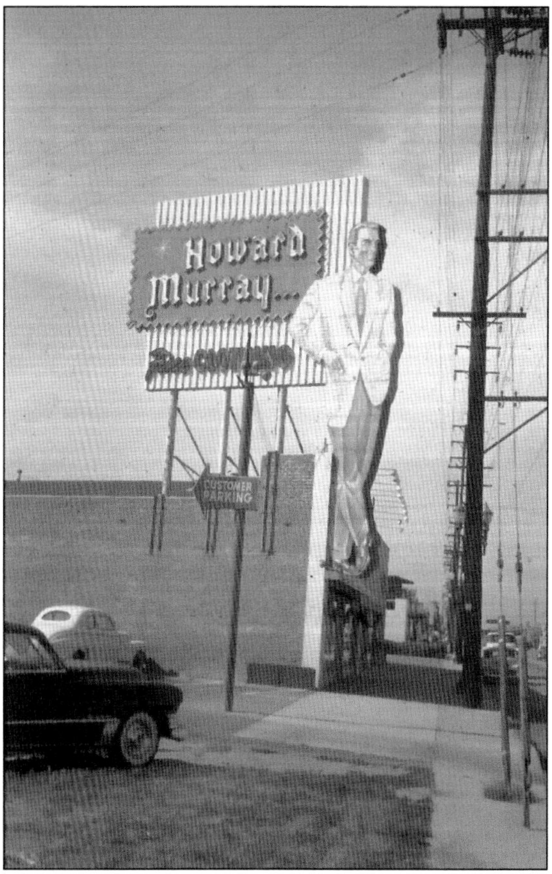

Howard Murray's Fine Clothing shop was located at 10135 Long Beach Boulevard and for years featured the unmistakably dapper gentleman signboard. Fine clothiers and tailors were common and well patronized in Lynwood. Howard Murray was known for an array of men's casual and formalwear. The store closed in 1962, after 15 years of business.

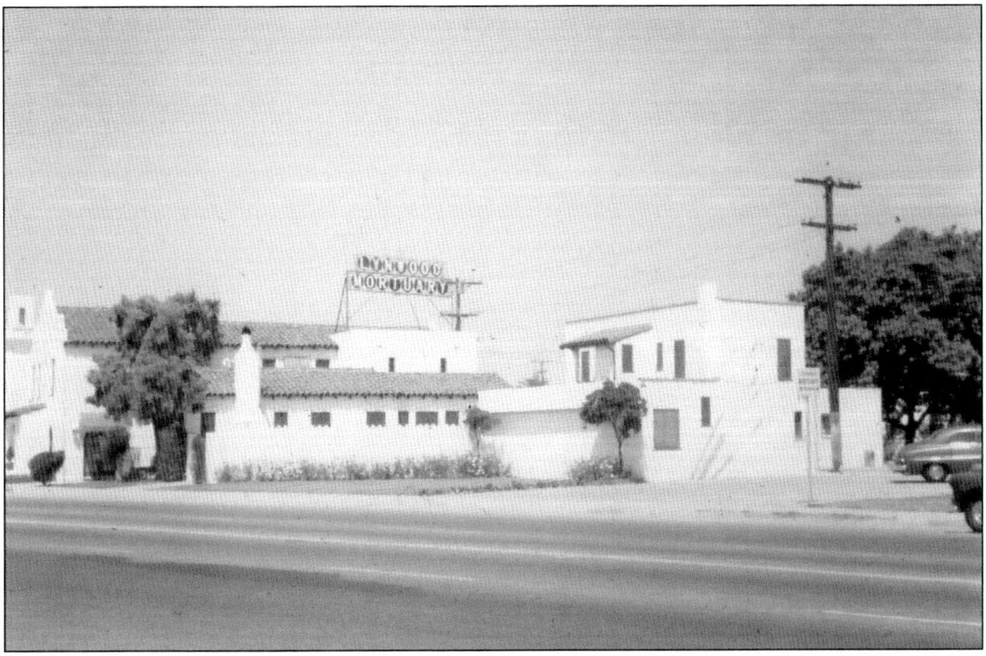

Shown here is the Lynwood Mortuary on Imperial Highway, which closed in 2006. The building was demolished, and the lot is currently vacant.

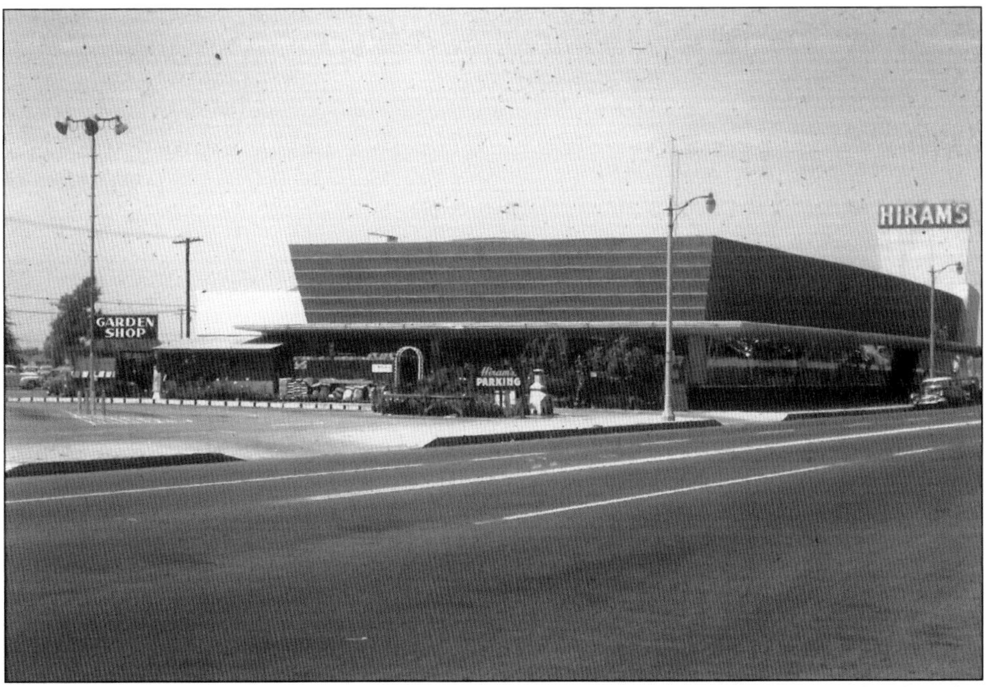

Hiram's was located at 10721 Atlantic Avenue and Abbott Road, now the site of Value Plus Grocery Market.

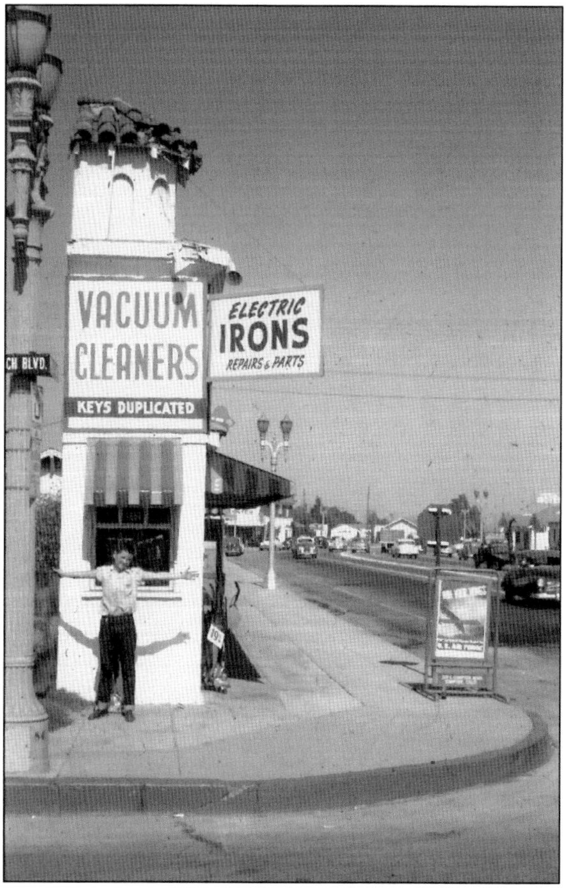

The Vacuum Cleaners and Repair Shop pictured here in the 1950s was known to many as the "Shoestring Building." (This is a side view compared to the picture below.) Renown for its narrow design, the building stood at the northeast corner of Long Beach Boulevard and Imperial Highway. The young man seen here with both arms extended demonstrates exactly how wide the building was. A few years later, the building was expanded to provide better use.

In 1930, when Imperial Highway was first developed, the owner of the property on the east side of Long Beach Boulevard wanted to retain frontage facing Imperial Highway but the owner of this property refused to sell his 5-by-128-foot building parallel to Imperial Highway. Eventually, the property was purchased by an enterprising real estate agent. A small retail plaza now occupies the site. Notice the single family homes on the far right. These homes are still standing and look the same as they did 80 years ago.

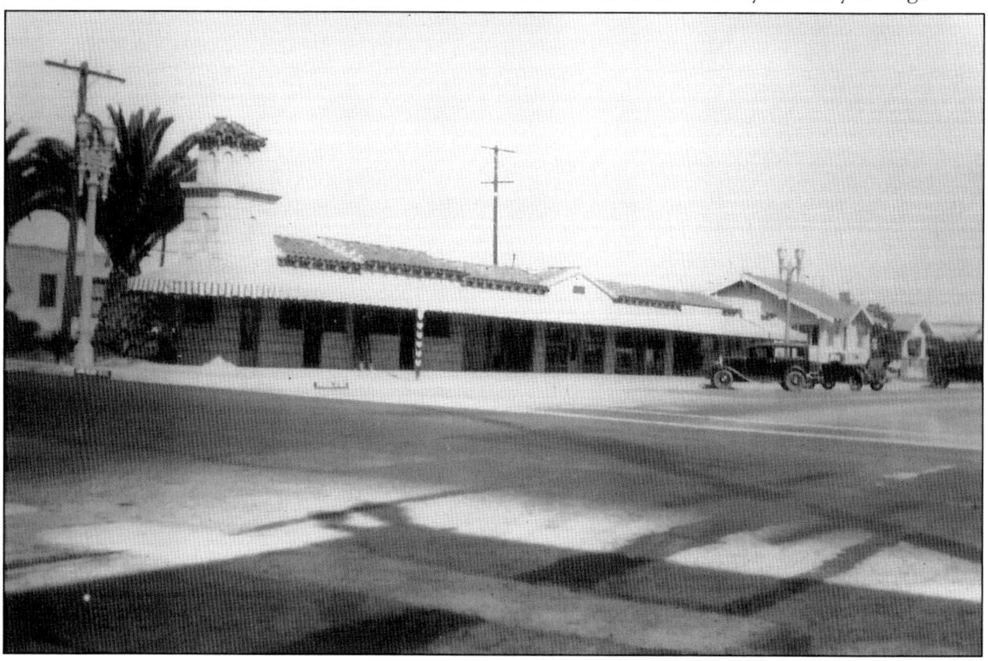

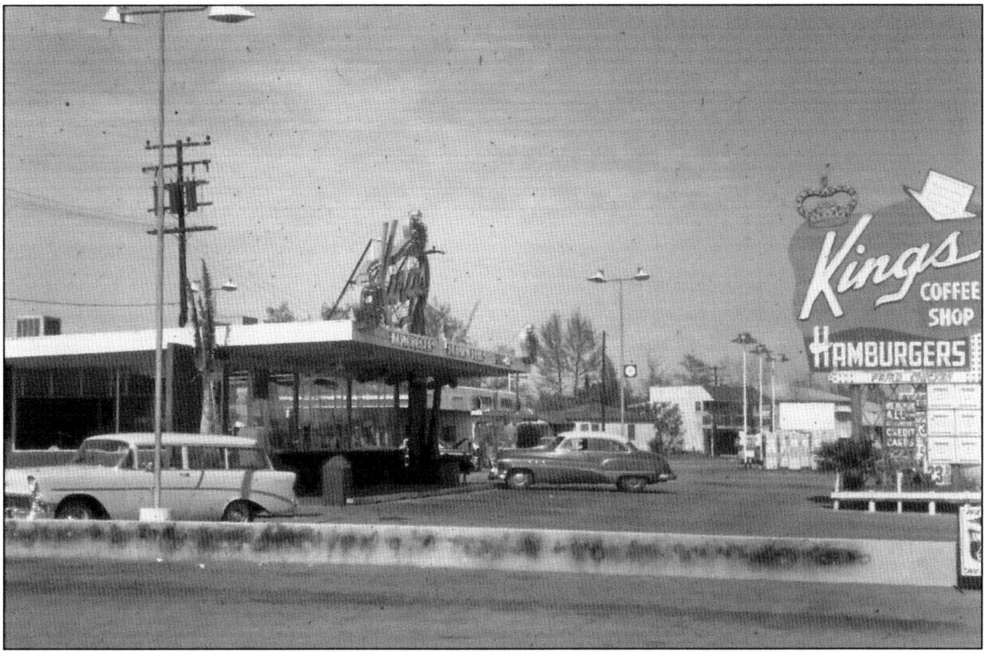

Shown here is Kings Hamburgers, which was a popular roadside eatery located on Imperial Highway at Century Boulevard east of St. Francis. Eateries similar to this were very common in the 1950s through 1970s across the nation.

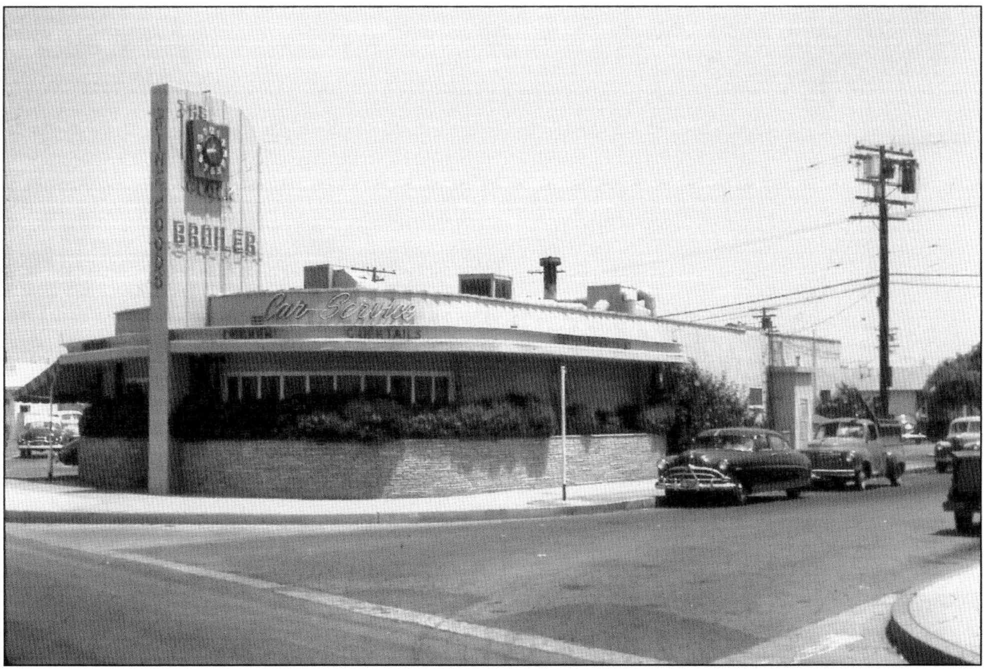

This photograph shows the Clock Broiler Restaurant near the intersection of Imperial Highway and Atlantic Avenue; the site is also the former location of Wendy's and El Pescador Restaurants.

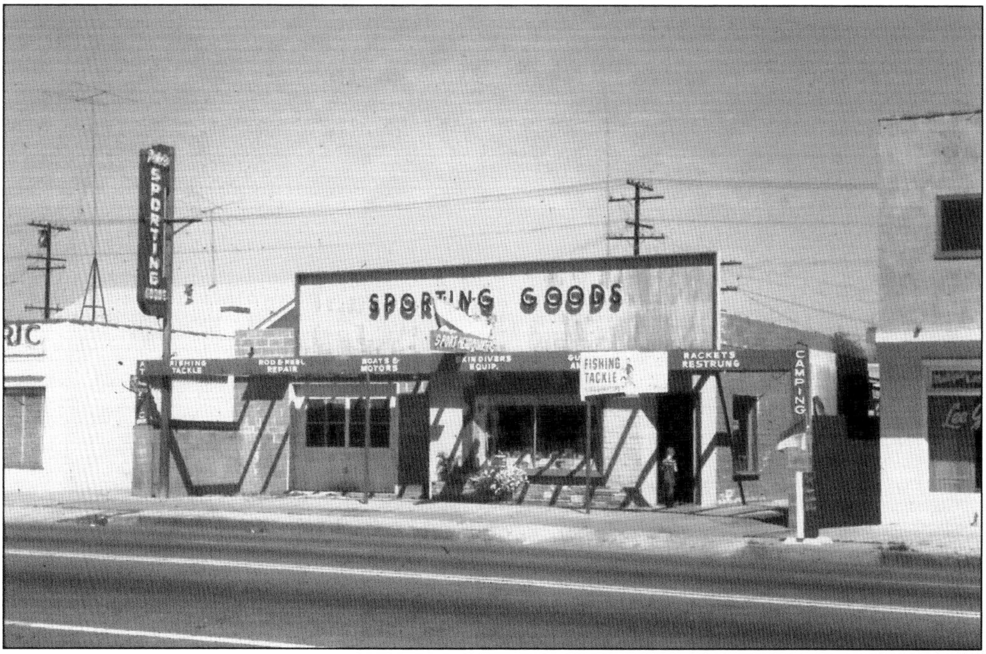

This 1950s photograph shows the Sporting Goods store on Long Beach Boulevard at Cedar Avenue. It specialized in sales and service of tennis racquets, fishing rods, scuba diving equipment, fishing tackle, and bait. It now houses a tire shop and liquor store.

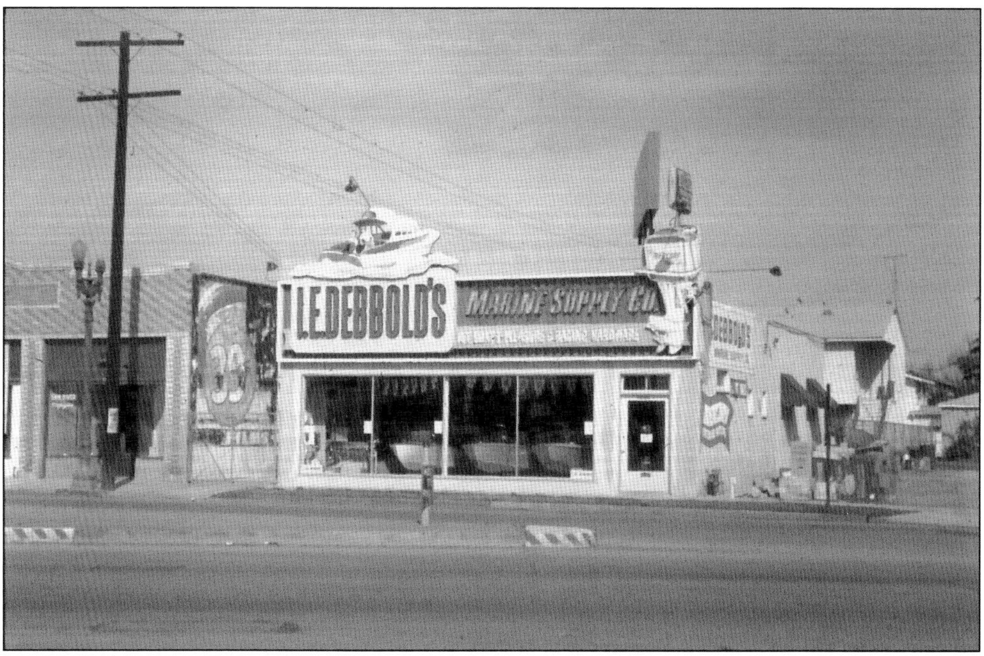

I.E. Debbold's Marine Supply is shown at the forked intersection of Long Beach Boulevard and State Street. Outdoor recreation activities are abundant in this area, and shops such as Debbold's were prevalent in cities like Lynwood, Compton, and Long Beach.

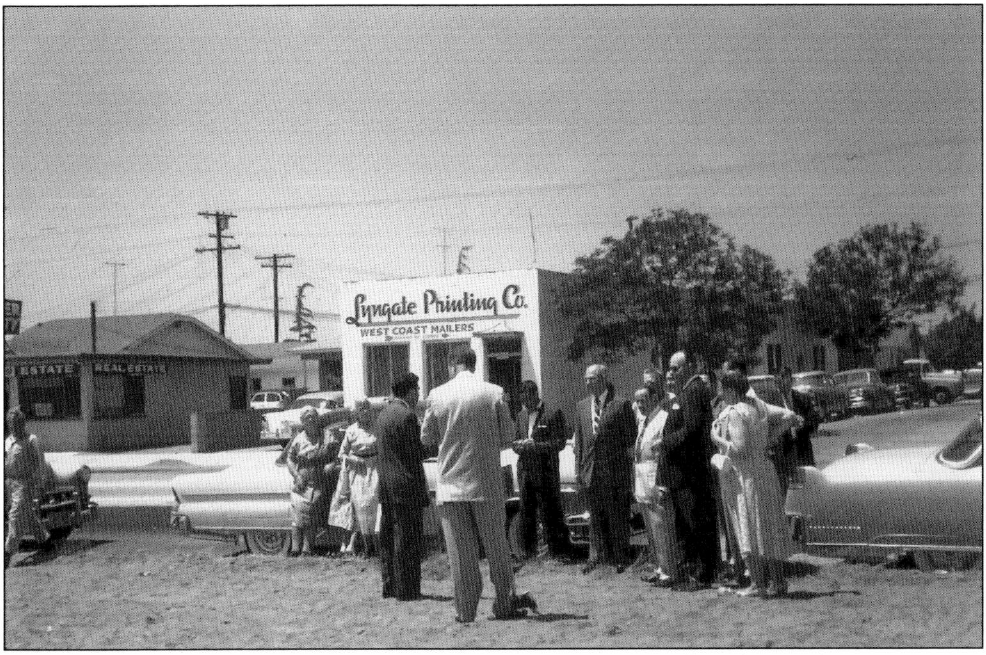

Lyngate Printing Co. and mail house was across from Stop's Coffee Shop and Restaurant on Abbott Road. The people shown here are believed to be attending the ground-breaking ceremony of Stop's Coffee Shop and Restaurant about 1957. This photograph is believed to have come from the *Lynwood Press Tribune.*

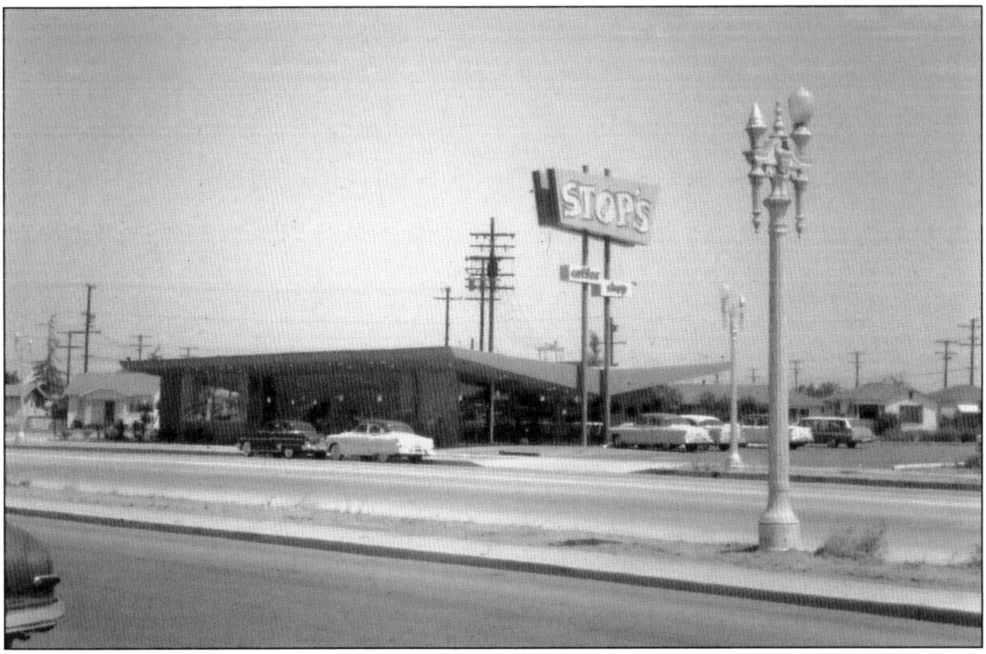

Stop's Coffee Shop and Restaurant was a roadside restaurant popular among local residents and passing motorists. This particular restaurant was located on Abbott Road and was the first development on the Century Square. The Alpha Beta Grocery Store would then occupy the area north of the restaurant.

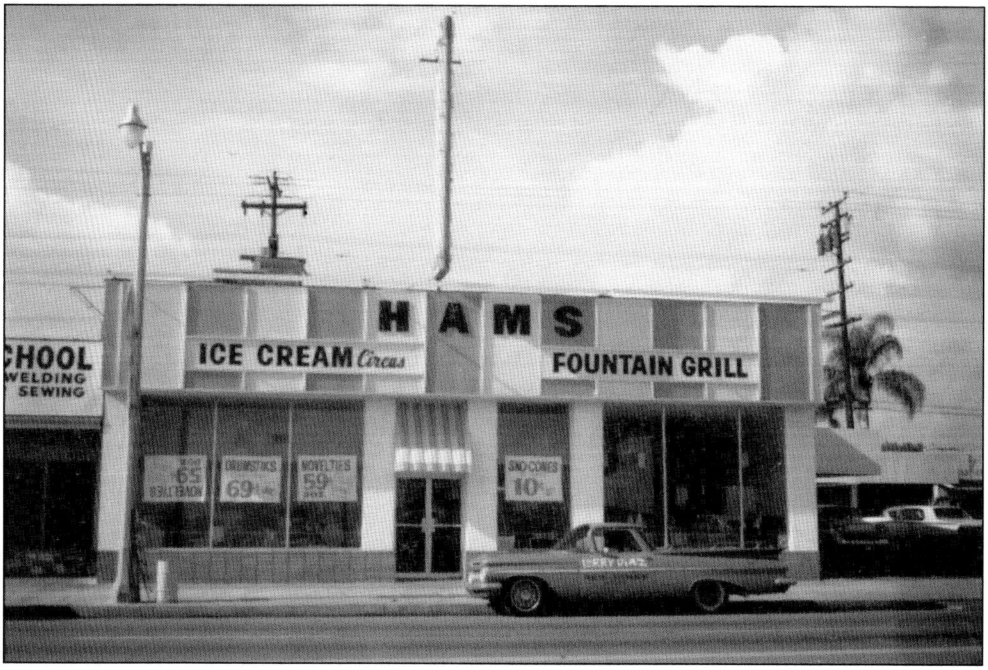

John Ham, better known as "Johnny Ham, the Ice Cream Man" to his Lynwood friends and patrons, owned Ham's Ice Cream and Restaurant, where he became locally famous for his family's ice cream and was widely respected as an honorable businessperson. In the early 1960s, he became a very popular Lynwood mayor and council member. (Courtesy of the Ham family.)

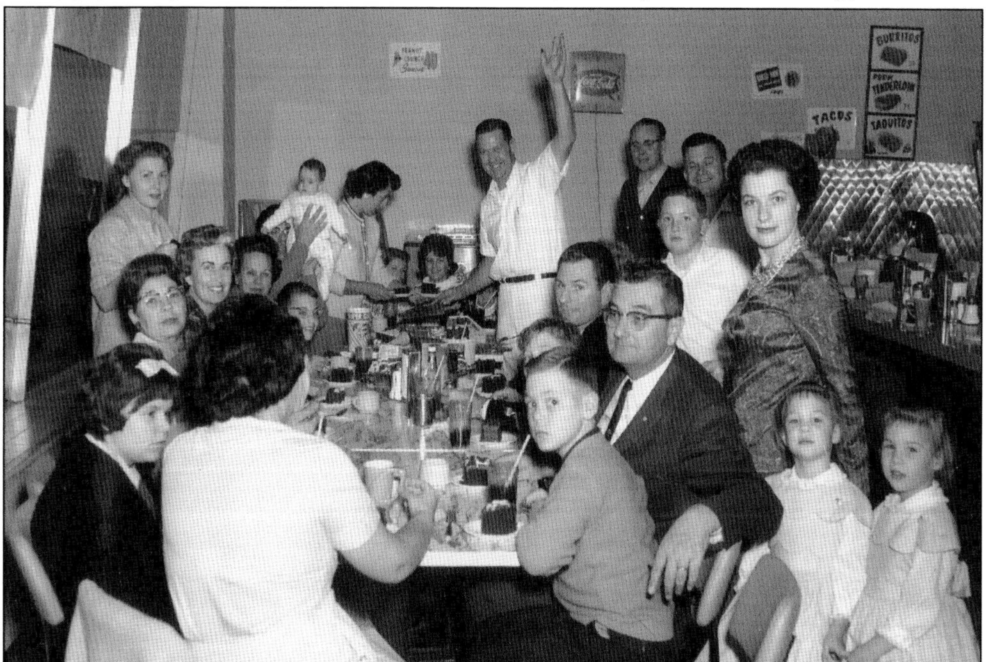

Members of the Ham family are pictured at a family gathering inside their restaurant in the late 1950s or early 1960s. (Courtesy of the Ham family.)

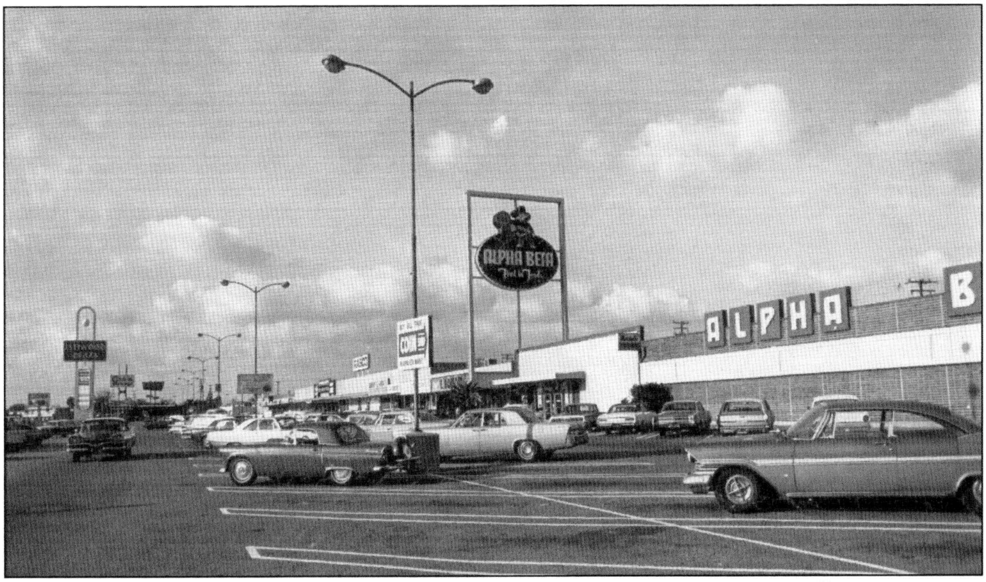

In 1958, Alpha Beta Grocery Store was constructed at the Lynwood Plaza on Century Boulevard and Abbott Road (now the site of Cesar Chavez Middle School). It opened on February 12, 1959. Alpha Beta was known for having clever advertising promotions to attract customers, such as Mother Goose Day and Valentine's Day, and on occasion sponsoring a small circus in front of the store. In 1961, the Plaza expanded to include Clark's Drug Store and J.J. Newberry's. Many Plaza stores were heavily damaged during the 1992 Los Angeles riots and never reopened. The shopping plaza site fell dormant until a new school was built in 2005.

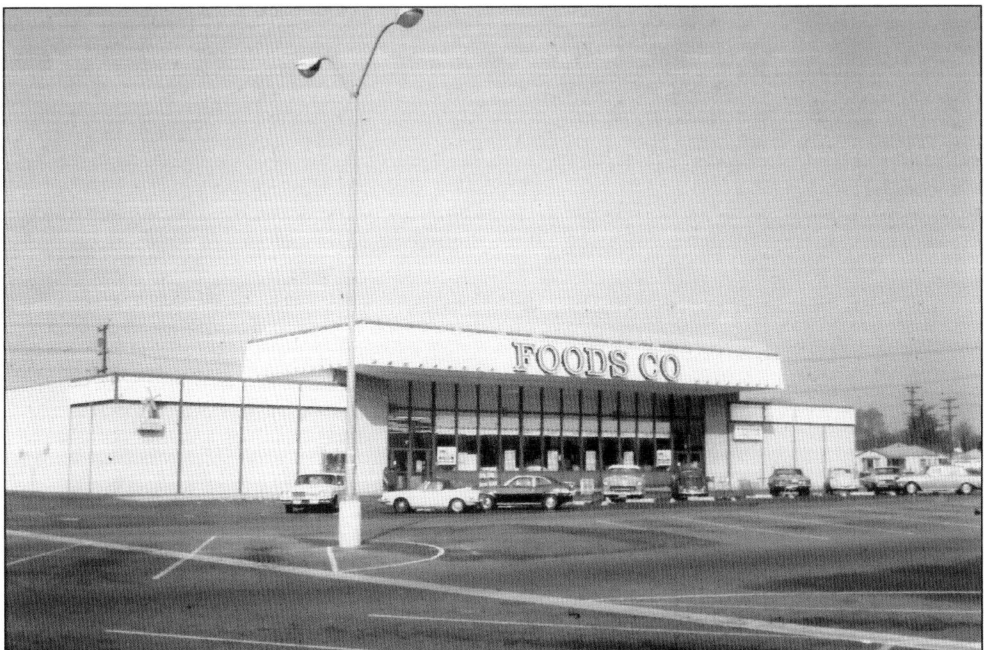

The Food Company, on Imperial Highway, is located on the site where Zody's Department Store stood in the 1960s. The site accommodated several grocery stores after that until 1998, when the Lynwood Unified School District built the state-of-the-art Lynwood High School.

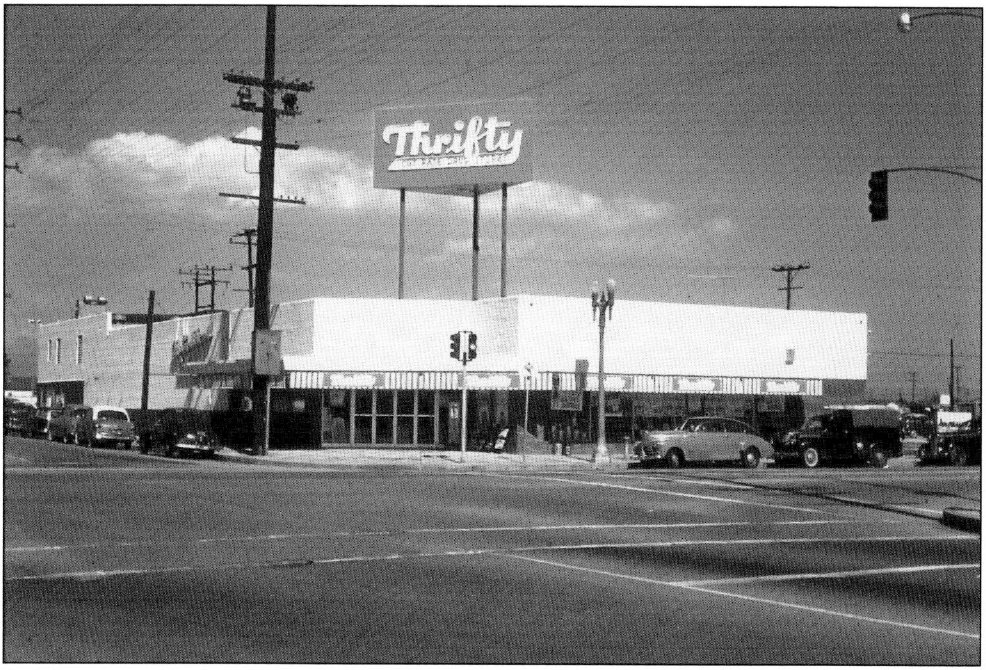

In February 1953, the Thrifty Drug Store opened its doors to Lynwood patrons. The store was built on the corner of Century Boulevard (Martin Luther King Jr. Boulevard) and Bullis Road. At the time, Thrifty's was one of the biggest drugstores in Lynwood. It was also the largest Thrifty store that had been built up until that point. Thrifty's was also popular in Lynwood for serving great ice cream. This site is now Superior Grocery Market's parking lot.

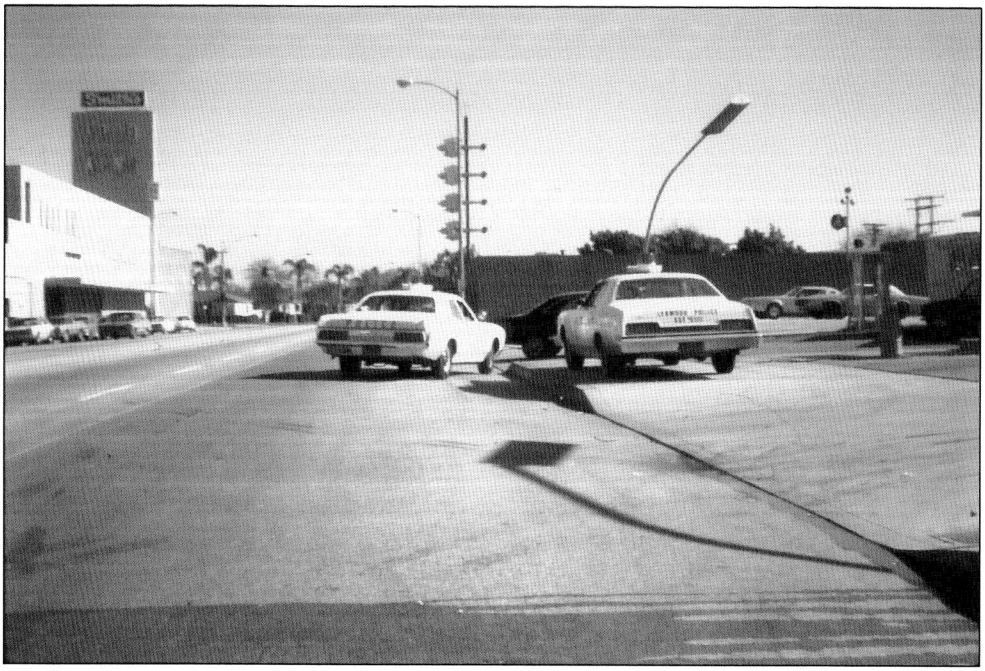

Food King was known for having events in its parking lot. It sold pancakes and other food, and proceeds often supported the Lynwood High School Library.

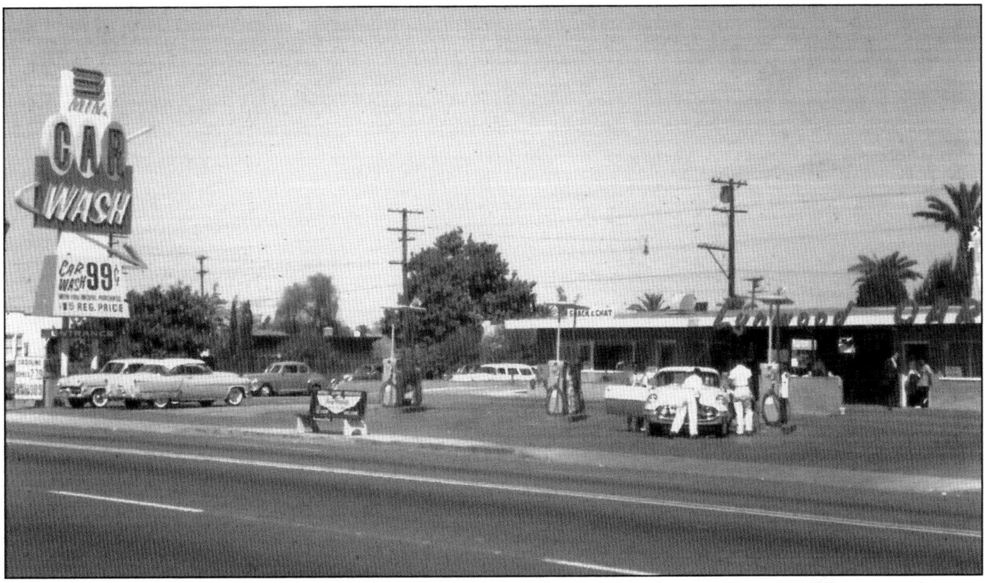

The Lynwood Car Wash, located on Long Beach Boulevard, has been a Lynwood business fixture for over 50 years. It only cost 99¢ for a car wash in the late 1950s!

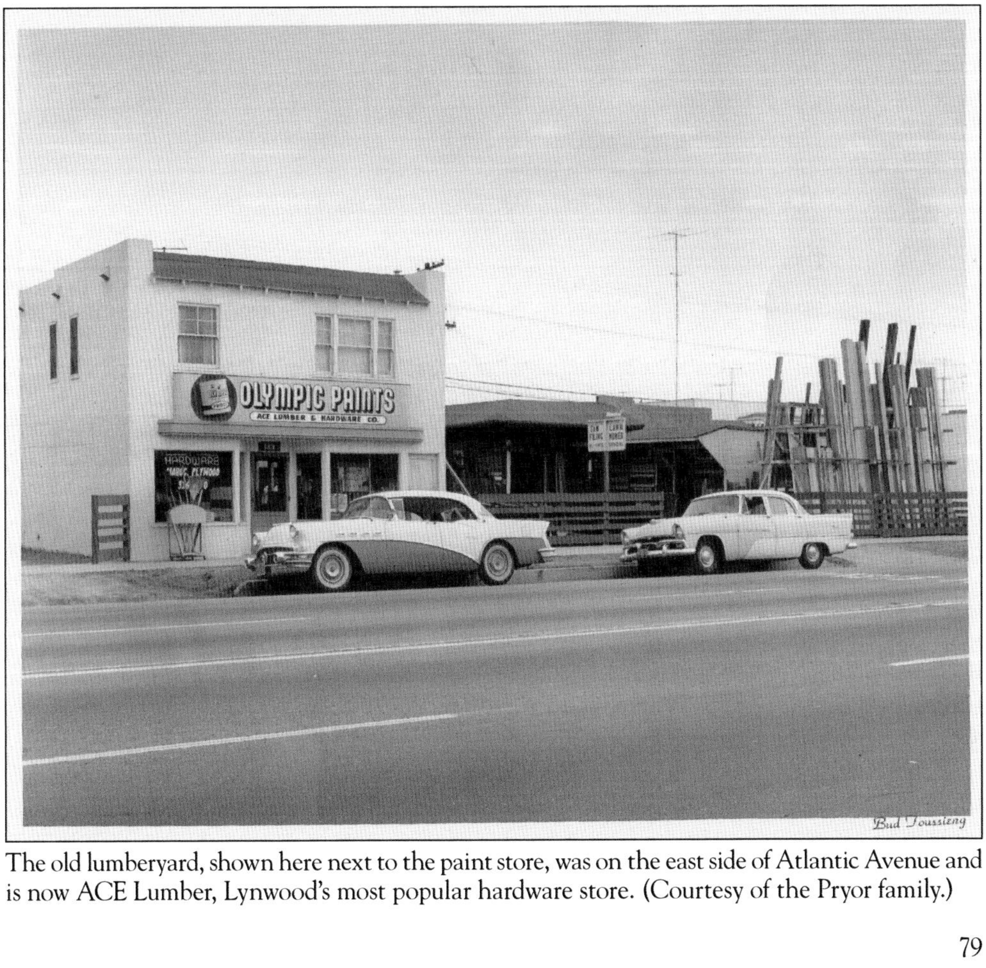

The old lumberyard, shown here next to the paint store, was on the east side of Atlantic Avenue and is now ACE Lumber, Lynwood's most popular hardware store. (Courtesy of the Pryor family.)

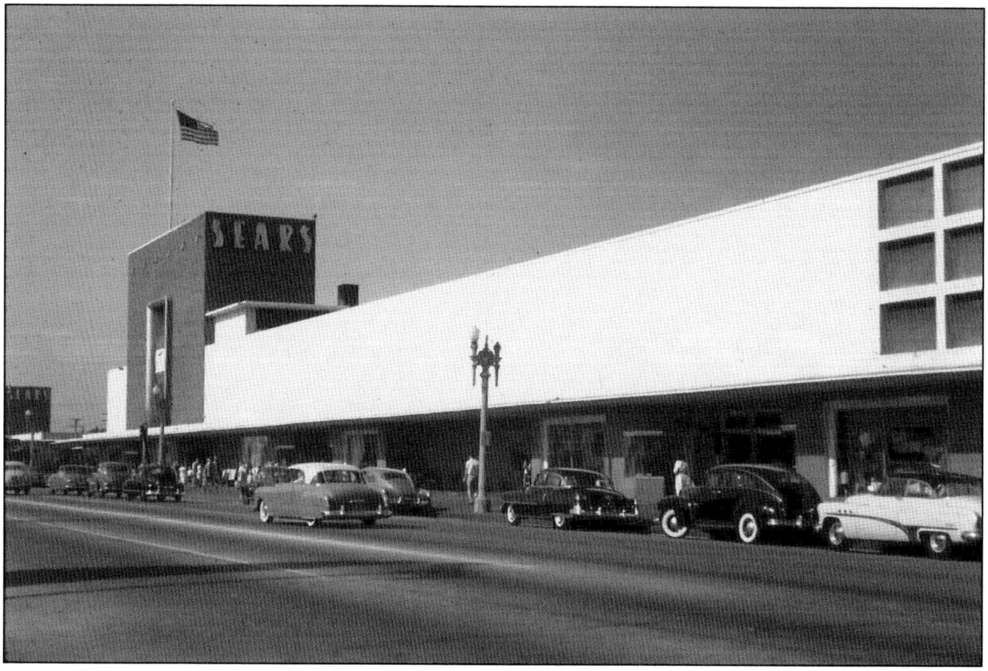

Pictured here is Sears Department Store on Long Beach Boulevard. The north end of the complex was a Sears tire maintenance shop that straddled the Lynwood-Compton border in the 1950s, when this photograph was taken.

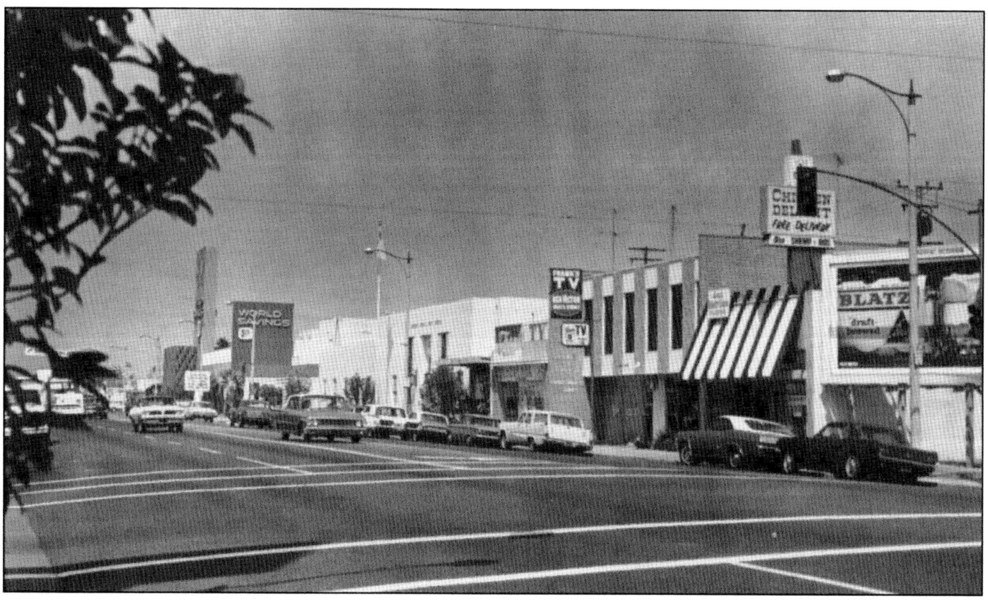

Long Beach Boulevard is shown, facing north toward Imperial Highway. The World Savings Bank (just left of center) was built in 1956 and was another highly successful business founded in Lynwood.

Pictured here is the Security First National Bank, which was built by Bernard Marks in 1961 (located at 11303 Long Beach Boulevard). When the bank opened in April 1961, its president was Russell Hodge. By the mid-1970s, the bank closed its doors and after several structural modifications is today used by several commercial tenants.

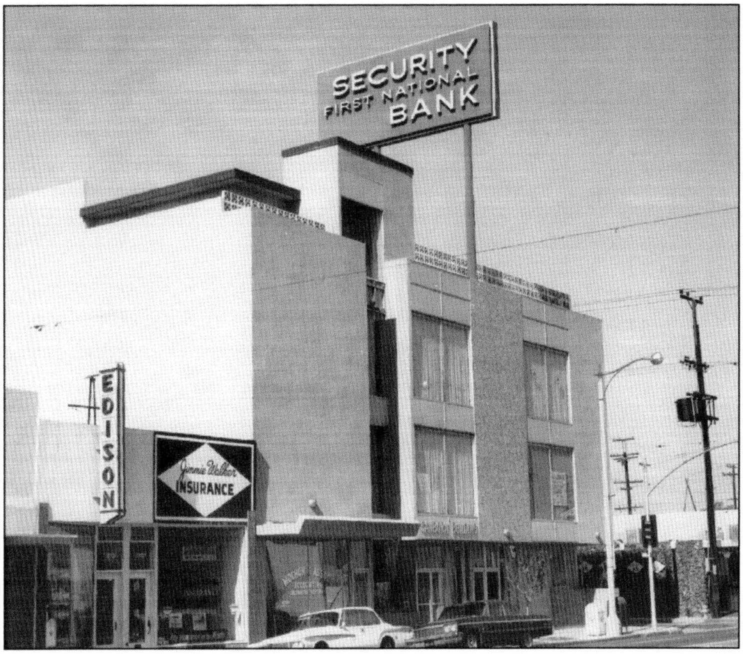

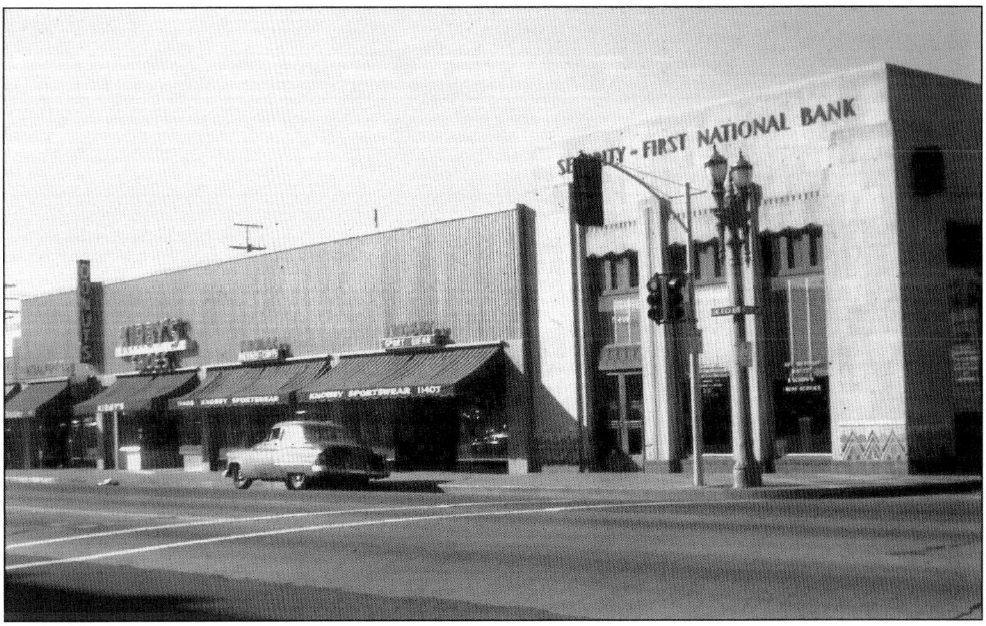

Lynwood's branch of the Security Bank was first opened in 1920, with quarters in the office of the Old Lynwood Company. The bank was then a small branch of the Farmers and Merchant Bank of Compton. The bank soon moved into its own building, located on Long Beach Boulevard and Mulford Avenue, to the two-story masonry building shown on page 37. That building was destroyed by an earthquake, and in 1933, the bank pictured here was built at 11330 Long Beach Boulevard. When the bank moved to the new building on the corner of Sanborn Avenue, the property was offered for sale or lease.

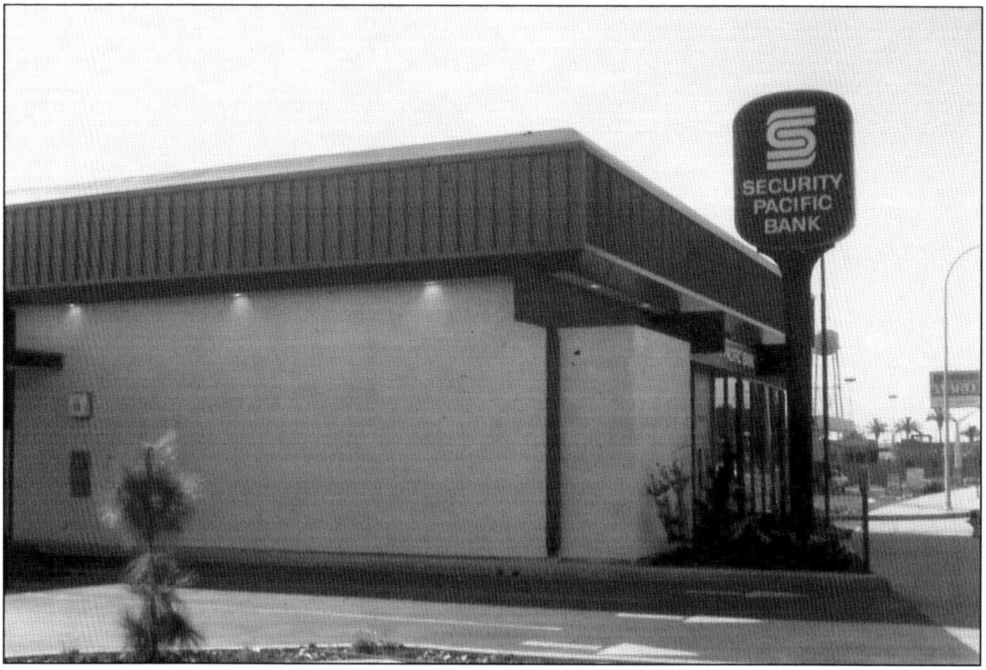

Shown is Security Pacific Bank on Imperial Highway, just west of Long Beach Boulevard. In 1967, Security First National Bank bought Pacific National Bank and became Security Pacific National Bank. In the early 1990s, Bank of America merged with Security Pacific Bank and the Lynwood branch was closed. The site pictured here is currently an auto parts store. In the background to the right is a view of the Montgomery Ward sign; the department store was situated on Imperial Highway and State Street, the present site of Plaza Mexico Shopping Center.

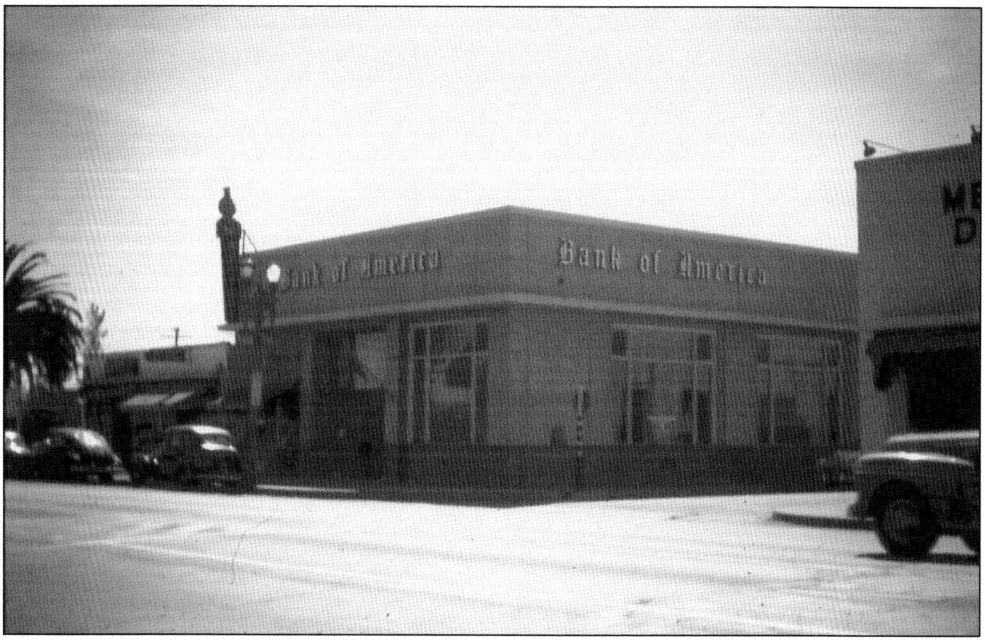

In 1946, the Bank of America stood on Long Beach Boulevard next to the old chamber of commerce building.

Five

Schools, Churches, and Hospitals

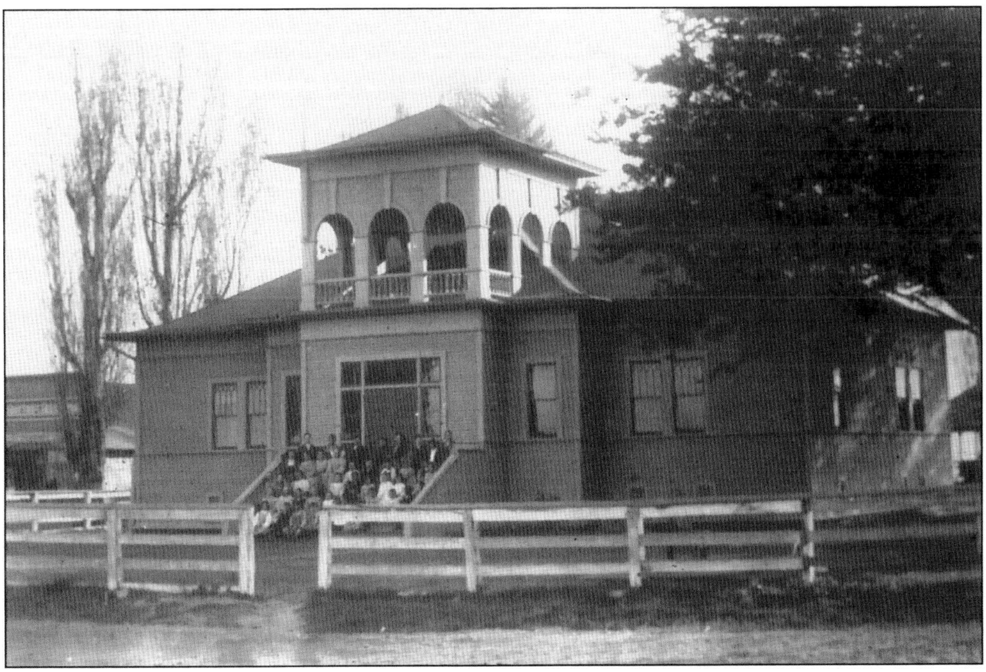

This is a photograph of the Lugo District School, built in 1895. The house had two rooms and a loft tower and accommodated eight grades. The school had two teachers; each taught four grades. In 1917, the Lugo District School closed and students were moved to the new school on Lynwood Road, named Wilson Elementary.

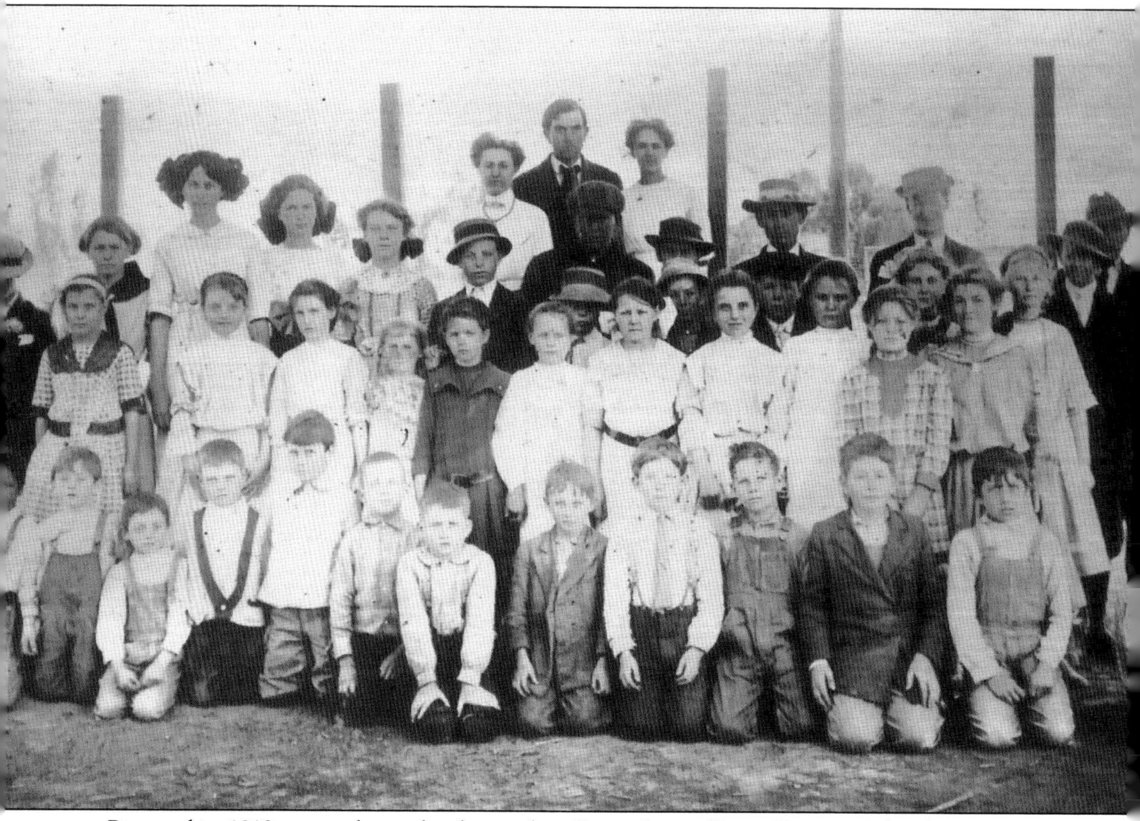

Pictured in 1912 are students, faculty, and staff members of Lugo District School.

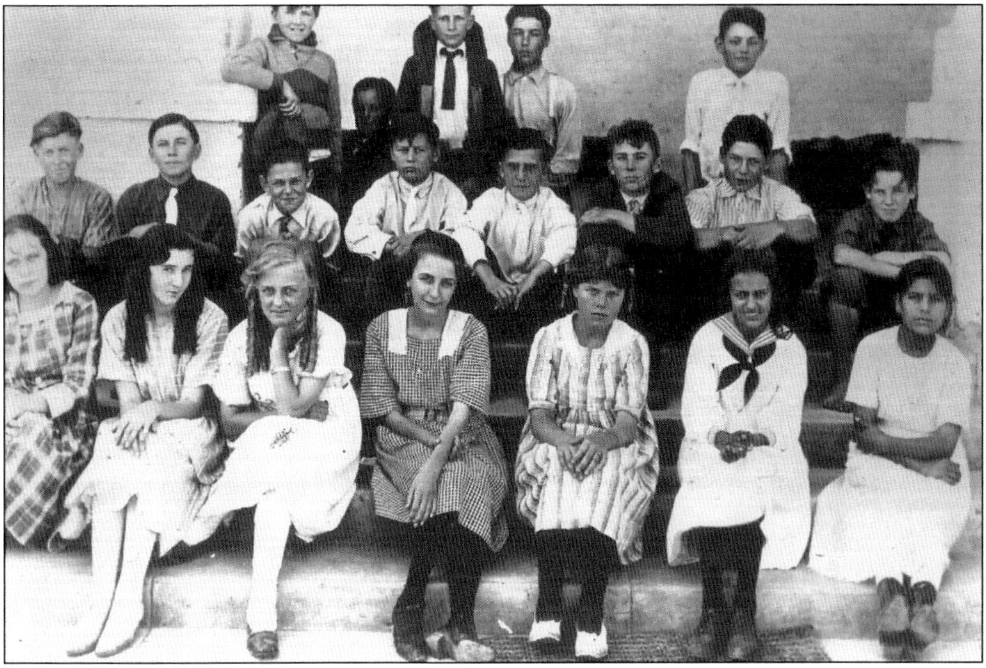

Photographed here in 1914 are the fourth and fifth grades of the old Lugo School. Many of the students in the classes were children of Lynwood's first families.

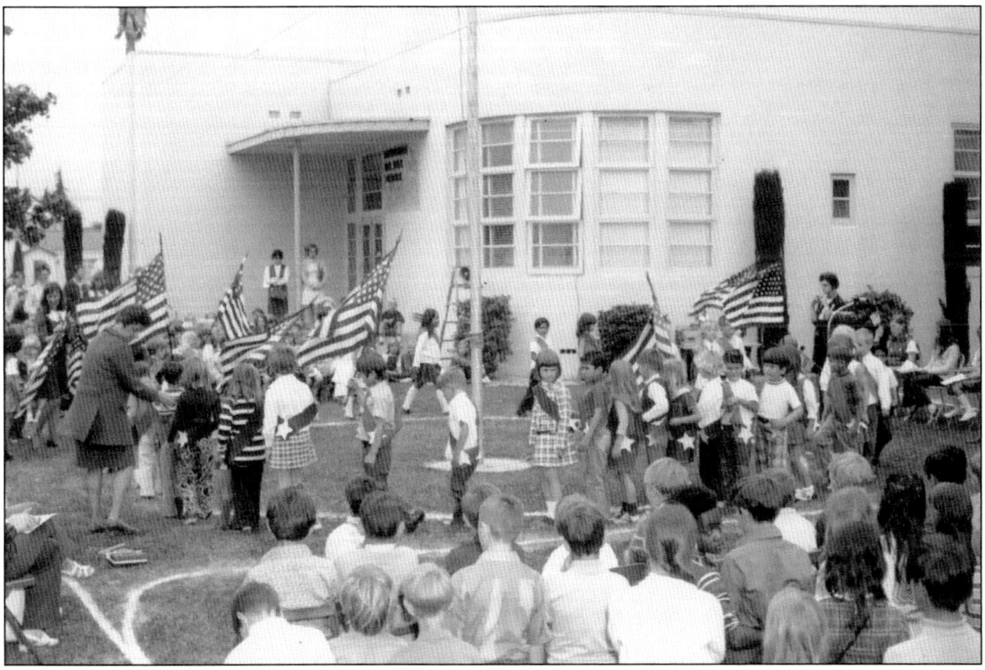

In 1917, the Lynwood District approved construction of a second school on Lynwood Road. The school was named Wilson Elementary. Students from the Lugo District School were moved to the Wilson School. This left the school building vacant, and the First Community Church made an offer to buy the school. Pictured here, Wilson students celebrate a national holiday in the 1950s. (Courtesy of Jean Hinojosa.)

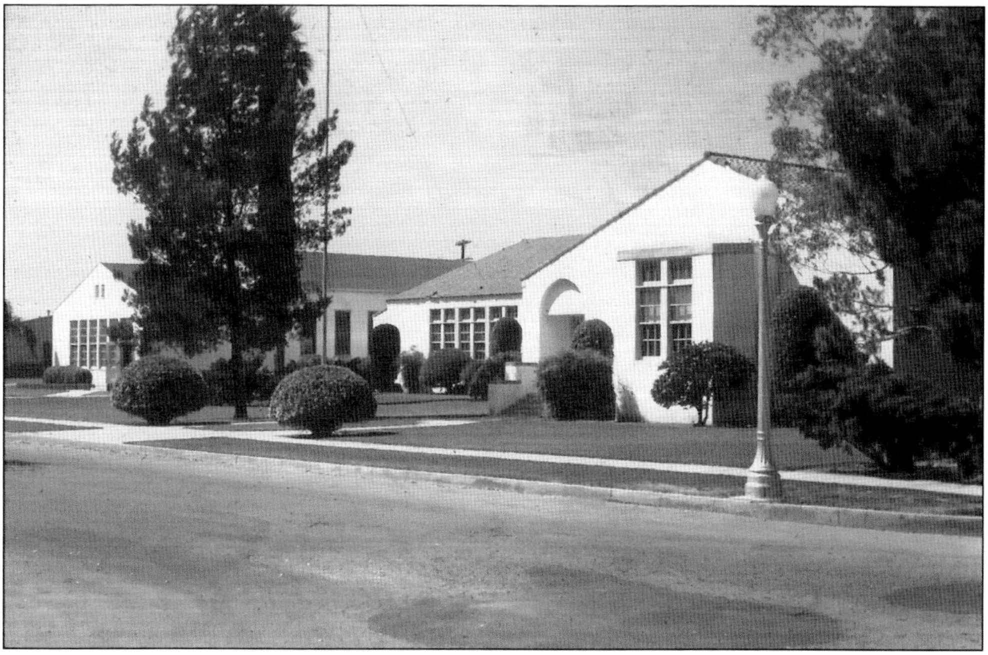

In 1929, Washington Elementary School, named in honor of the nation's first president, was the fifth school built in Lynwood.

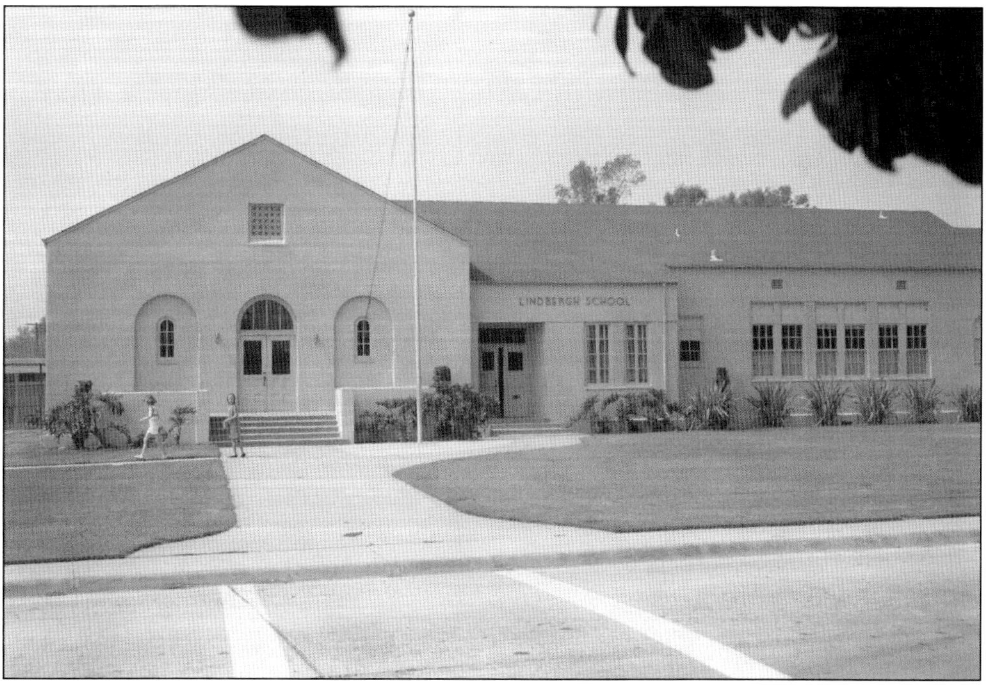

This photograph is Lindbergh Elementary School, which was built in 1926 at the same time as Lincoln Elementary. The only original part of the school existing today is the front entrance and library; the remaining sections have all been renovated over time.

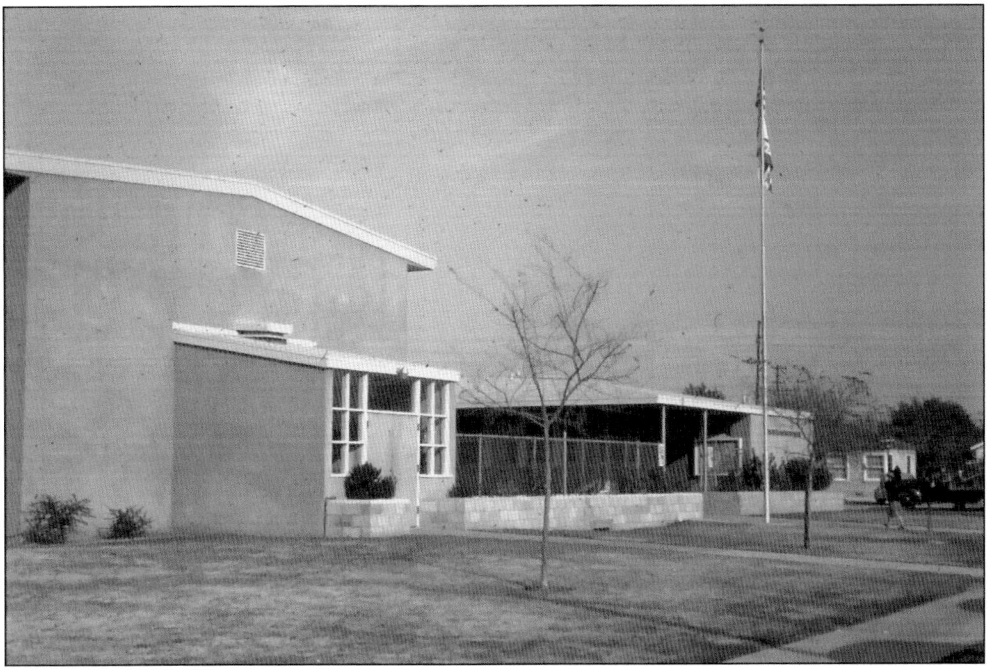

Roosevelt Elementary, built in 1924 and shown here, was named after Pres. Franklin D. Roosevelt. The school site is at Mallion and Abbott Avenues.

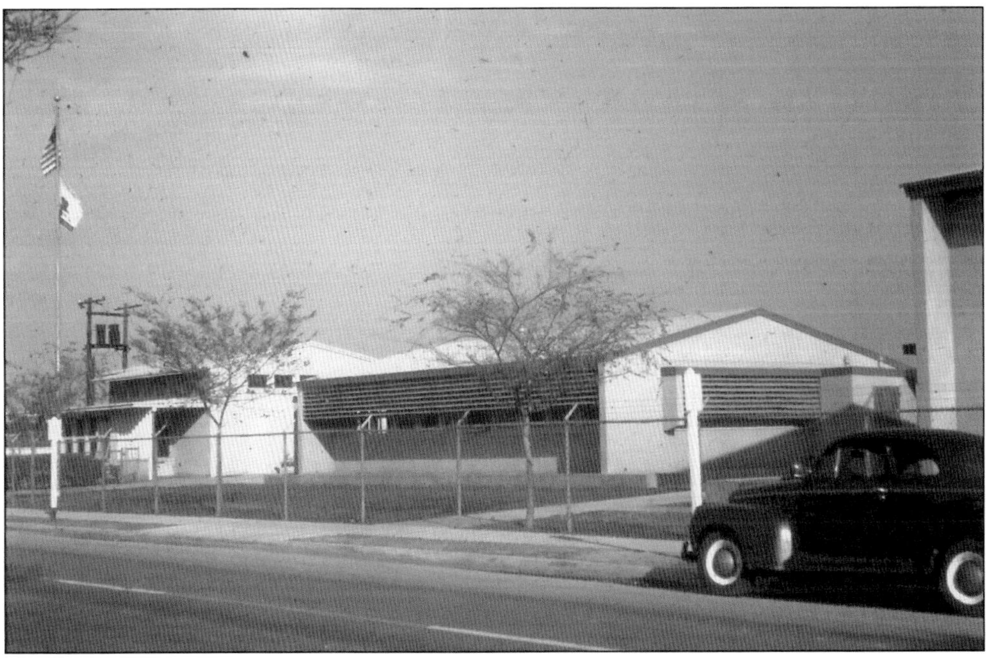

Will Rogers Elementary School was built in 1930 on Wright Road and was named after the famous American cowboy, writer, and performer. By this time, the city's population was steadily growing and more schools were needed as communities developed and expanded. The school was later moved to a nearby location, and the old campus pictured here serves as a continuation high school.

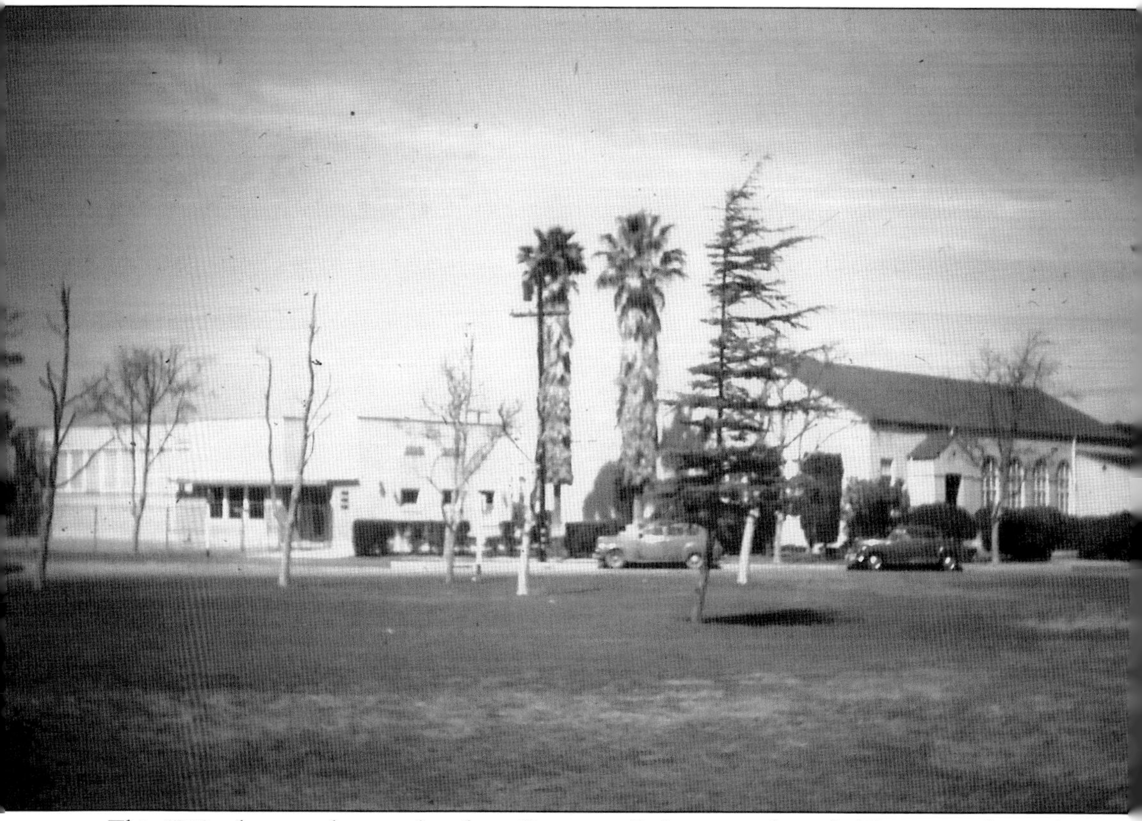

This 1940s photograph was taken from Carnation Park viewing Lincoln Elementary, located at State Street; note that the park is not landscaped with palm trees as it is today.

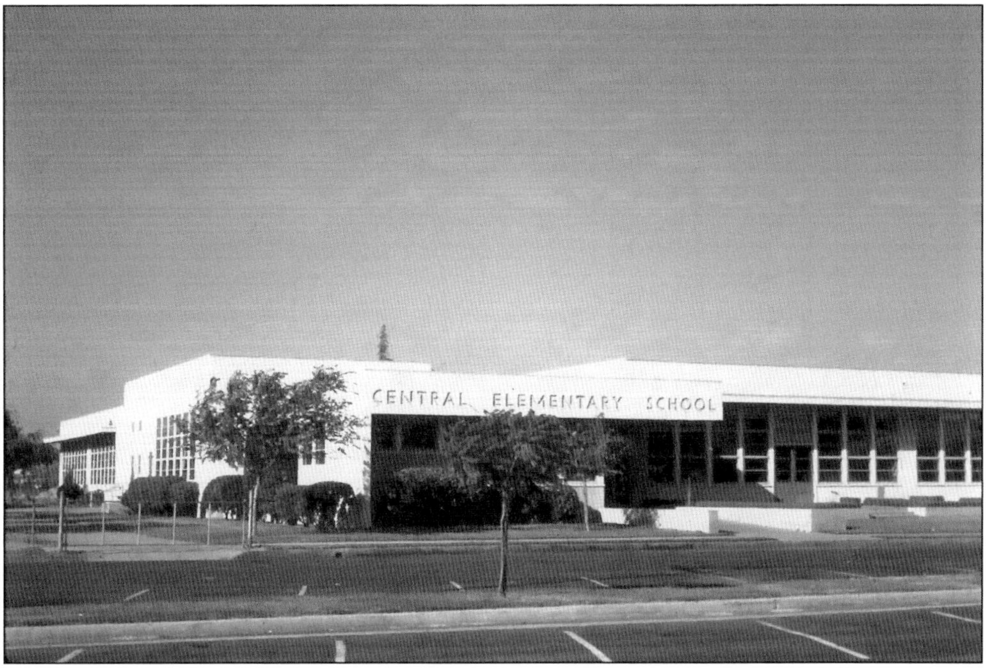

Central Elementary School was built in 1936 and was originally part of the Compton Union School District. The school was converted into a middle school in the 1950s and renamed Hosler Jr. High School after Dr. Fred W. Hosler.

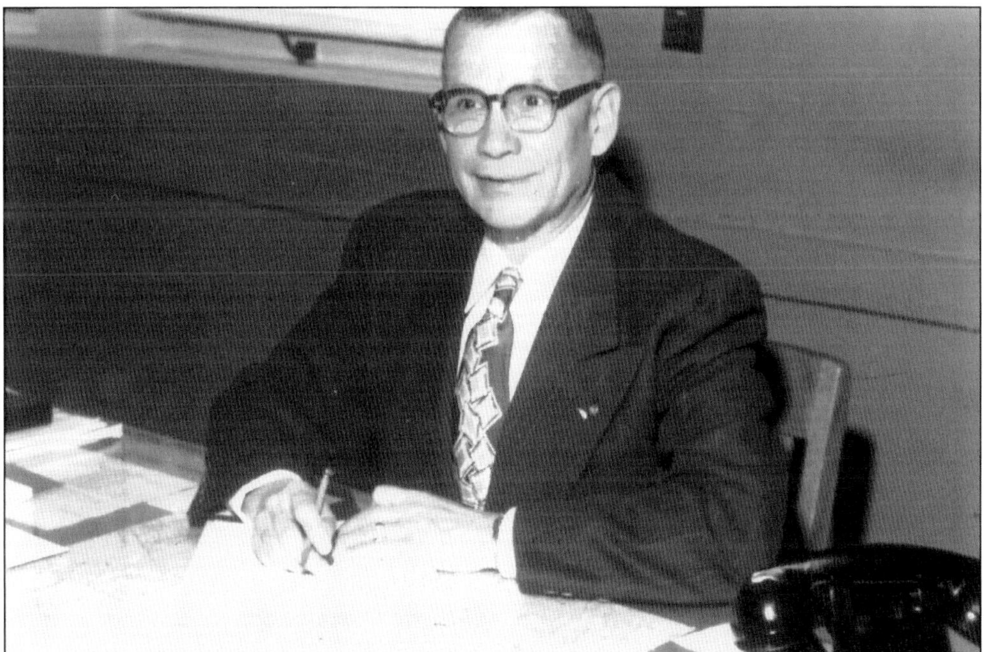

Fred Hosler was a popular administrator in the Lynwood School District who served in many positions, including superintendent, until his death in 1952. The legacy of Hosler remains in Lynwood, as the school district named a middle school in his memory.

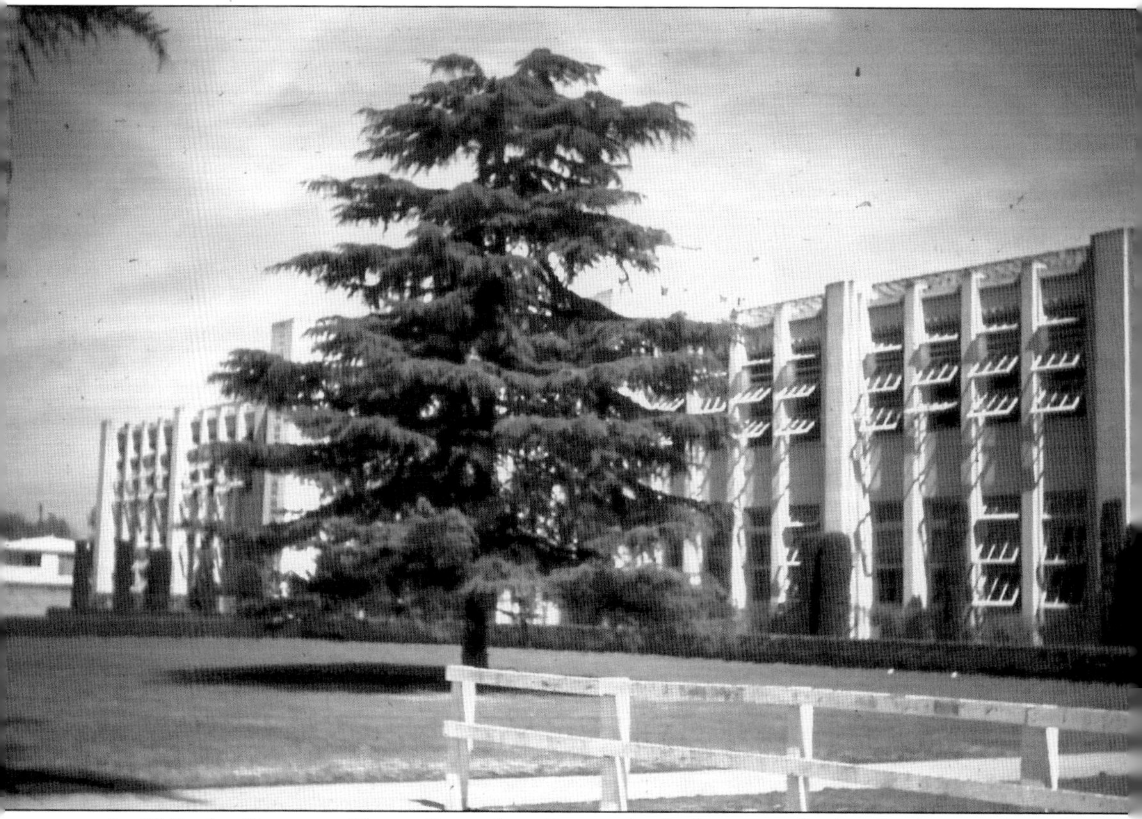

In 1941, the Compton Union Secondary District built this junior high school on Bullis Road and Carlin Avenue that later became Lynwood High School (known informally as *the Castle*). In 1998, the high school moved to a new facility on Imperial Highway, and Lynwood Middle School has occupied the building since then.

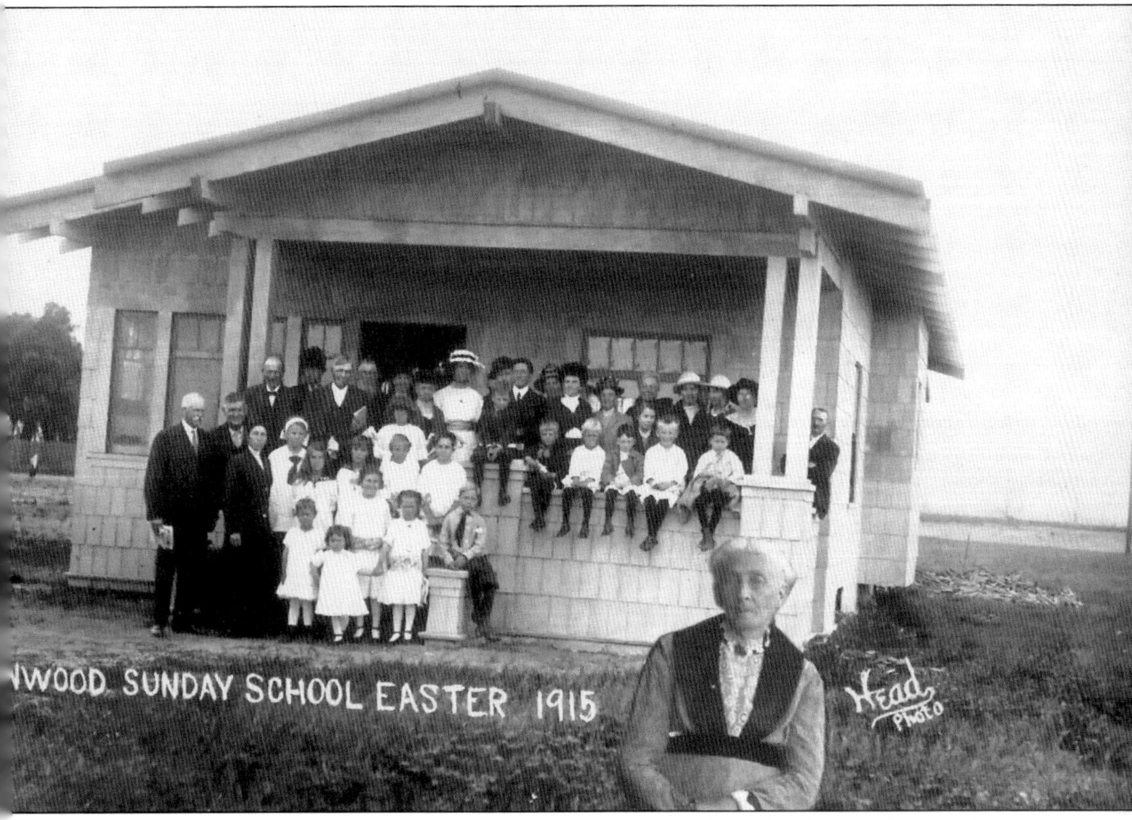

This photograph of a small church congregation attending Sunday School was taken on Easter Day in 1915. The building originally housed the Lugo District School around 1894.

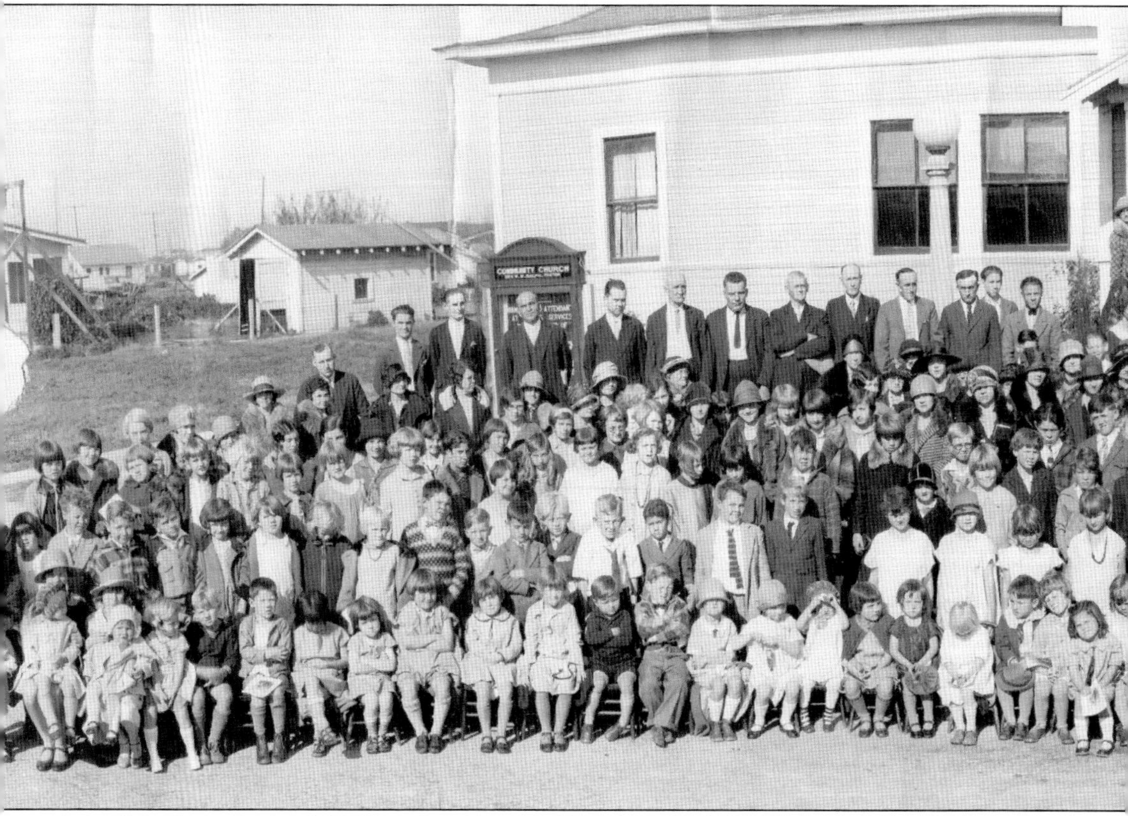

This photograph of the First Community Church was taken on January 23, 1927. The entire

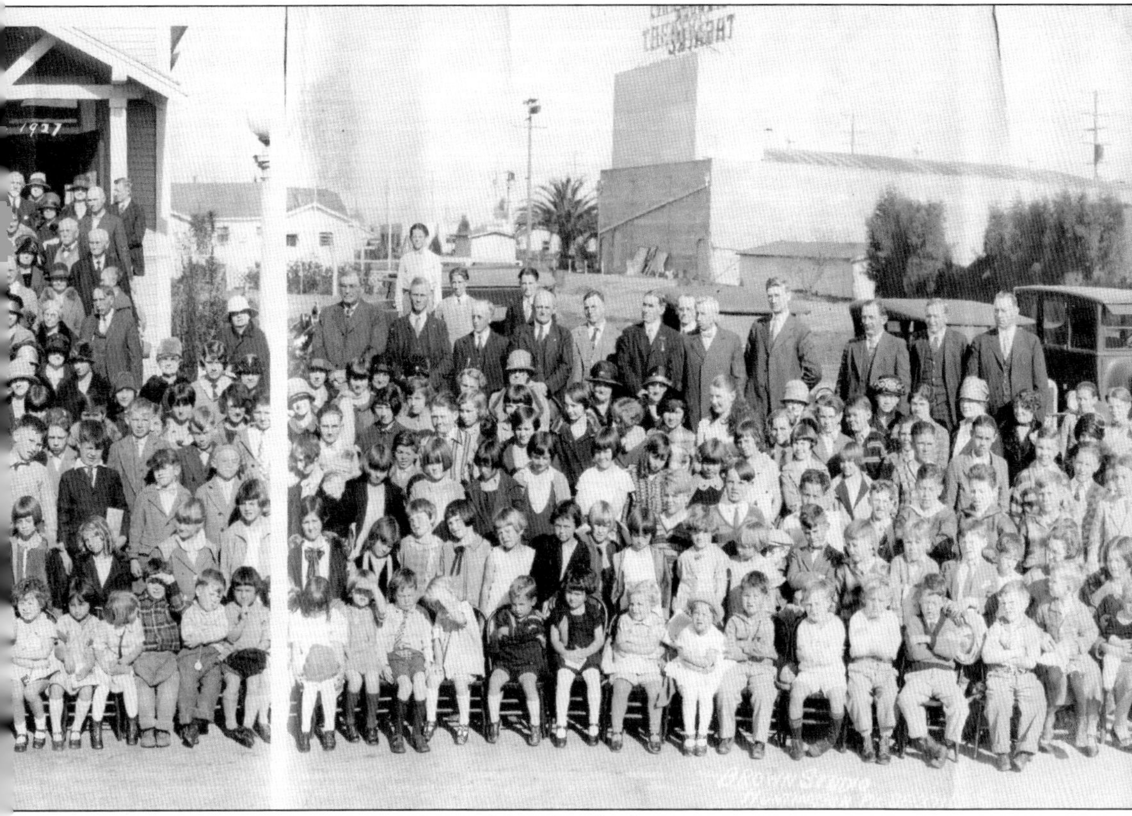

congregation is seen here posing in front of the church after morning services.

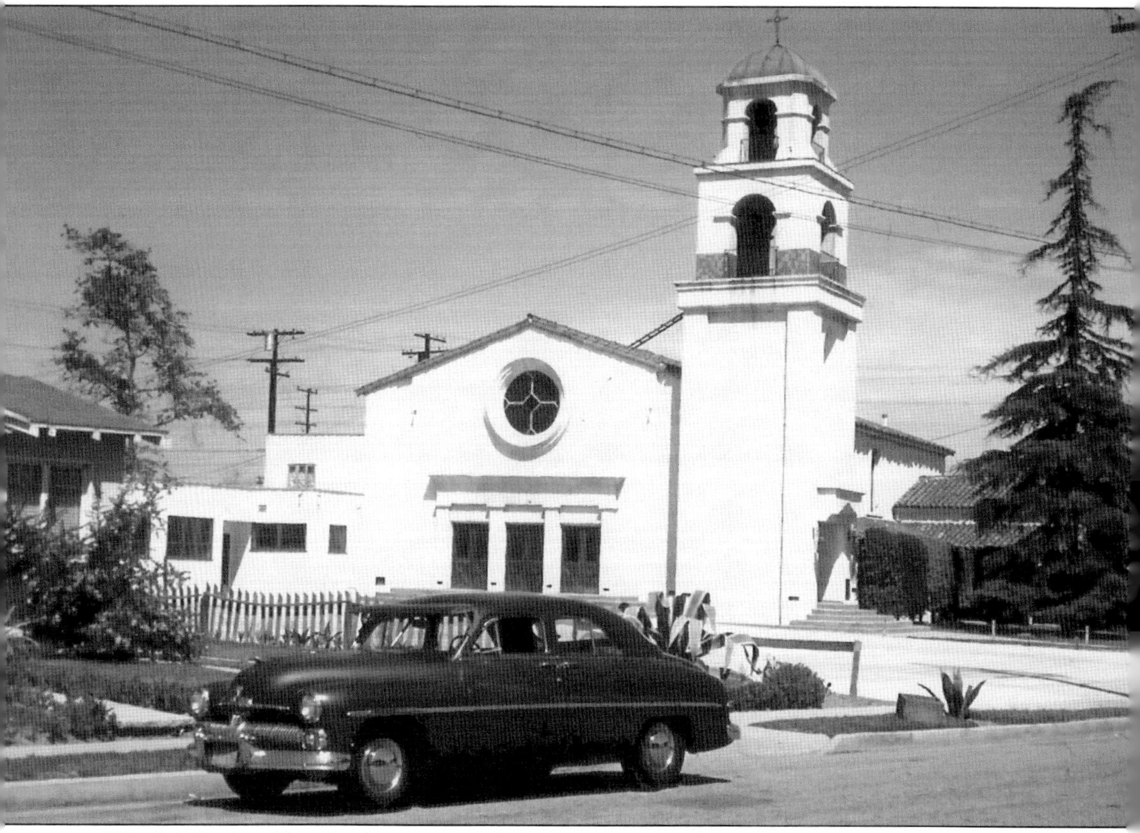

The Methodist Church, shown around 1940, was on Beechwood Street, just west of Long Beach Boulevard. The church now is home to Lynwood Grace Hispanic Church of the Nazarene. The building is largely unchanged today.

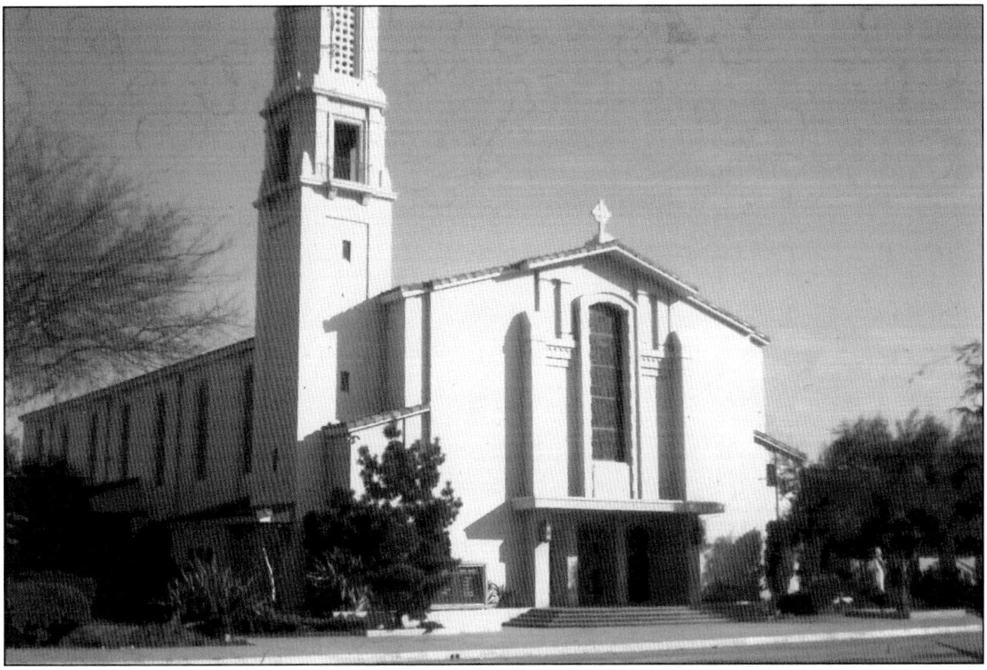

Before moving here to its present-day site, St. Emydius held services in the old city hall. A church was built at the corner of California and Mulford Avenues that served St. Emydius from the 1920s until 1951. Thereafter, the church occupied the current building on California Avenue, pictured here in 1958, and continues services today.

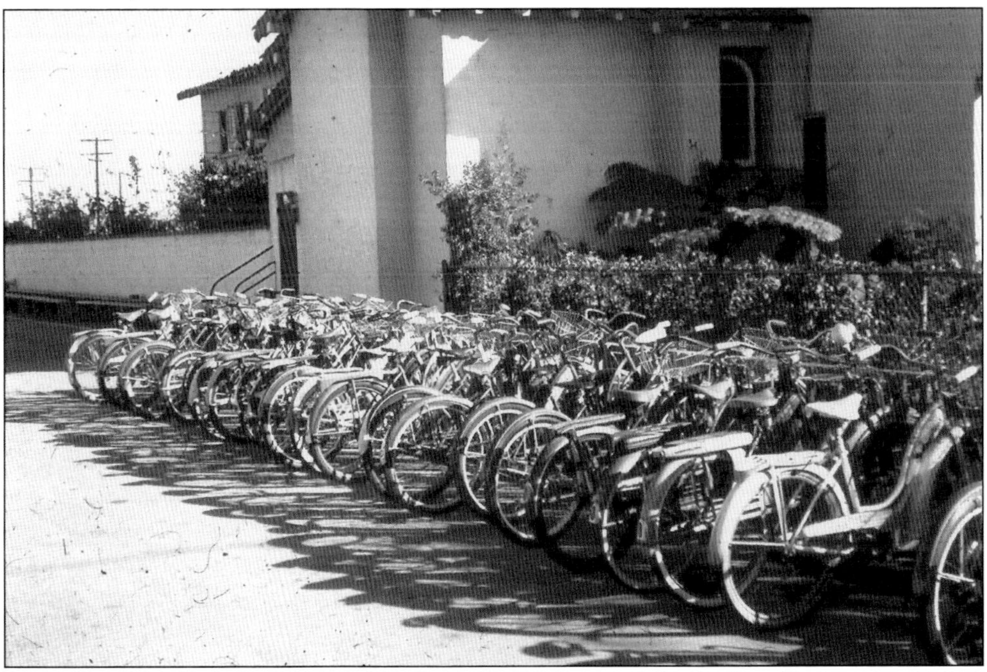

This photograph shows the back of the St. Emydius Elementary School. The school was established in 1947, with the help of Father O'Carrol, at the present-day California Avenue location. The school had five teachers, and the first principal was Sister Lucy.

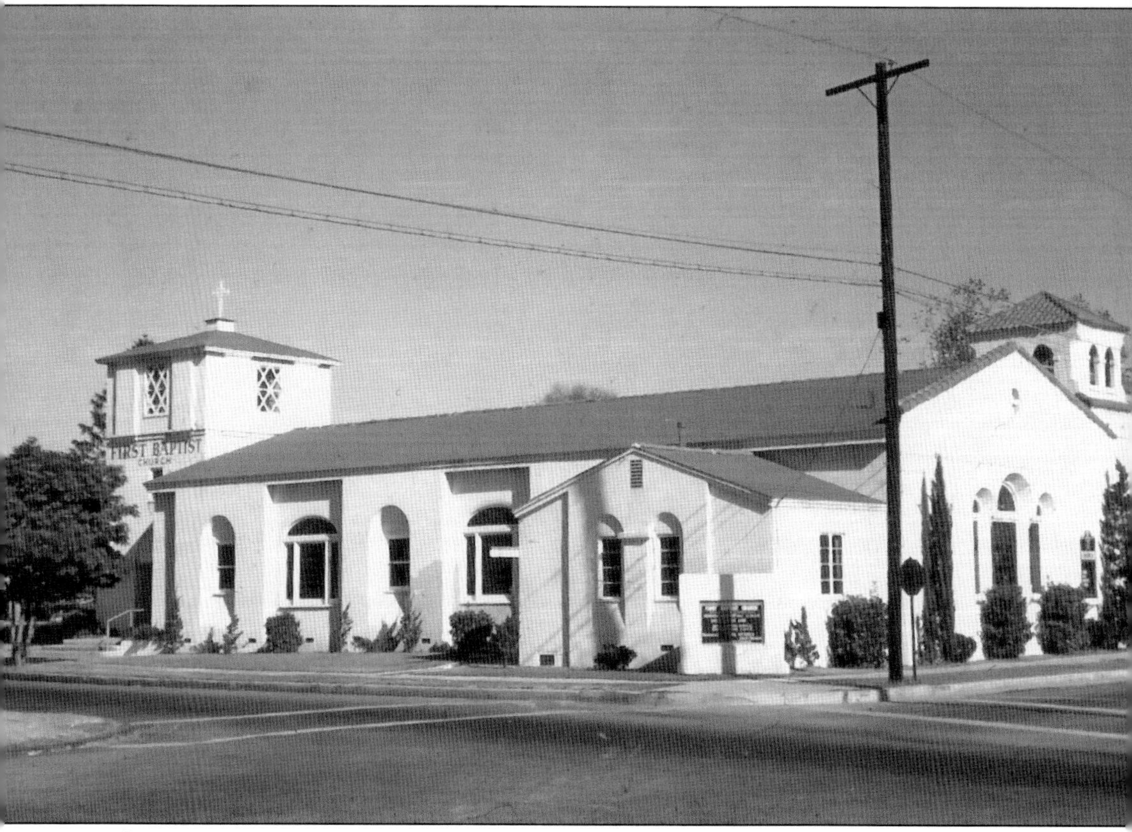

The First Missionary Baptist Church was built on March 26, 1925, on what is present-day Lynwood Road and State Street. The Reverend Van Dyke Todd served as pastor for the First Missionary Baptist Church. By the 1950s, the Baptist church had vacated. It is now home to an Apostolic church.

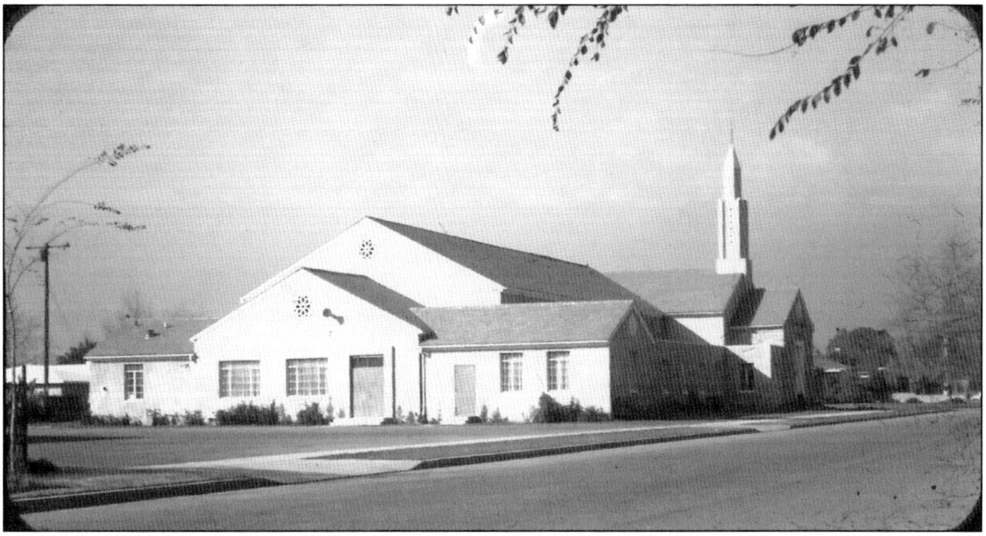

This 1951 photograph shows the Mormon church on Bradfield and Magnolia Avenues.

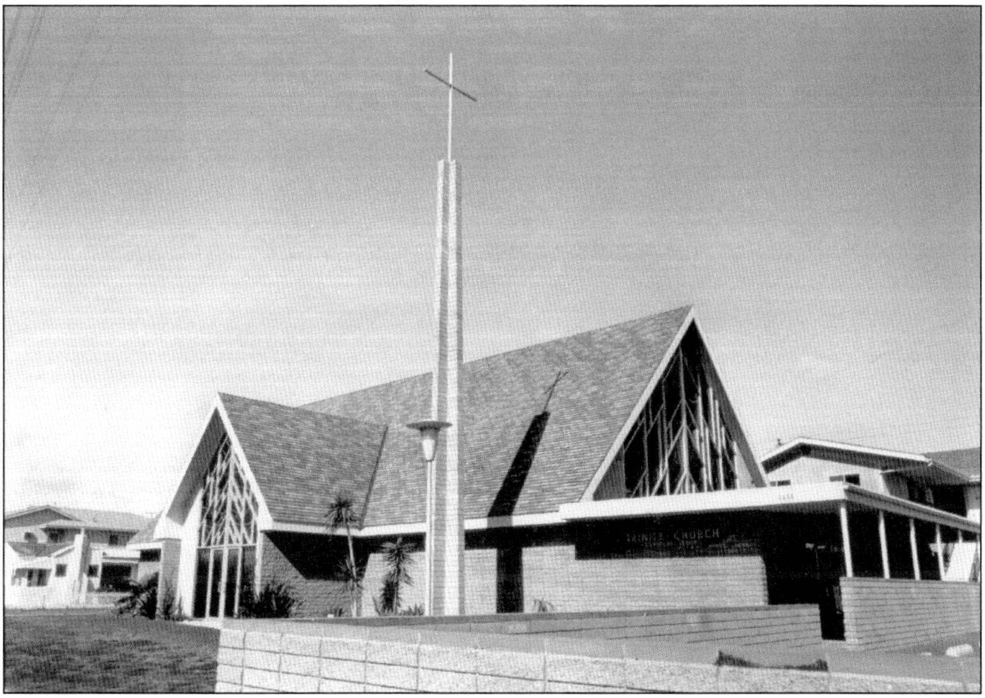

Shown here is Lynwood Foursquare Church, organized in 1928, with the Rev. L.W. Schultz serving as the first pastor. In 1938, the church purchased the Women's Club building on Fernwood Avenue and Fir Street.

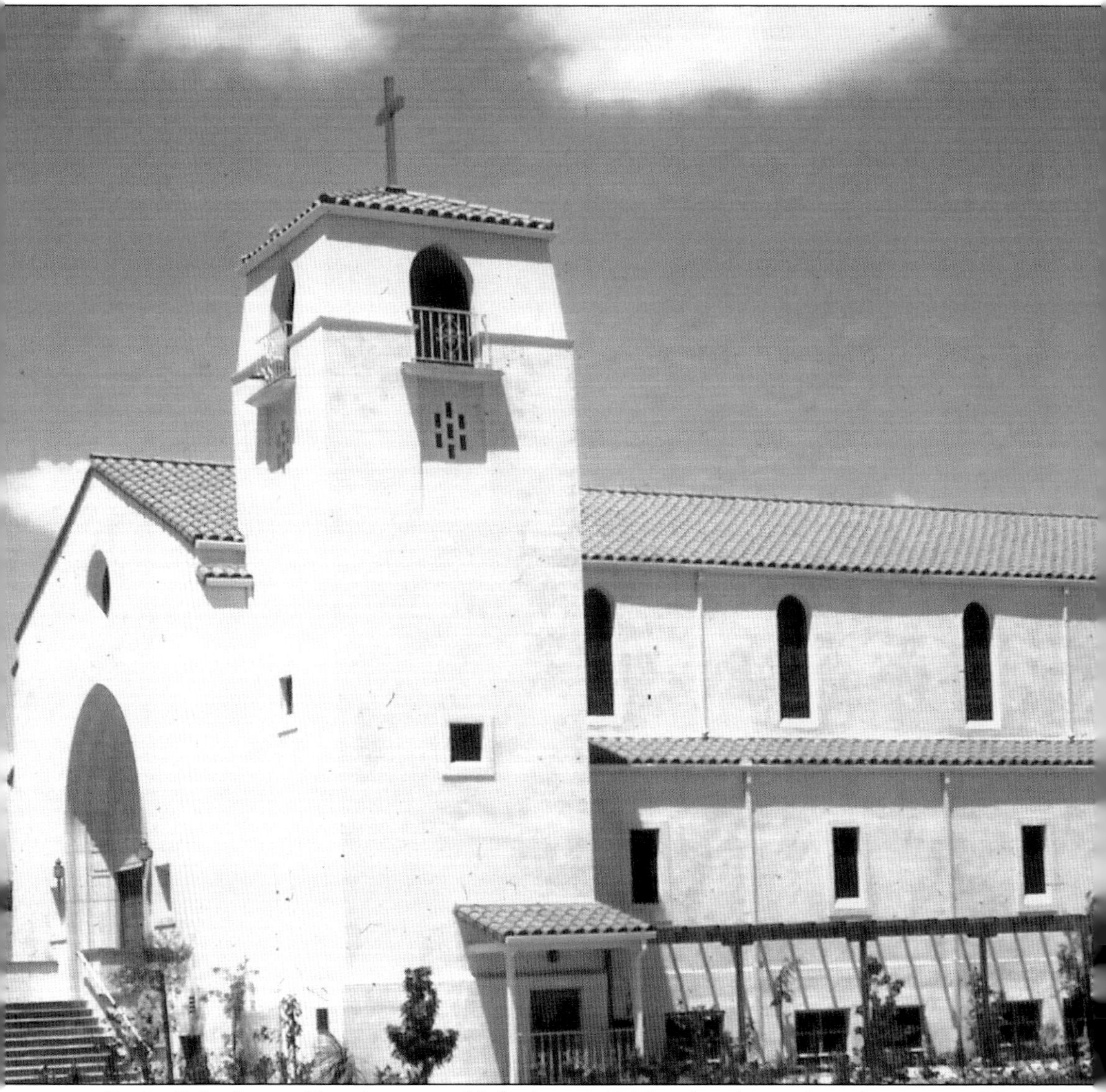

St. Paul's Lutheran Church was established in 1945. The church stands at the corner of Carlin Avenue and Cortland Street. Dr. Kent Johnson and the Reverend Alvin O. Pinke led worship services in the 1970s.

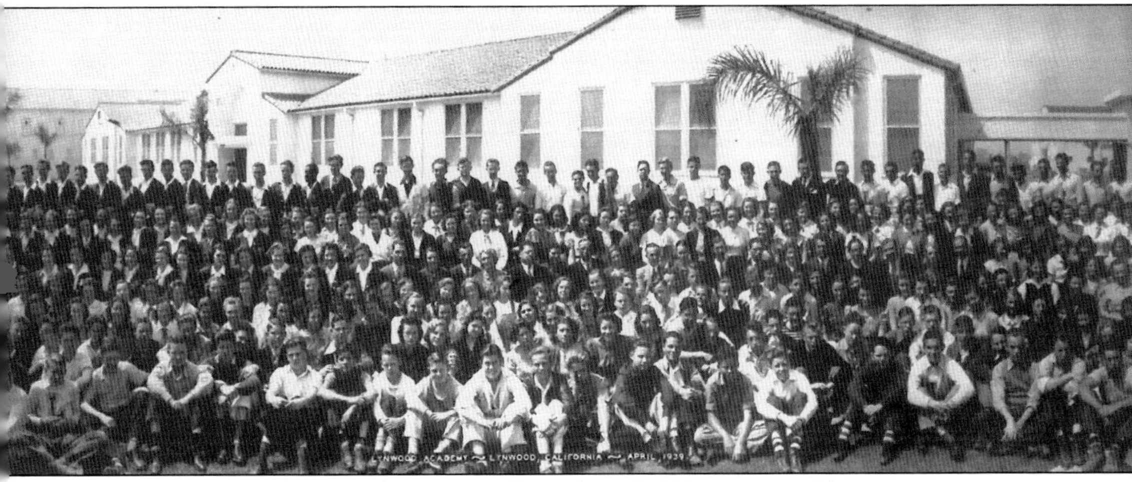

Members of the Seventh-Day Adventist Academy class of 1939 are pictured here.

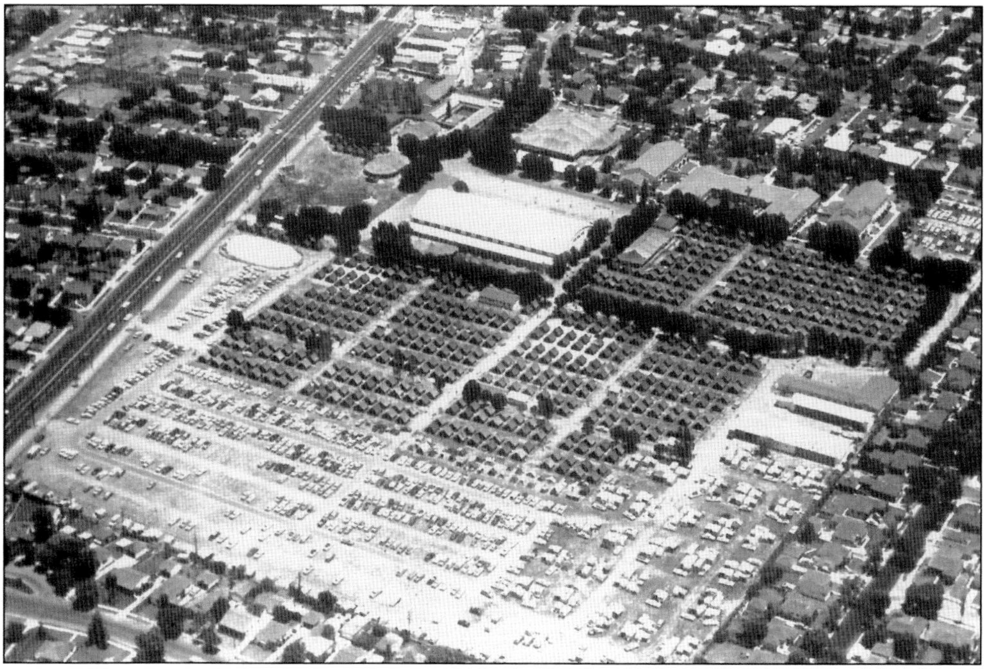

This aerial view of the Seventh-Day Adventist Academy was captured facing west toward Bullis Road from Atlantic Avenue. The entire campground area in the scene comprises nearly 46 acres.

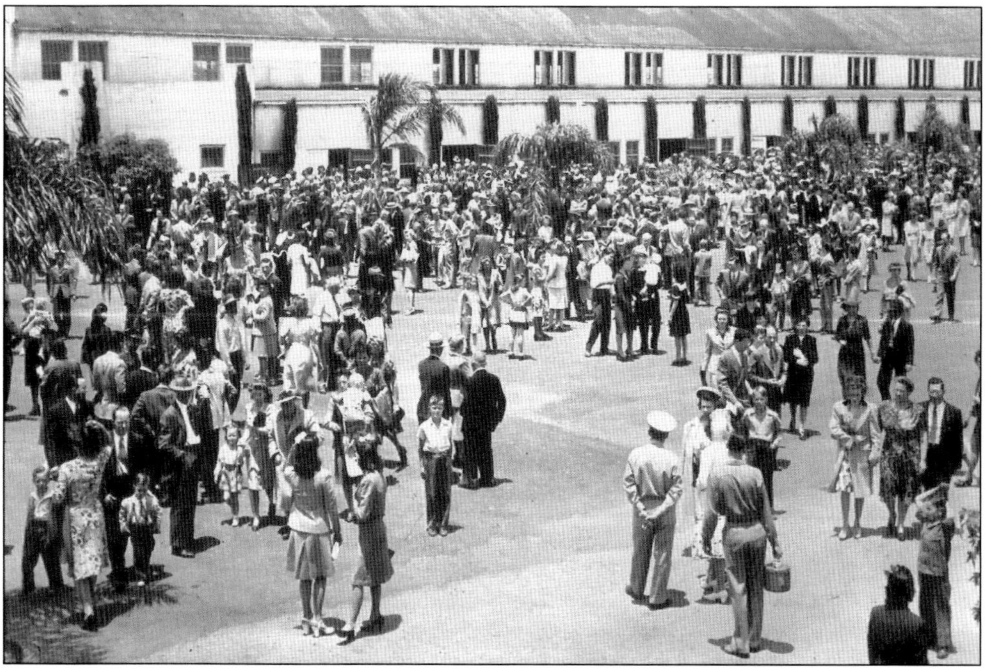

In 1961, the Seventh-Day Adventist Conference was held in Lynwood. Nearly 10,000 people came to the weekend event. Hundreds of tents were used to cover the area—the present-day site of Lynwood High School.

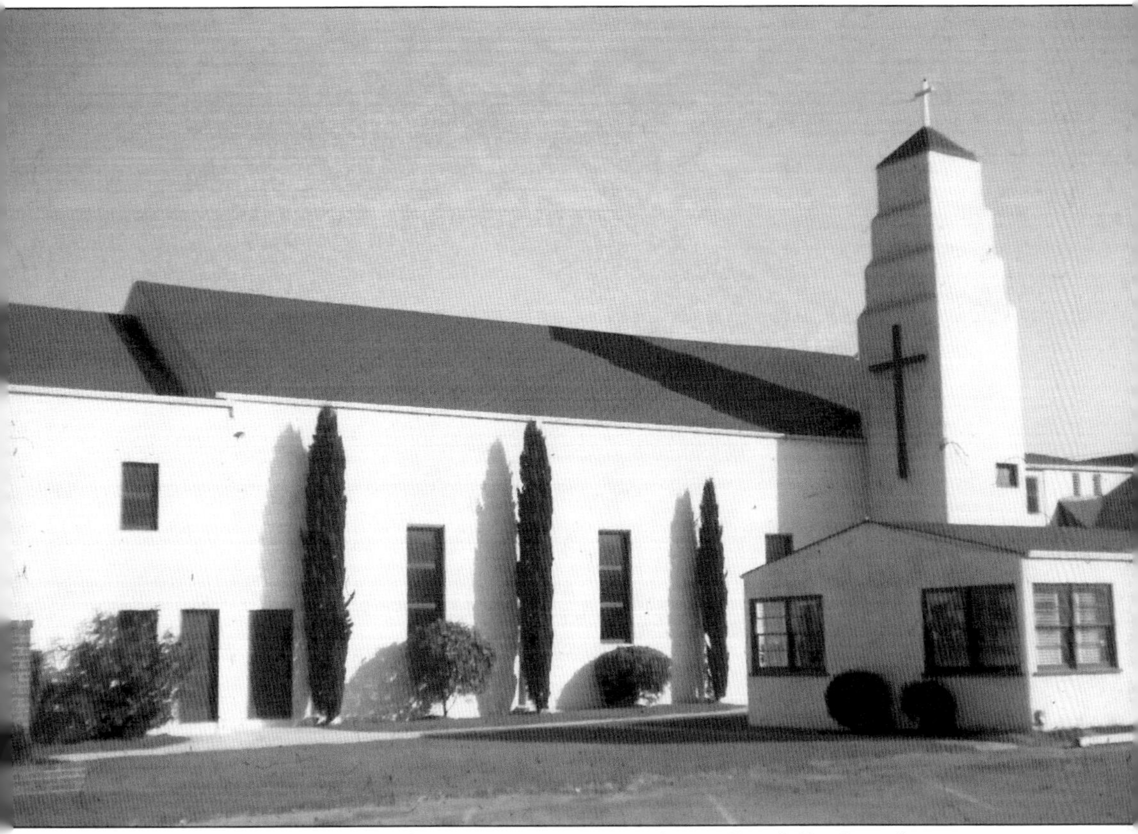
Pictured here is the church on Sanborn Avenue, just east of Long Beach Boulevard.

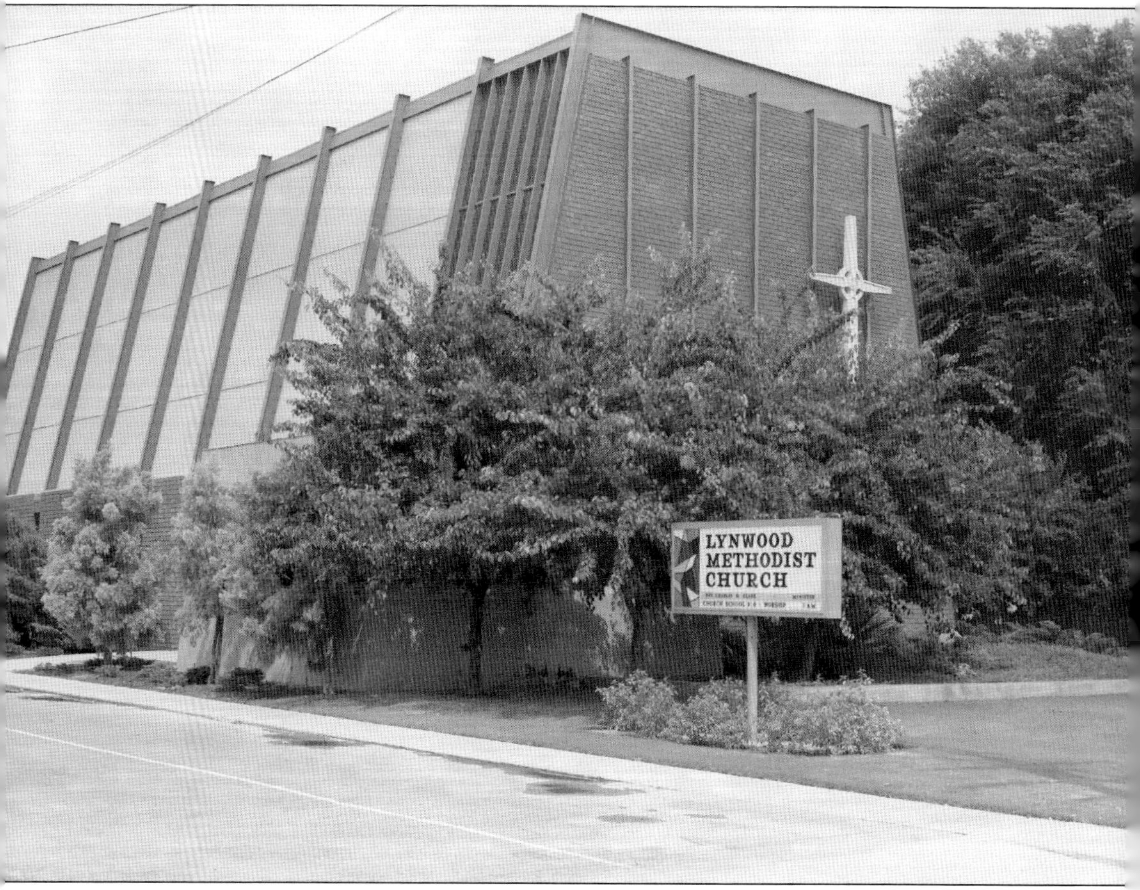

Located on Carlin Avenue and Thorson Street, the Lynwood Methodist Church building pictured here was completed in 1953. At one time, the church used the old Lugo District School building, constructed in 1917, to hold services. After the 1933 earthquake, however, damage was too extensive for use.

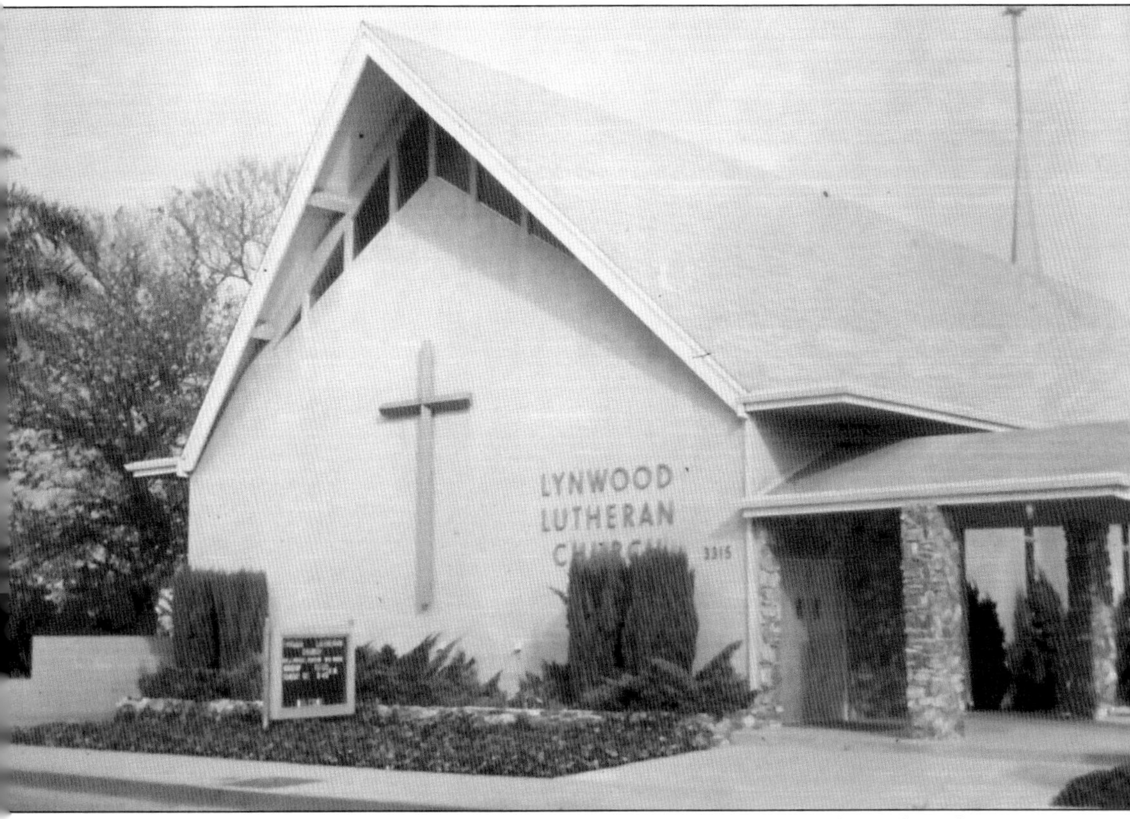

This Lutheran church is located on Magnolia Avenue just west of Long Beach Boulevard.

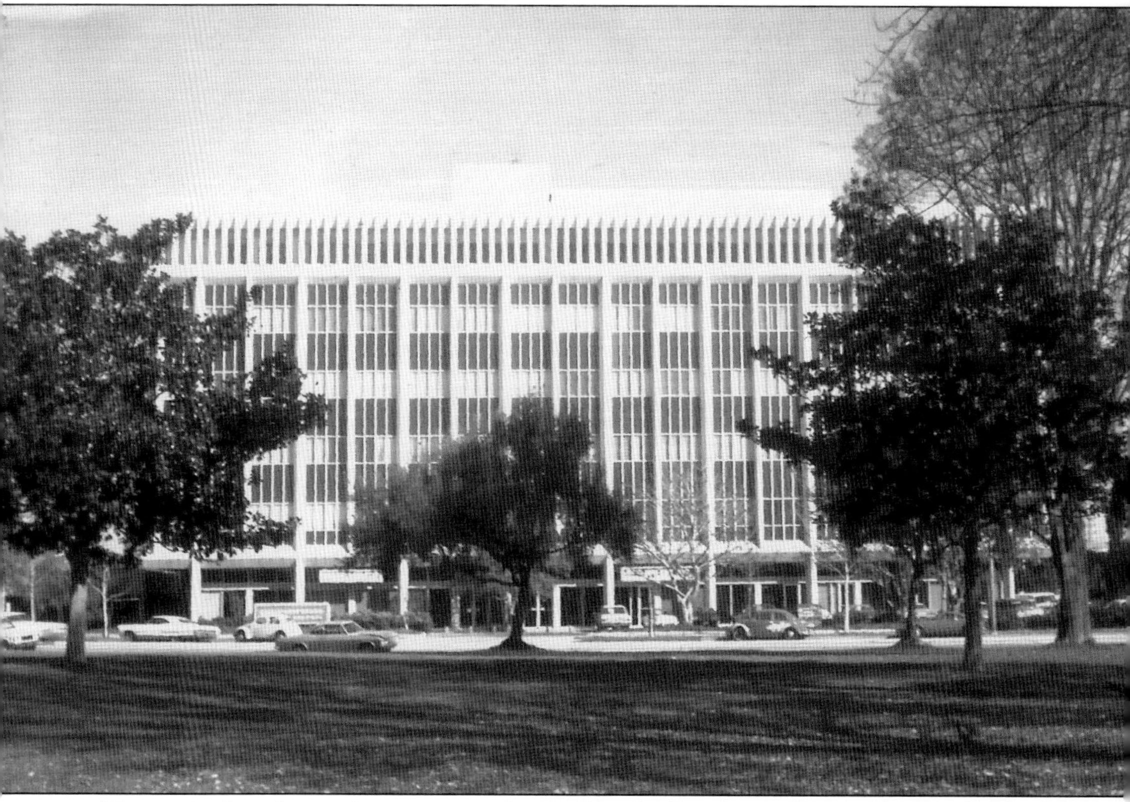

The medical professional center opened in 1963 and still accommodates various medical offices today. The building is located on Martin Luther King Jr. Boulevard, formerly Century Boulevard, just across the street from Lynwood City Park. This building was the largest in the city at the time. St. Francis Medical Center later expanded and is now the largest complex.

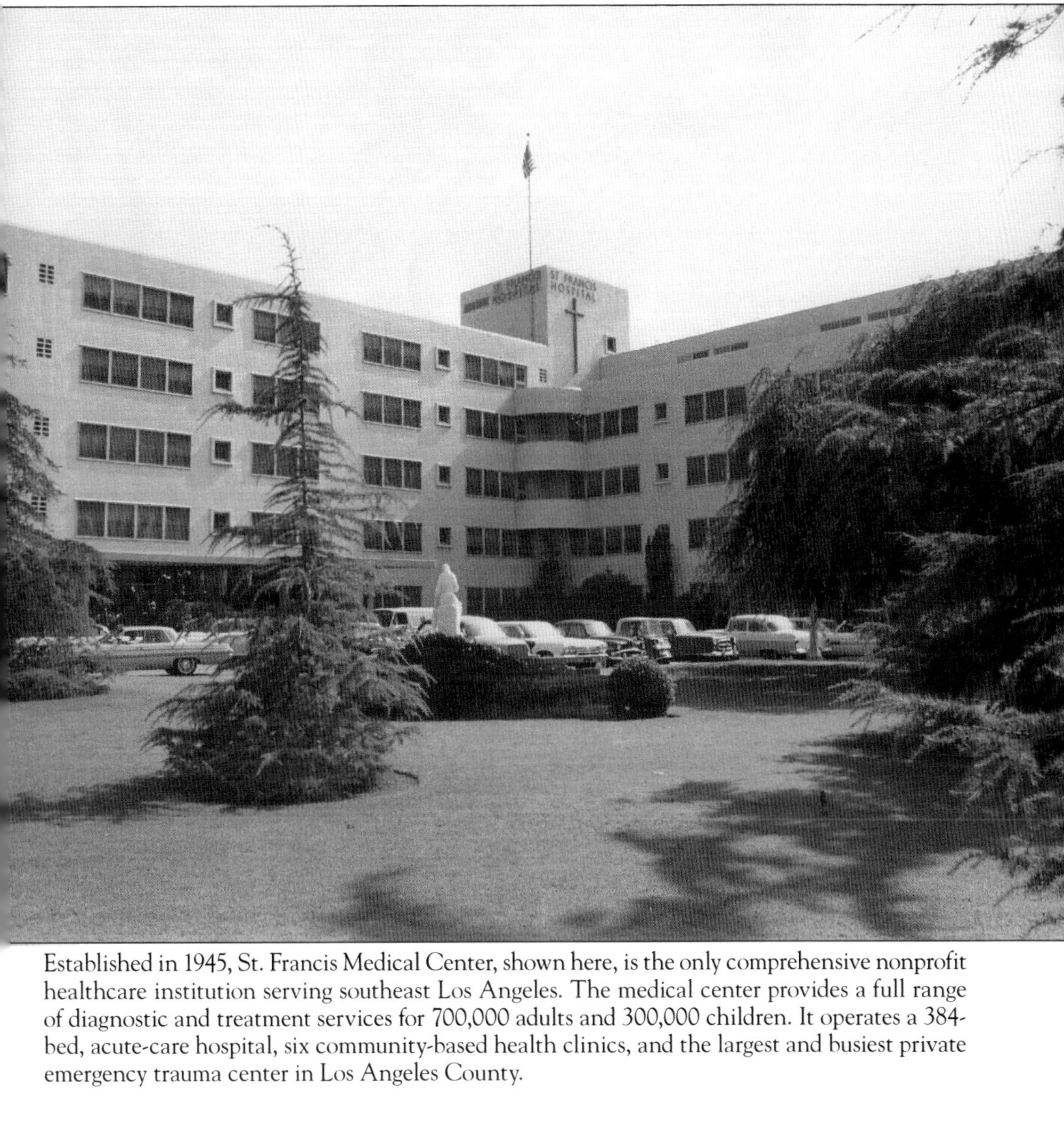

Established in 1945, St. Francis Medical Center, shown here, is the only comprehensive nonprofit healthcare institution serving southeast Los Angeles. The medical center provides a full range of diagnostic and treatment services for 700,000 adults and 300,000 children. It operates a 384-bed, acute-care hospital, six community-based health clinics, and the largest and busiest private emergency trauma center in Los Angeles County.

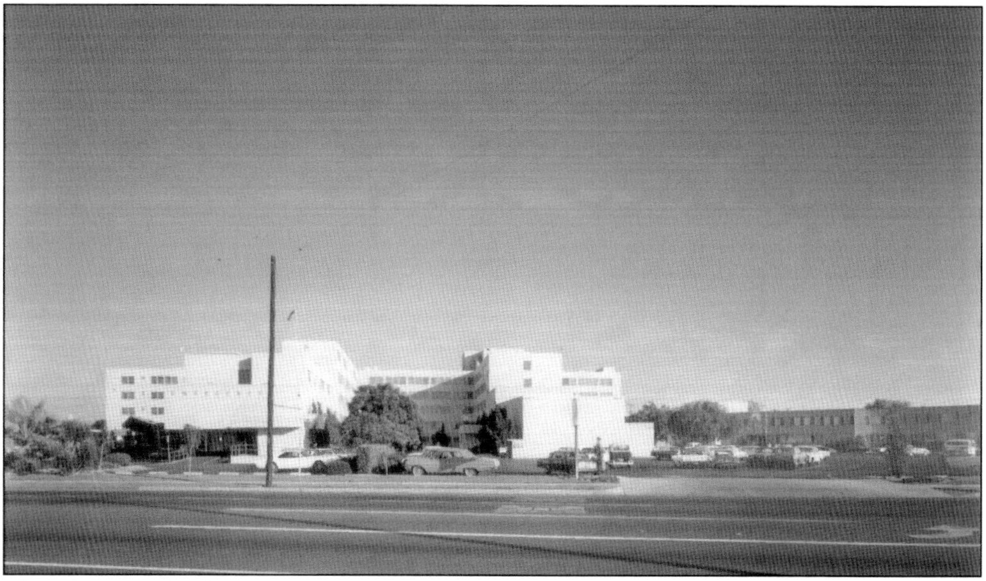

This photograph of St. Francis Medical Center was taken from across the street, on Martin Luther King Jr. Boulevard.

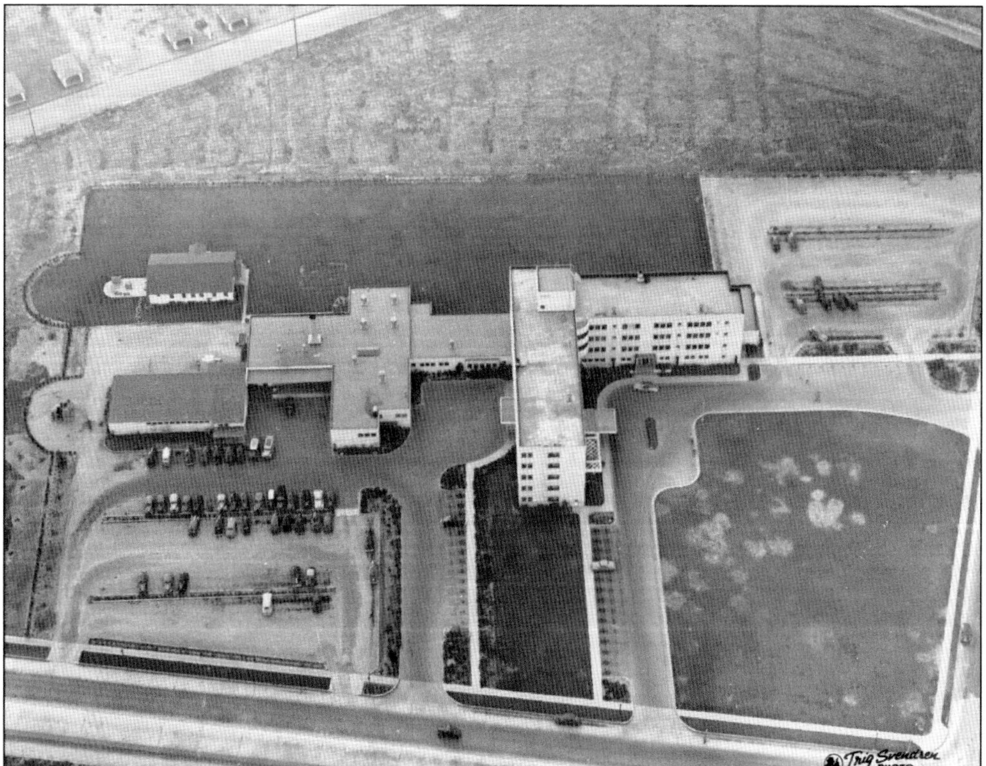

This is an aerial view of the St. Francis Medical enter in the mid-1950s. The five-story building in the background was constructed in 1944. The campus covered 14 acres, adjoining Lynwood City Park on its south side.

Six

Civic Pride and Recreation

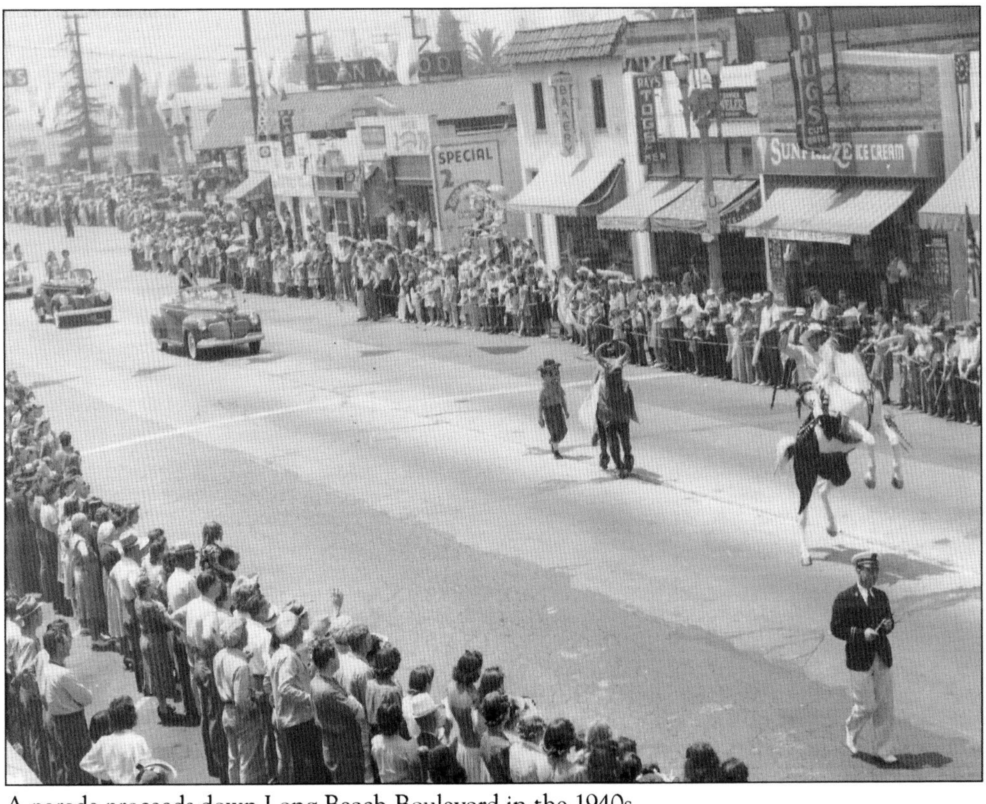

A parade proceeds down Long Beach Boulevard in the 1940s.

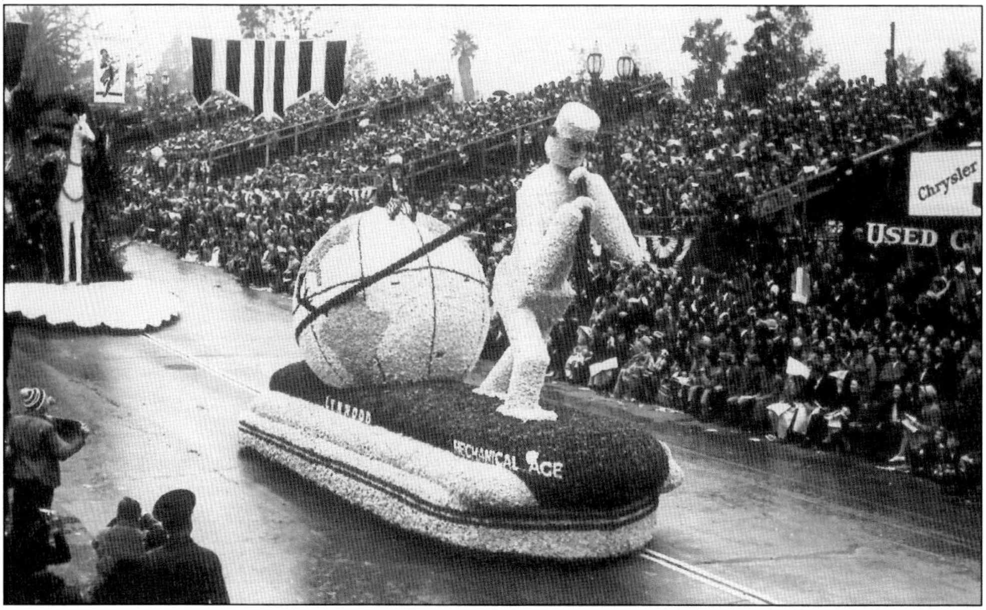

In 1940, Lynwood entered the float pictured here in the Pasadena Tournament of Roses Parade and placed third in its category. Titled "The Mechanical Age in Flowers," the globe showed the continents in a variety of colors and flowers. Sitting atop the globe in an Uncle Sam costume is five-year-old Rolland Jack.

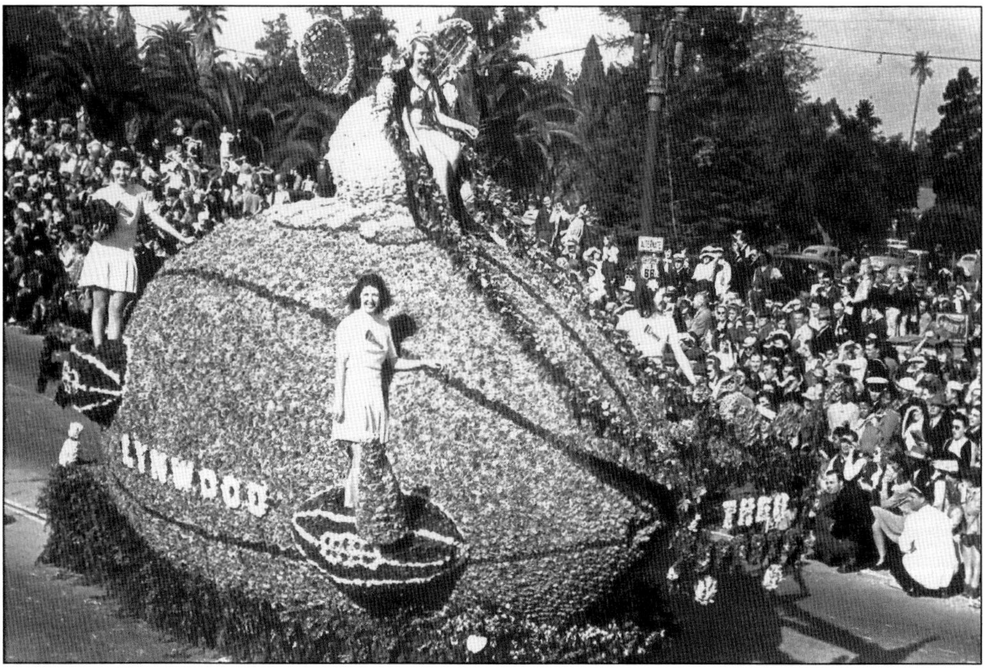

Lynwood's first float entry in the Pasadena Tournament of Roses Parade was in 1937. The float shown here is not dated, but it may be the one entered that year. At the time, a parade committee actively sought money from merchants and citizens in town. The city also donated funds. The committee then built the float at cost, usually about $2,500 per float. After 1945, it became too costly for the city to sponsor parade floats.

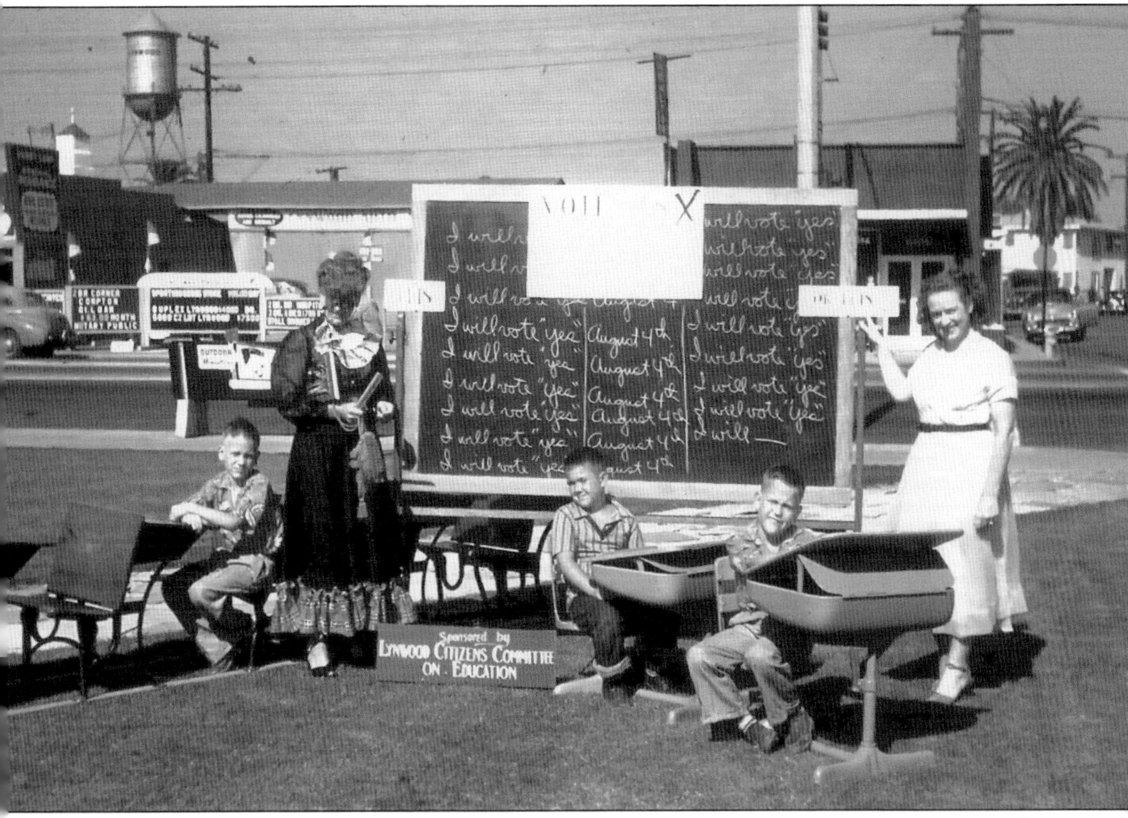

This is a photograph from the 1950s showing two women believed to be part of the Lynwood senior committee displaying "I will vote" signs to travelers on Long Beach Boulevard.

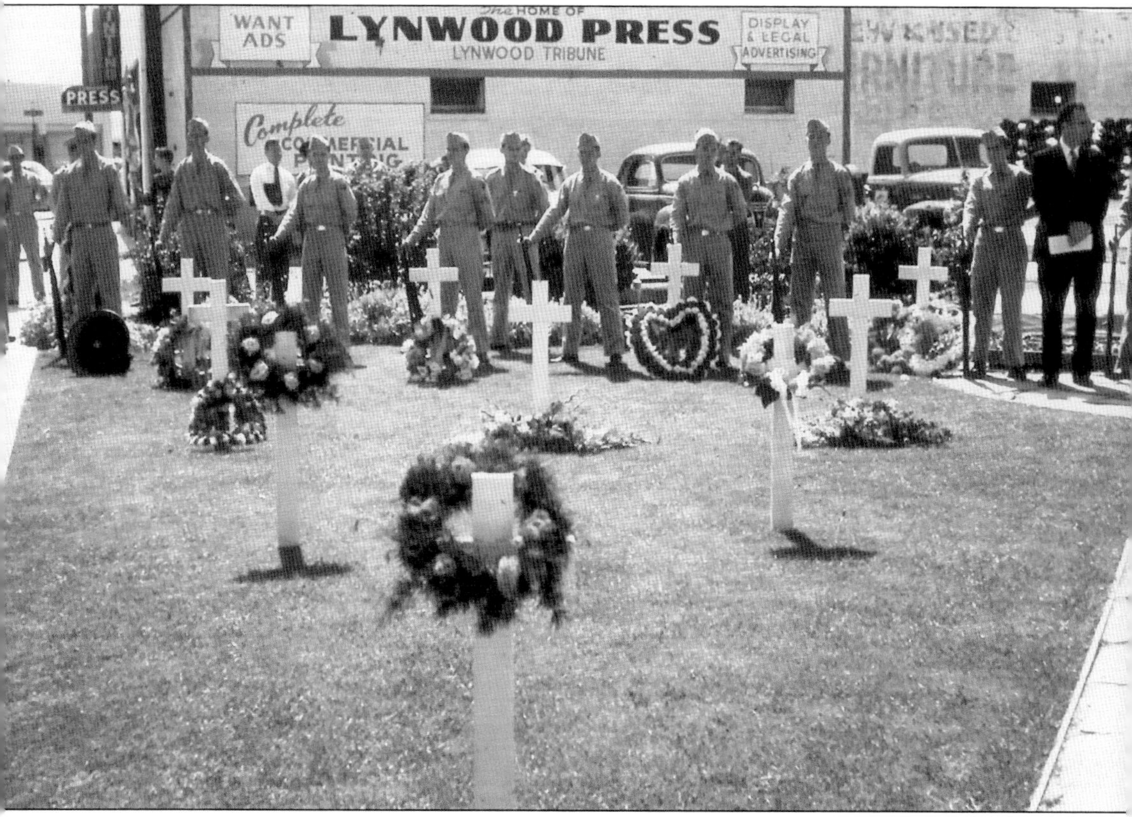

The annual Veterans Program Ceremony was photographed from the corner of Mulford Avenue and Long Beach Boulevard. The yearly program is held on the lawn of the present-day city hall on Bullis Road.

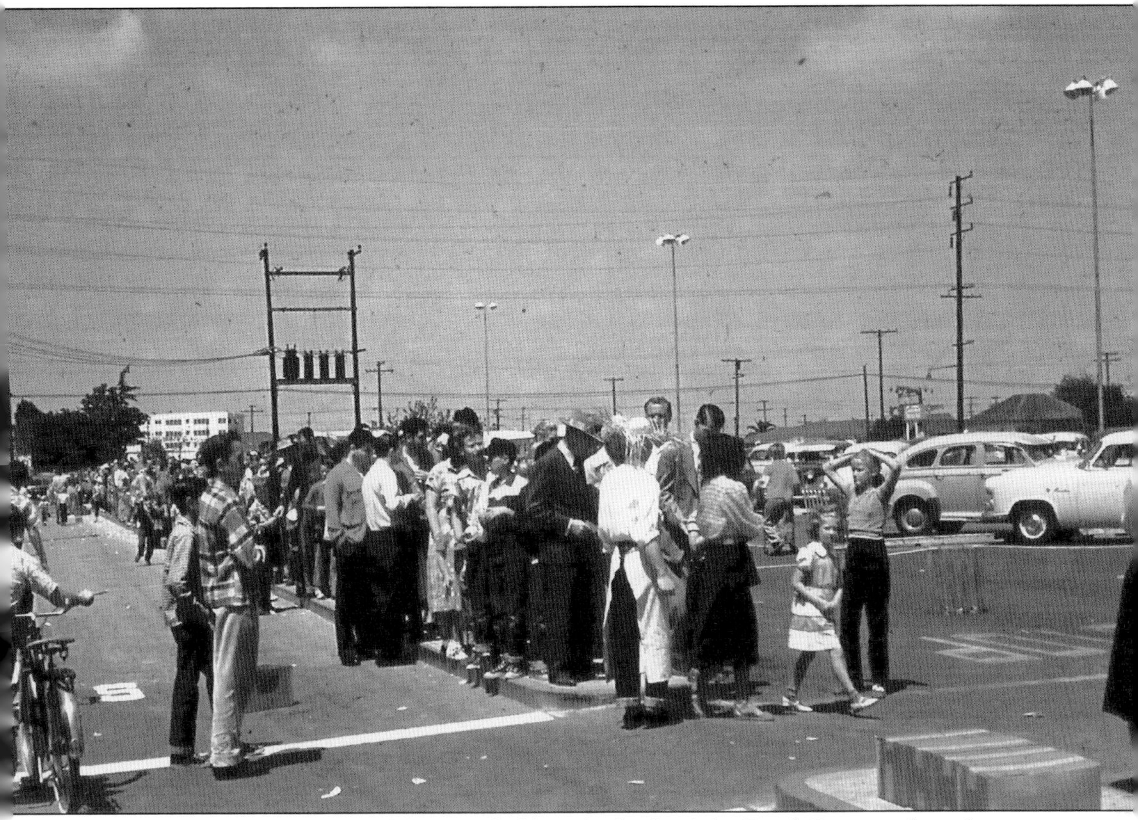

In the 1950s, a 10¢ benefit breakfast was held at the back of the Food Giant parking lot on Century Boulevard, now Martin Luther King Jr. Boulevard and Ernestine Avenue. The project, which helped raise money to buy books for the Lynwood High School library, was led by the Lynwood Junior Women's Club.

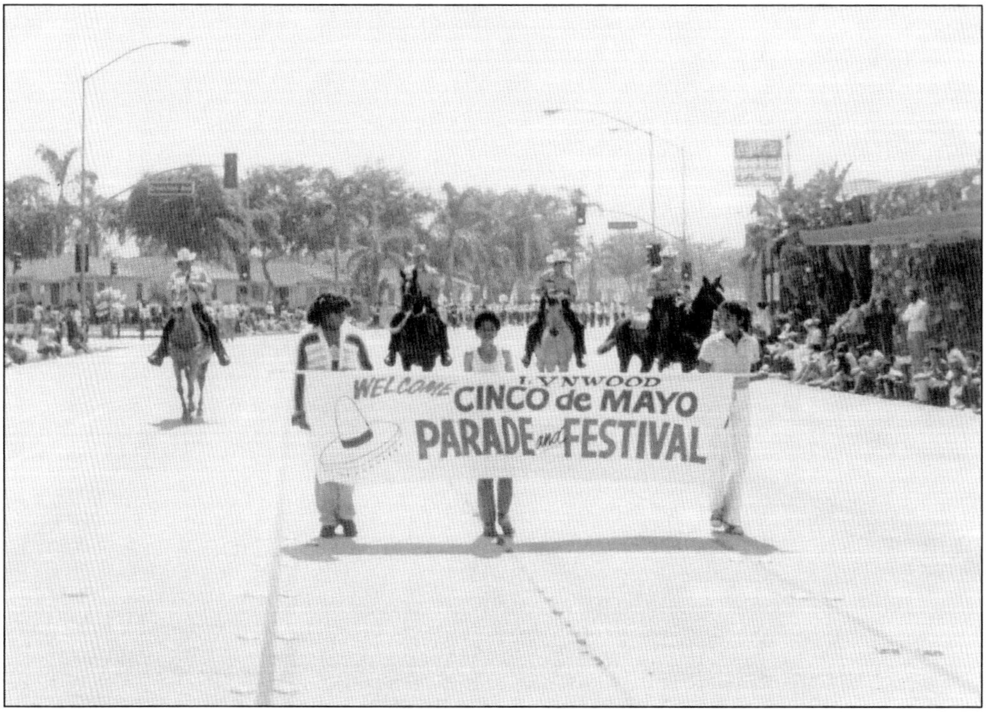

A Cinco de Mayo Parade travels down Martin Luther King Jr. Boulevard (formerly Century Boulevard) in the early 1990s. Celebratory parades have always been part of Lynwood's makeup and today include the annual Candy Cane Lane Christmas Parade.

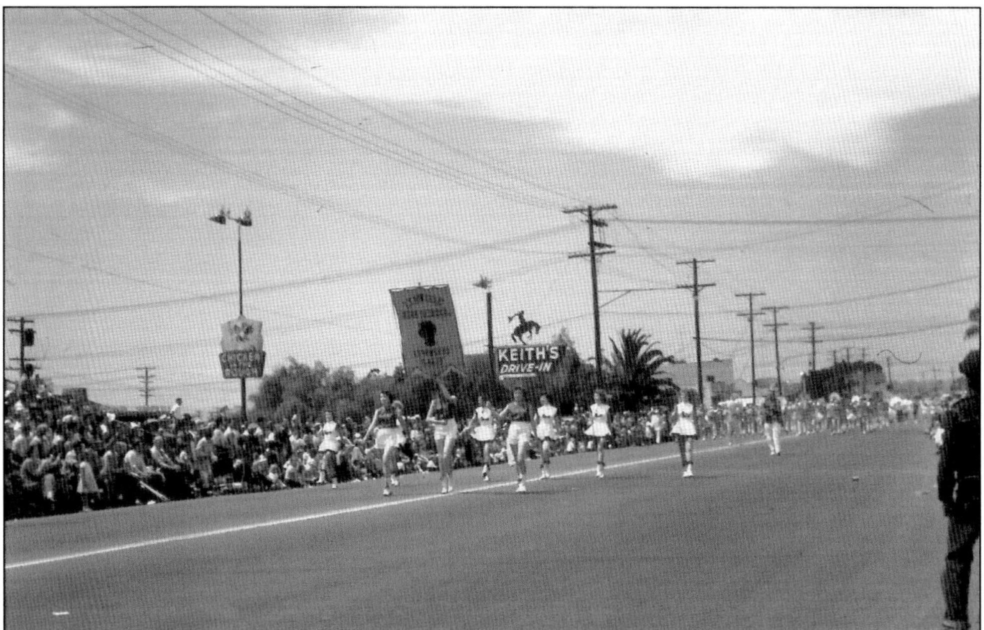

Local high school students are shown marching in a Lynwood parade. Lynwood residents have a strong tradition of staging, participating, and attending town parades.

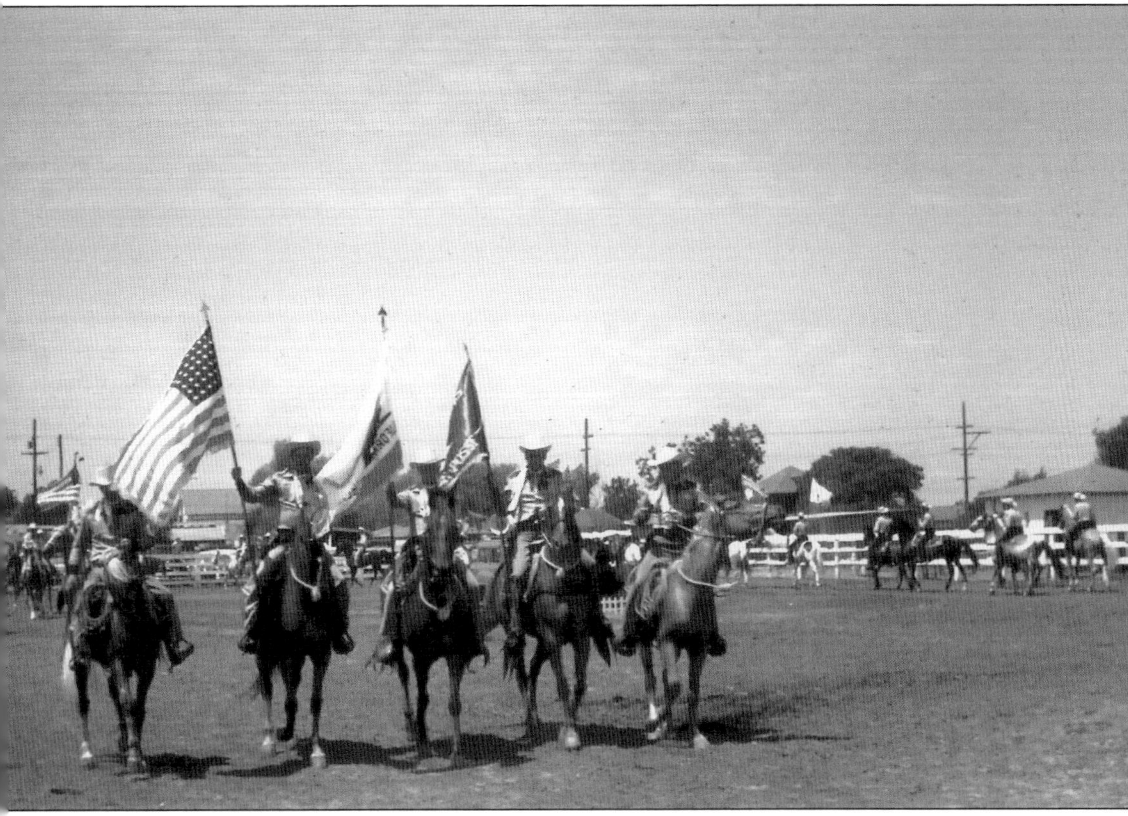

A horse-mounted police unit presents colors at an event held at the horse stable located on the corner of Abbott Road and Century Boulevard.

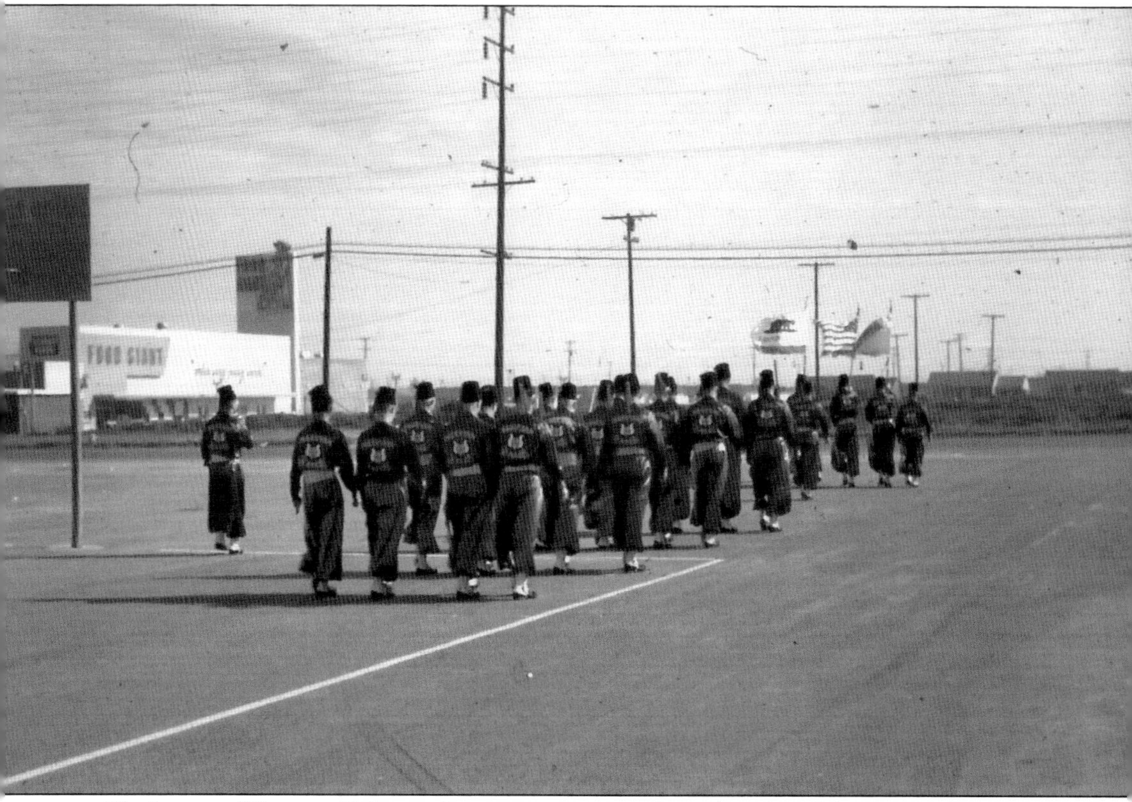

The Lynwood Kiwanis Club marches in procession in the parking lot of the Lynwood Community Center. The club comprises dedicated men who volunteer their time helping others. The street facing the vacant lot is Bullis Road. A CVS Pharmacy is now located on the site.

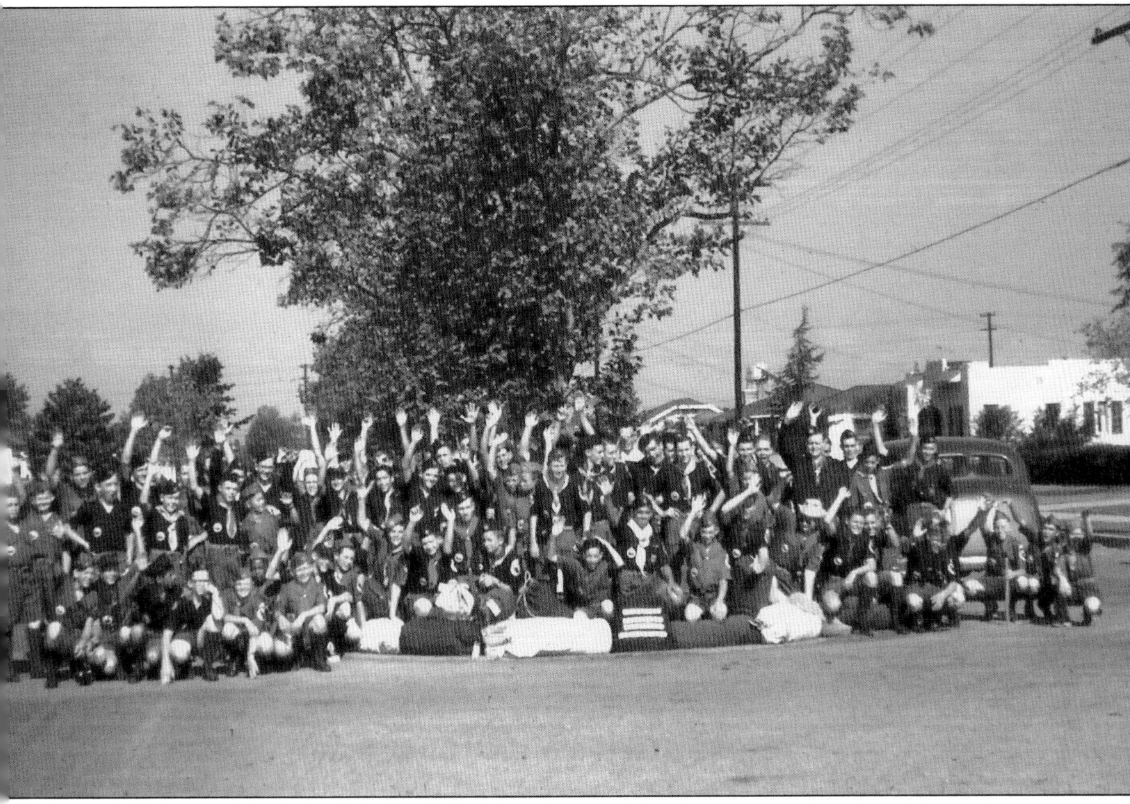

Photographed here are some 60 Boy Scouts preparing for a camping trip, judging from the tent bags on the ground. This gathering took place at Flower Street by Constitution Park (now Carnation Park) in the late 1940s.

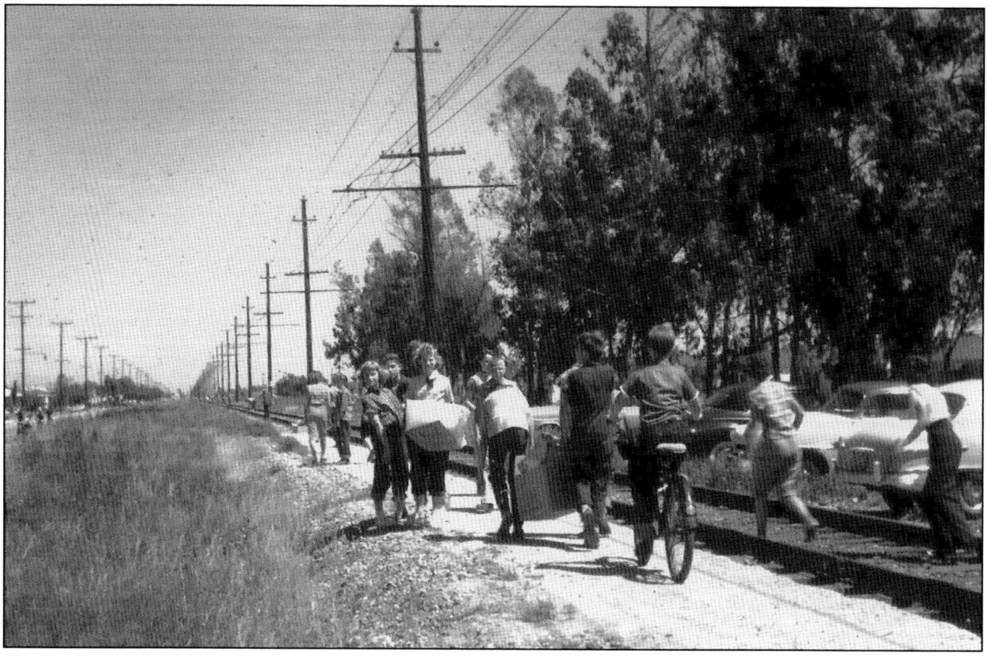

Here, the City of Lynwood stages a summertime clean-up campaign. Several hundred students from high schools turned out to collect trash along the railroad tracks.

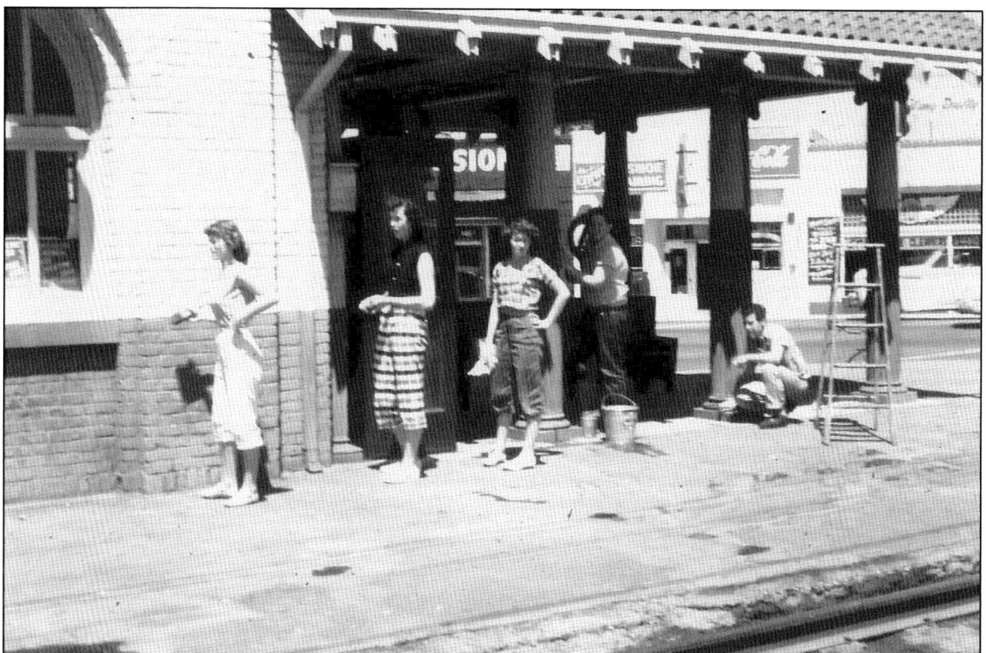

Community youth volunteers painted the Pacific Electric depot as part of Lynwood's summer clean-up project.

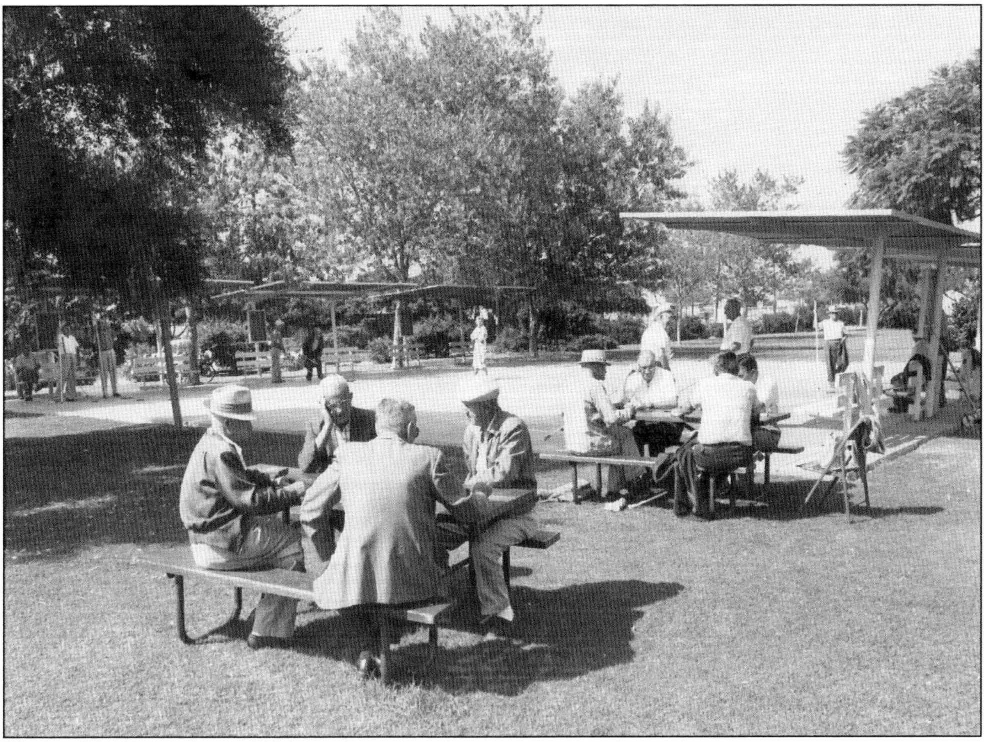

Shuffleboard and checkers were popular games among senior citizens who frequented Lynwood City Park. The shuffleboard area was fenced and located in the middle of the park, where the soccer fields are now located.

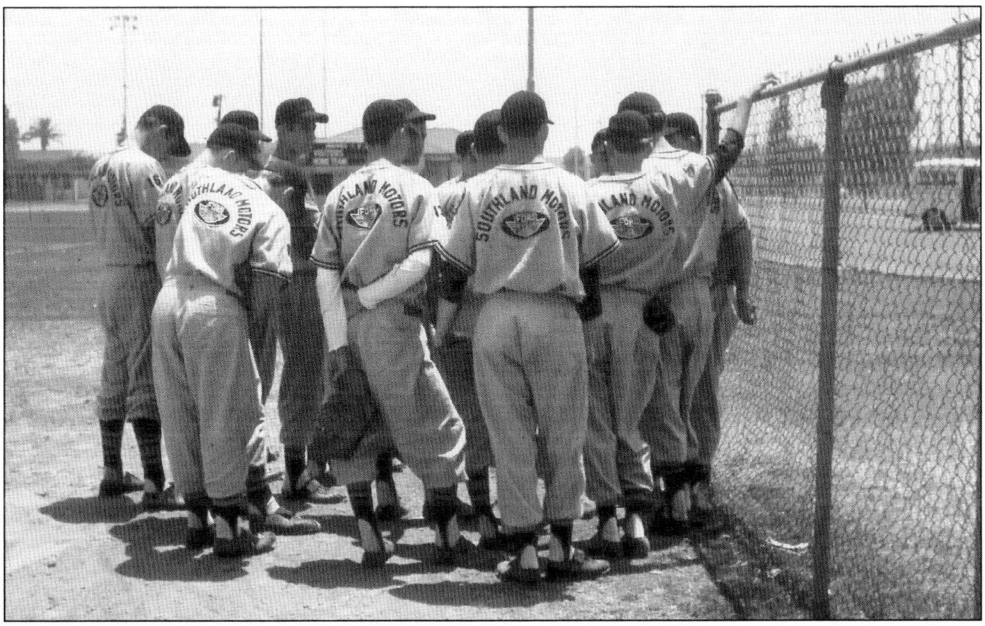

Sporting activities were primary recreational choices among Lynwood's youth, especially baseball, softball, soccer, and basketball. Shown here are local baseball team members preparing for game play. In those days, uniforms displayed sponsor names; this team's uniforms say "Southland Motors."

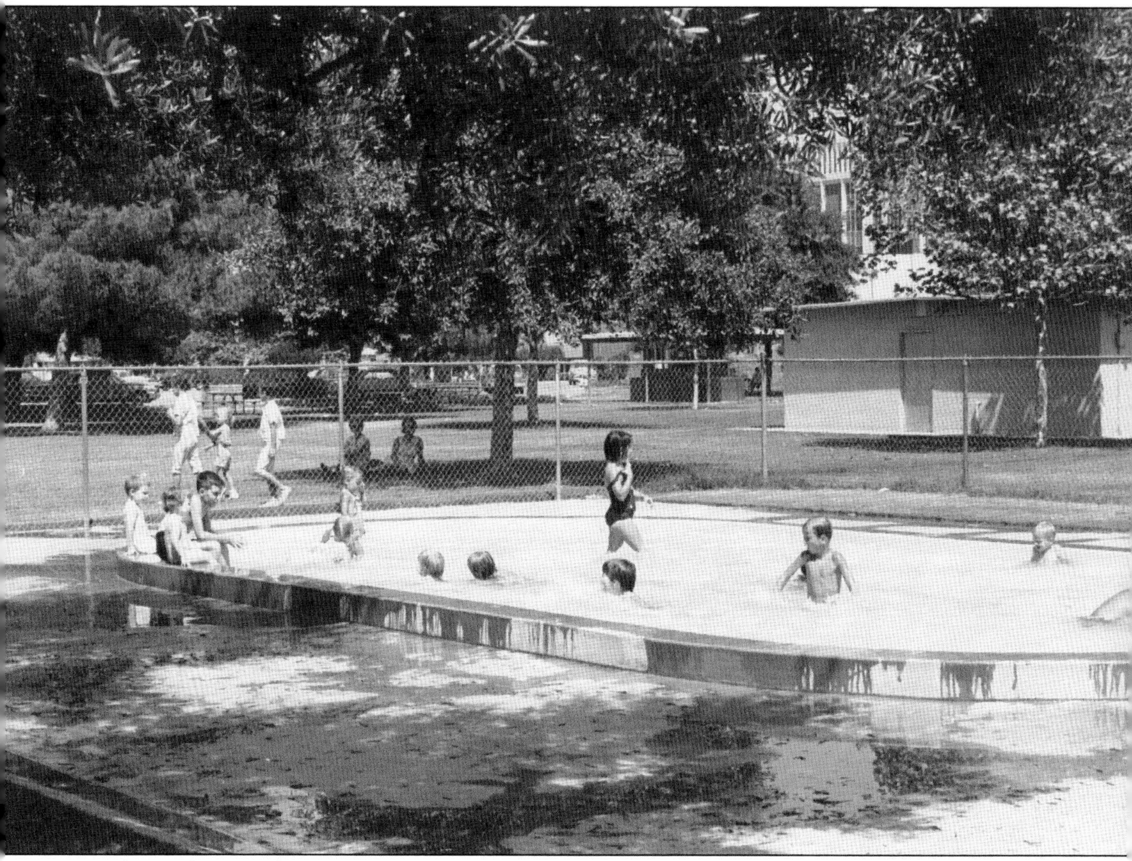

The wading pool at Lynwood City Park saw heavy traffic during the summer months. The pool was in the middle of the park, where soccer fields are located today.

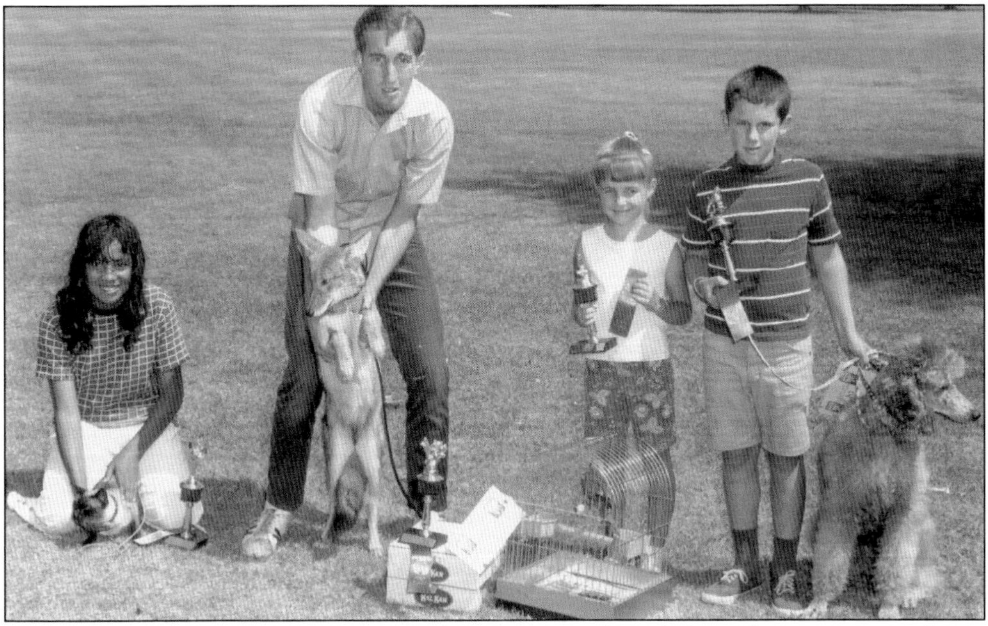

Pet shows were routinely held at Ham Park and continued until the park was repurposed for a new high school in 2005. Here, young participants pose with an impressive array of creature-contestants and ribbons from a contest held in the late 1960s.

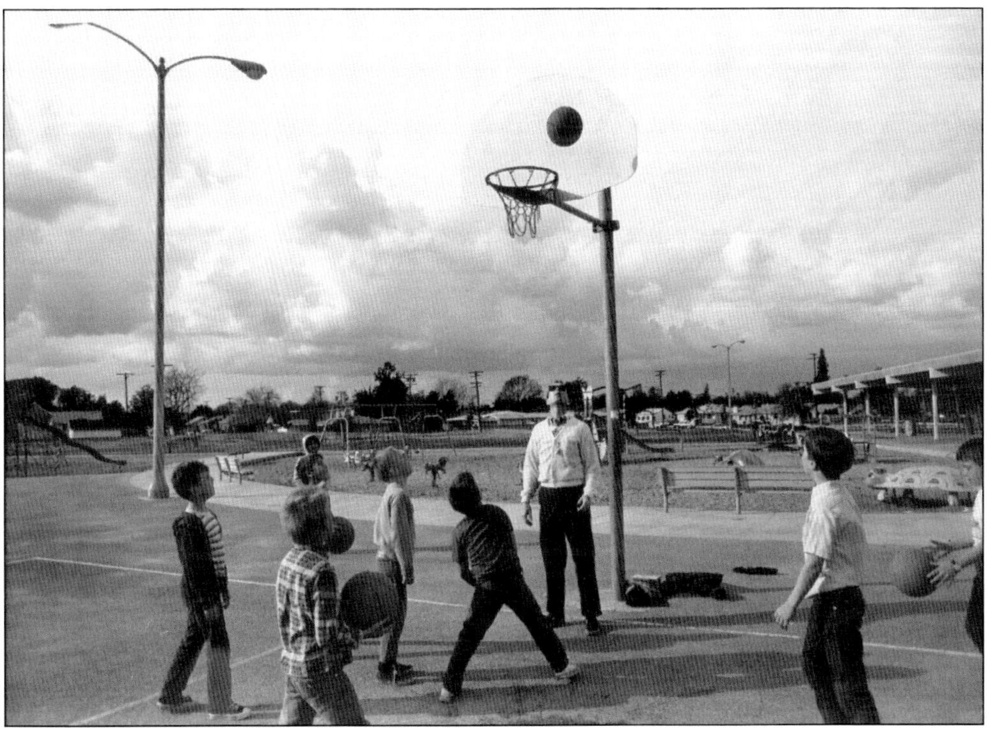

This 1960s image shows boys playing basketball at Ham Park.

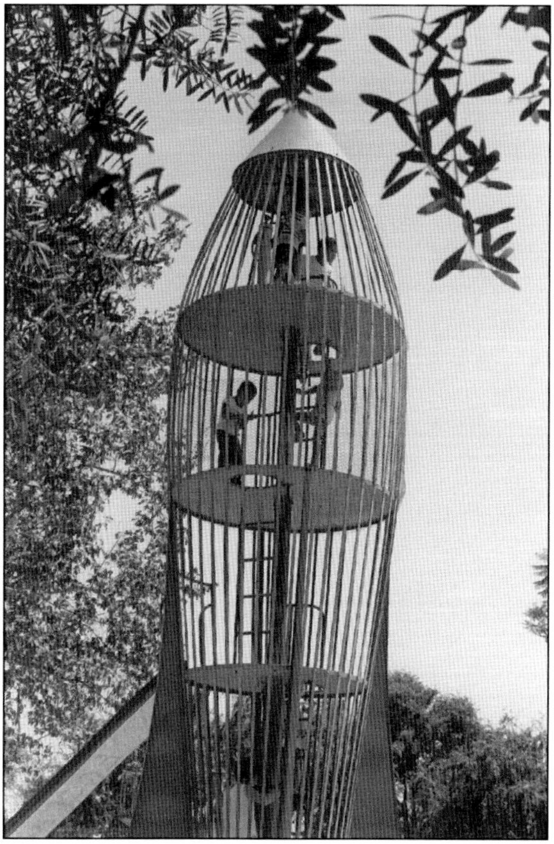

In 1963, Lynwood dedicated this space-age rocket shuttle at the Lynwood City Park playground. The space-themed playground was located in the large play area at the northwest end of the park by the cannon.

Kids are shown enjoying the playground at Ham Park. Part of the former community center is visible in the background. Many programs and activities took place at the site, including summer day camp. The park was named in memory of John D. Ham in 1965. Ham had served as mayor and council member in Lynwood, and his ice cream store on Atlantic Avenue endeared him to many citizens of Lynwood. The park, originally called Lugo Park, was built in the late 1950s.

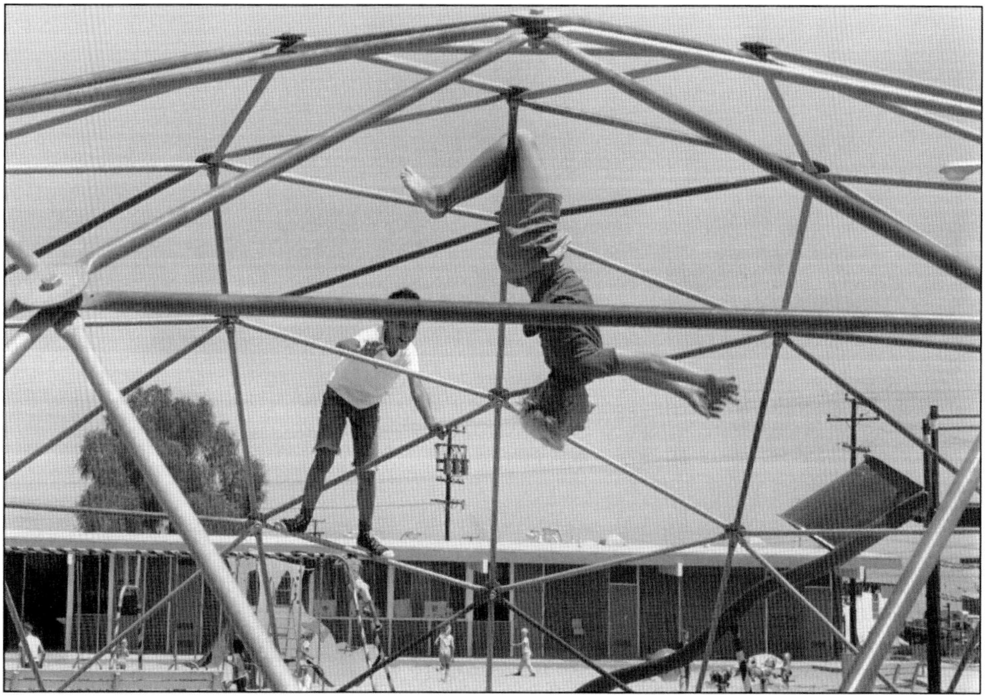

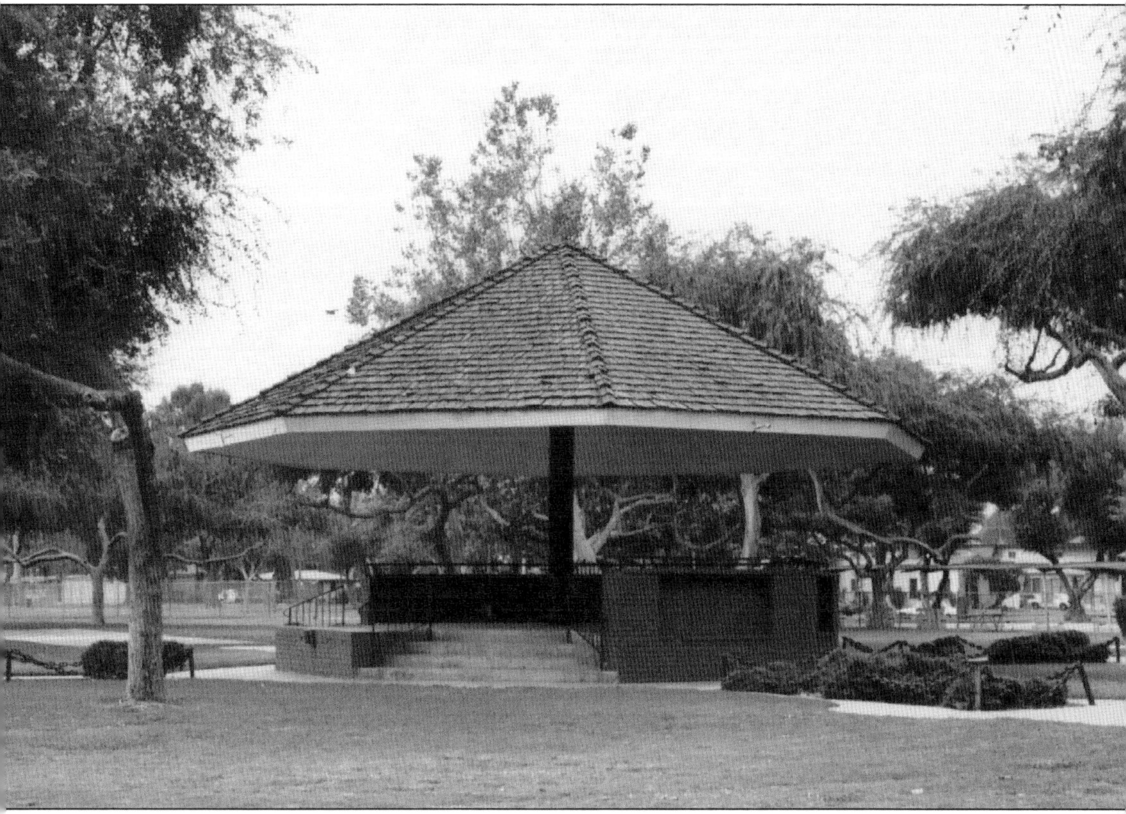

This hexagonal band shell was placed in Lynwood City Park around 1966. The shelter was built to honor Lynwood sons who lost their lives at war. Many city events and celebrations were staged at this site.

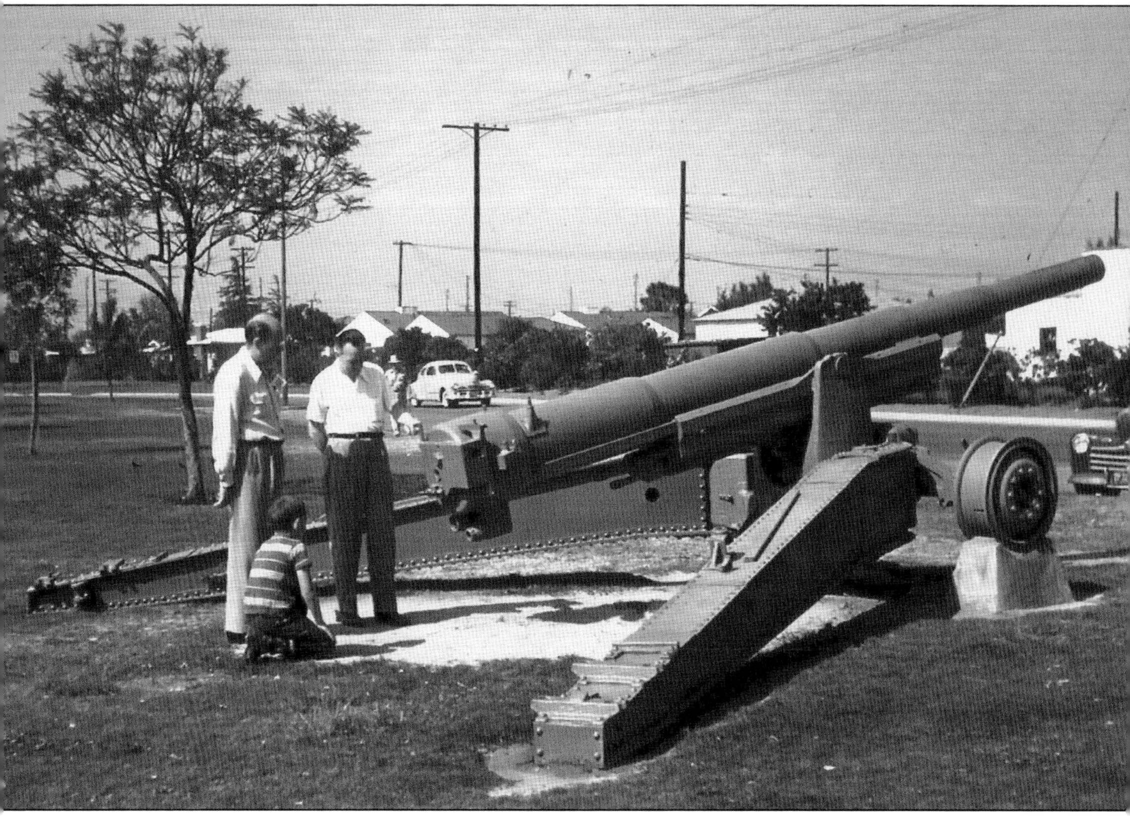

In 1969, weapons of war were converted to memorials of war and placed in parks. The cannon pictured here was installed at Lynwood City Park at the east end of the park near the playground.

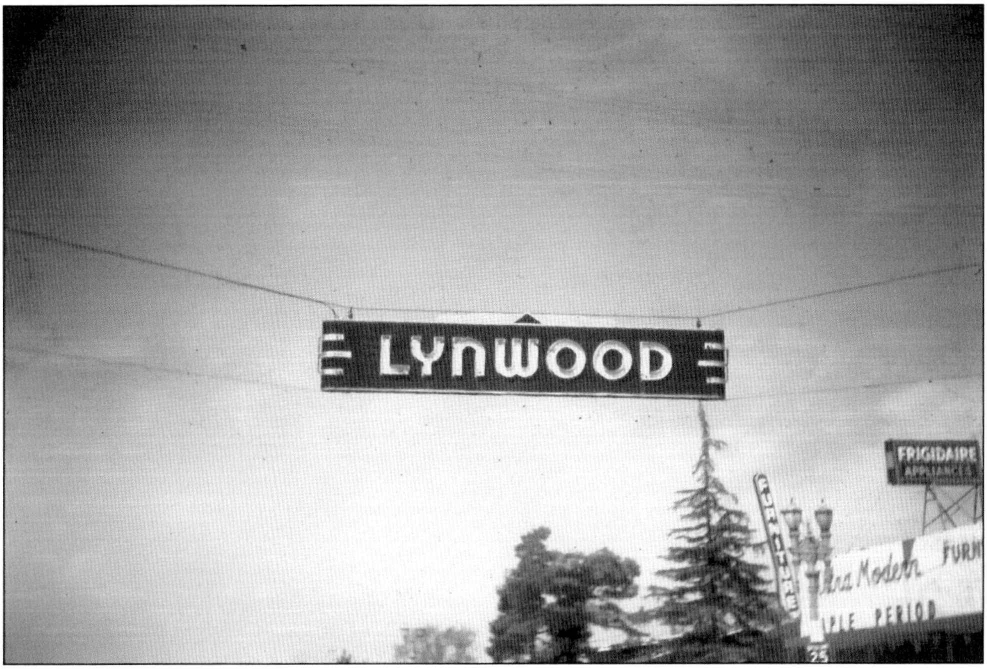

In 1937, new signs greeted motorists at the north and south entrances to Lynwood, along Long Beach Boulevard. "Welcome," "Farewell," and "Lynwood (shown here)" signs appeared.

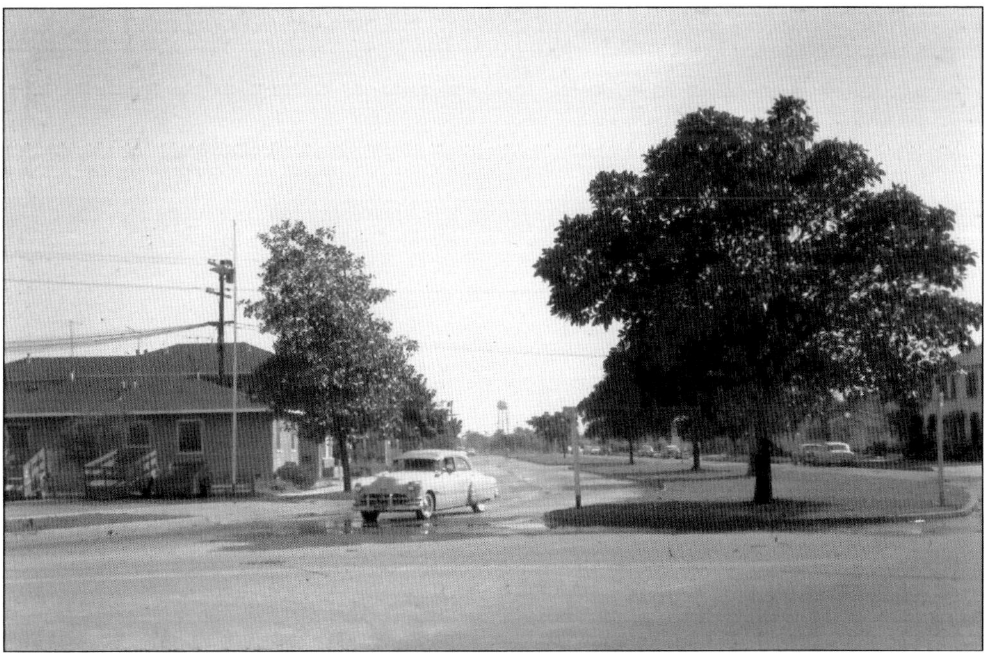

This grassy, oak-lined median area was a pleasant welcome for residents and visitors.

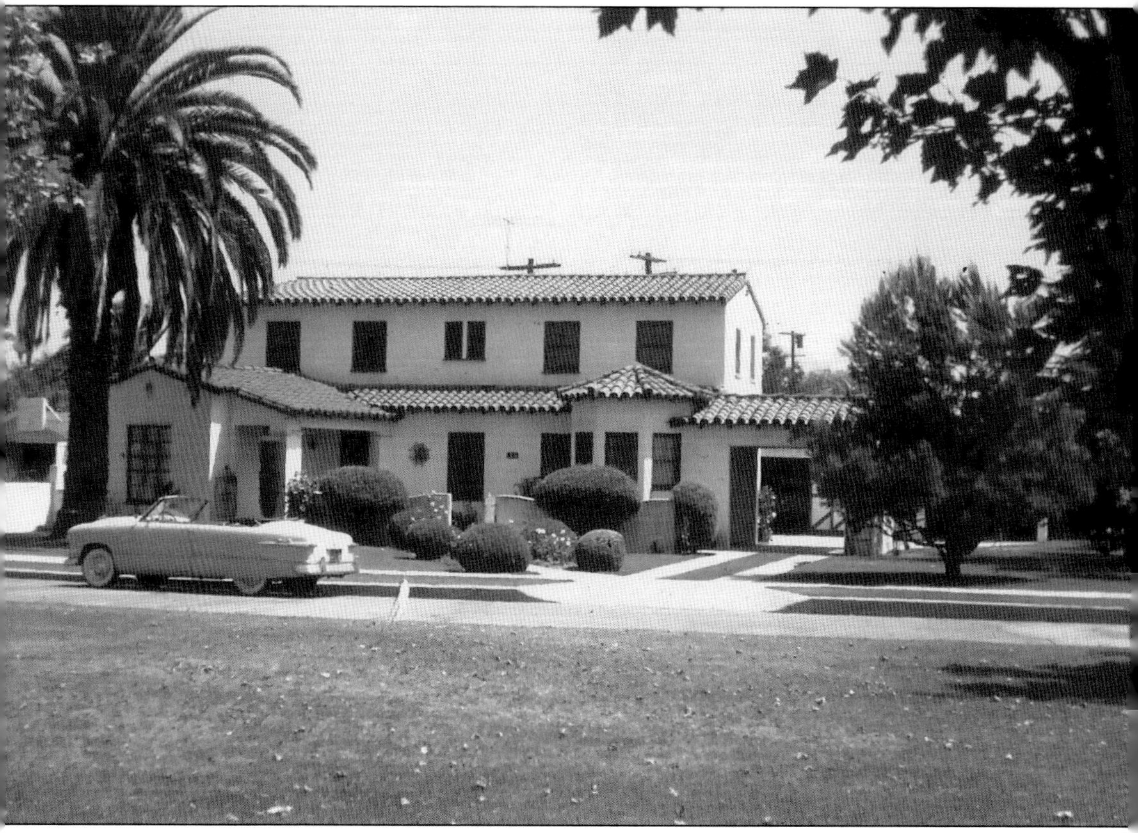

The Spanish-style home on Los Flores Street was built in the 1930s. Many of the homes in that area featured Spanish-style architecture and were surrounded by palm trees.

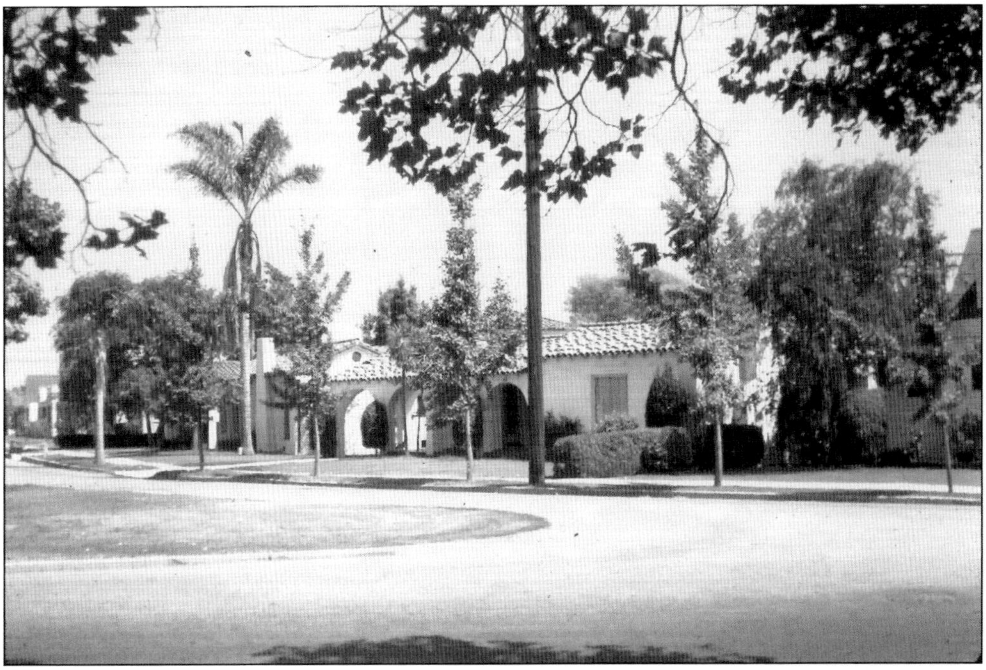

Shown here is a picturesque home from the early 1930s located in the former Modjeska Park Tract on Flower and State Streets. The home looks much the same today.

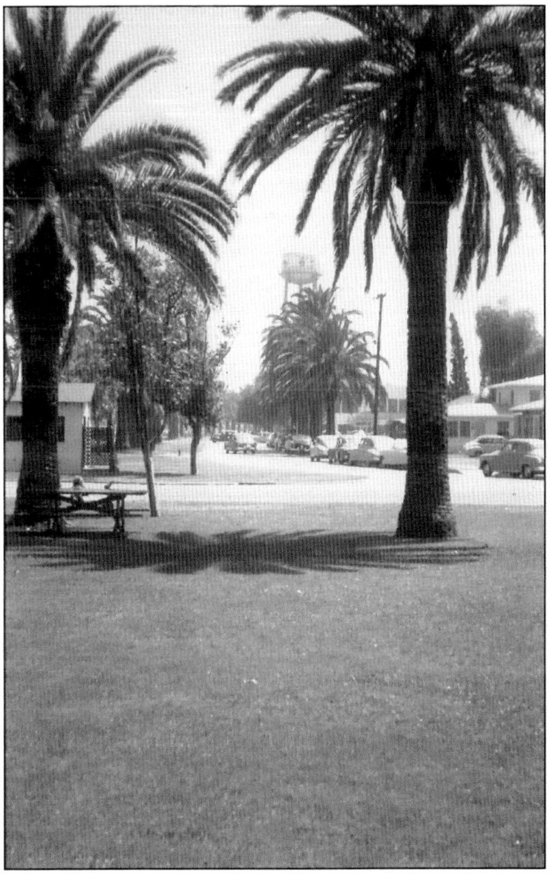

This photograph was taken from Constitution Park (now Rose Park) facing west toward Alameda Street. The small shed seen in the background was used by the city to store street maintenance equipment and materials. The building has since been removed.

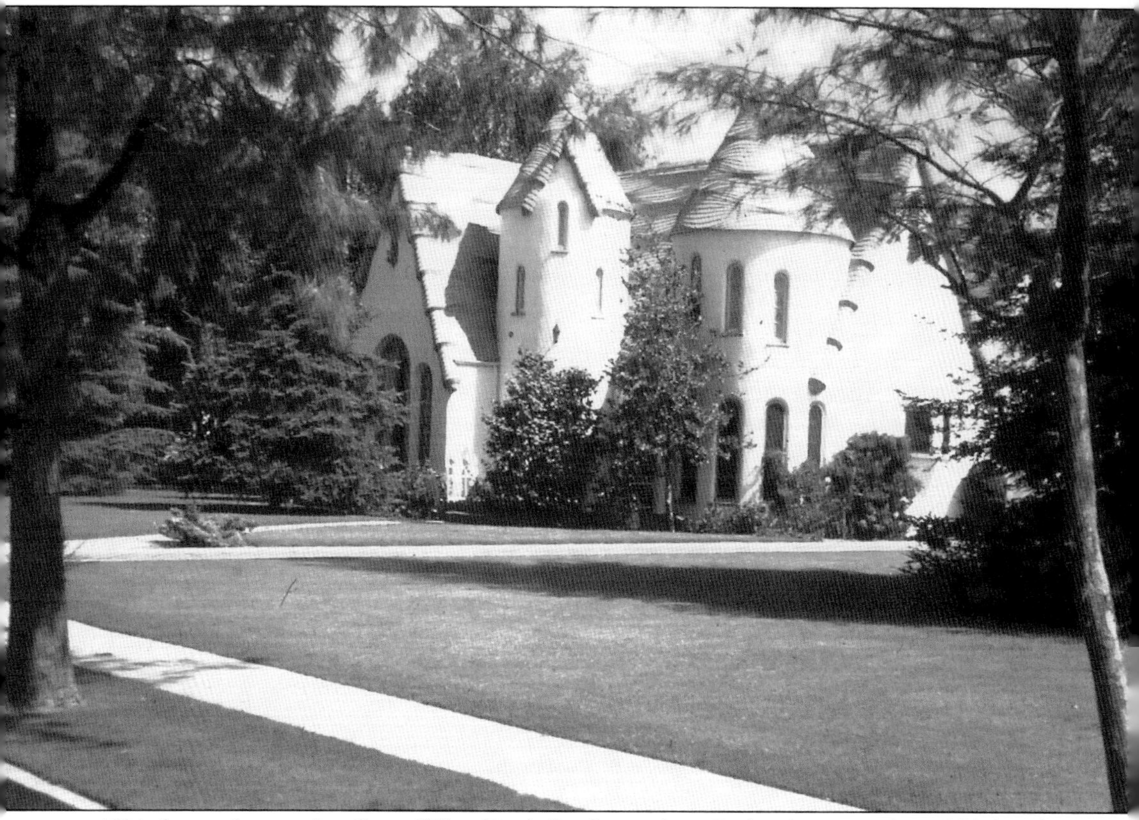

This home, known locally as "The Castle," is located on Cedar Avenue, about 300 feet from Bullis Road and near Lynwood Middle School.

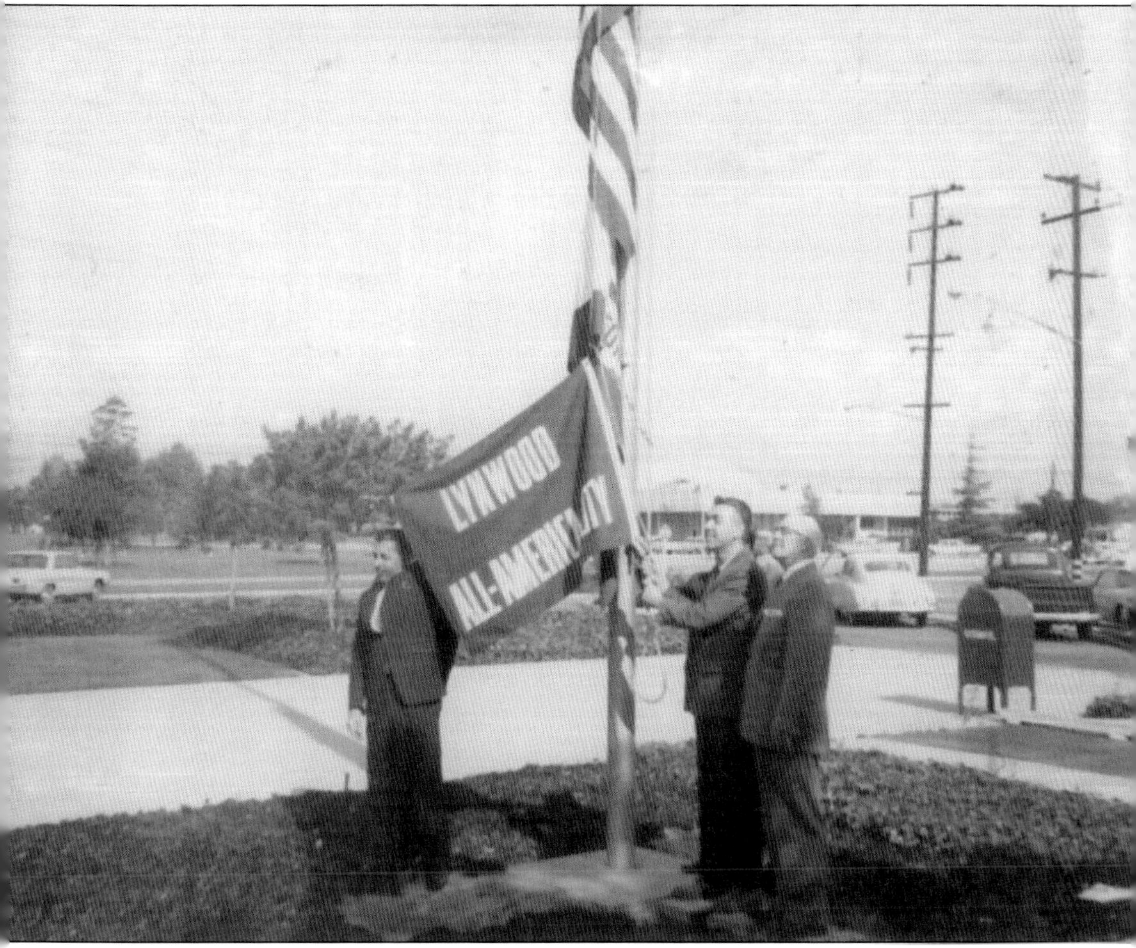

Lynwood's outstanding civic accomplishments were recognized nationally when it won the prestigious All-America City Award in 1961 and 2010. Lynwood had the distinction of being the only city in Southern California to receive the awards. To win, communities demonstrated an ability to address challenges with innovative, grassroots strategies that promote civic engagement and cooperation among public, private, and nonprofit sectors.